Arms Control and Defense Postures in the 1980s

Also of Interest

† *The Soviet Union in World Politics*, edited by Kurt London

† *The Soviet Union in the Third World: Successes and Failures*, edited by Robert H. Donaldson

† *The Domestic Context of Soviet Foreign Policy*, edited by Seweryn Bialer

† *NATO—The Next Thirty Years: The Changing Political, Economic, and Military Setting*, edited by Kenneth A. Myers

† *Eastern Europe in the 1980s*, edited by Stephen Fischer-Galati

† Available in hardcover and paperback.

About the Book and Editor

Arms Control and Defense Postures in the 1980s
edited by Richard Burt

The current standstill in U.S.-Soviet arms limitation negotiations has raised a number of questions about the effectiveness of arms limitation treaties, whether it is possible to negotiate an arms control agreement that would actually cut back on U.S. and Soviet strategic arsenals, and how such an arms reduction could be accomplished.

The authors of this book explore the problems of arms competition in the 1980s and stress the need for a complete reassessment of U.S. security interests lest negotiations become curiously disconnected from defense policy. To protect national interests, they assert, future arms limitation talks must allow for effective unilateral response to new classes of military problems and technologies. Each contributor addresses a specific area of arms negotiations, identifying various options, outlining potential outcomes, and discussing whether the talks actually are focusing on the right military issues. The book also provides an overview of previous U.S. arms limitation strategies and describes the Soviet approach to integrating national security with arms control policies.

Richard Burt, formerly a Washington-based correspondent for *The New York Times*, is now director of the Bureau of Politico-Military Affairs in the U.S. State Department. He is also an associate at the Washington Center of Foreign Policy Research, School of Advanced International Studies, Johns Hopkins University.

Arms Control and Defense Postures in the 1980s

edited by Richard Burt

Foreword by Robert E. Osgood

Westview Press • Boulder, Colorado

Croom Helm • London, England

This book is included in Westview's Special Studies in National Security and Defense Policy

Published in 1982 in the United States of America by
  Westview Press, Inc.
  5500 Central Avenue
  Boulder, Colorado 80301
  Frederick A. Praeger, President and Publisher

Published in 1982 in Great Britain by
  Croom Helm Ltd.
  2-10 St. John's Road
  London SW ll

Library of Congress Catalog Card Number: 81-21913
ISBN (U.S.): 0-86531-162-5
ISBN (U.K.): 0-7099-0624-2

Printed and bound in the United States of America

Contents

Foreword

American foreign policy was powerfully shaped in the 1970s by shifting premises concerning the nature of the international environment and America's role in shaping it. One large shift, prompted by reaction to the excesses of the Vietnam war, was marked by a revision of some of the key premises that underlay the global affirmation of American power and American commitments that preceded our involvement in the war. Another shift followed in the late 1970s, which has been marked by a reassessment of post-Vietnam premises in the wake of reviving aspects of the familiar Cold War outlook. In both cases different approaches to the management of East-West relations have been central to the shift.

Prominent in recent evaluations of détente is the question of the utility of arms control as an instrument of Western security. This question has been generated largely by American reaction to the adverse shift in the East-West military balance and to the expanding reach of Soviet power and influence in vulnerable areas of the Third World. The issue is more deeply rooted in our disappointing experience with arms control negotiations and agreements following our high expectations that were seemingly confirmed by the Nuclear Test Ban of 1963. The reality of that experience stands in sad contrast to the widespread confidence that arms control could regulate and moderate the military competition that disarmament, as embodied in the ill-fated Baruch Plan, had proved unable to stop.

The arms control concept that underlay the Nuclear Test Ban and subsequent negotiations and agreements was formulated most authoritatively by American economists and political analysts like Thomas Schelling in the early 1960s. According to this concept, arms control, unlike disarmament, functioned not to abolish or even to reduce arms, but rather to restrain and regulate competition for military power by making that competition, through mutual agreement, more stable and predictable; less provocative; safer for human health (a primary motive behind the atmospheric nuclear test ban); and less expensive. Moreover, effective arms control could make the actual use of arms more humane, less destructive, and more susceptible to political control. The theory was that properly conceived arms agreements would be a complement, not an alternative, to defense policy. Blended together, arms control and defense policy would be integral parts of national security policy.

In practice, although arms control has made some distinctive contributions, it has fallen far short of achieving most of its objectives. This is not only because of the obvious obstacles imposed by East-West tensions. In part, the disappointing results stem from inherent political and technical difficulties involved in trying to control arms competition by mutual agreement. Misconceptions about the relationship of arms control to defense policies, reflecting the tendency of arms control to become an end in itself, have also been a hindrance. This study notes two additional limitations on the efficacy of arms control in American practice: the institutional impediments and the lack of a coherent consensus on military strategy.

Nevertheless, although arms control negotiations and agreements have failed to meet all of the high expectations invested in them, even the most critical skeptics concede that arms control has become an enduring feature of international politics. In many countries the conspicuous pursuit of arms control is regarded as an indispensable concomitant of security policies, if only for domestic political reasons. The realities of international and domestic politics indicate that arms control—in one way or another, and for better or worse—will play a significant role on the international stage in the 1980s. It is important, therefore, that the current review of arms control theory and practice examine this role objectively and constructively.

To this end, the Washington Center of Foreign Policy Research (subsequently succeeded by the Foreign Policy Institute), a research arm of the Johns Hopkins School of Advanced International Studies, undertook to study how the relationship of arms control to defense policy may enhance U.S. security. Under the Center's auspices Richard Burt, then Washington diplomatic correspondent of *The New York Times*, conducted a series of seminars based on papers dealing with several aspects of postwar arms control experience. He organized the edited papers, along with his own analysis and synthesis in Chapter 1, to form this volume. We are particularly grateful to the Ford Foundation for giving us the grant that made the volume possible.

Robert E. Osgood
Director of Studies,
Johns Hopkins Foreign Policy Institute

1
Defense Policy and Arms Control: Defining the Problem

Richard Burt

Few concepts have gained greater allegiance from political elites around the world in the last two decades than arms control, or more specifically, formal diplomatic negotiations aimed at limiting military forces. It is curious, then, that after the two superpowers succeeded in achieving a second strategic arms limitation accord (SALT II), arms control seems to have fallen into disrepute. In national politics, negotiations and their outcomes have become the subject of intense controversy. In the analytical community, meanwhile, thinking about arms control suffers from an unmistakable malaise.

However, it is not really so difficult to explain this state of affairs. During the last decade, we have learned that negotiating for East-West arms control can be an exhausting and time-consuming process. Following the conclusion of the first SALT accords in 1972, it was widely assumed that a follow-on agreement would be obtained in a few years at most. Yet SALT II took nearly twice as long to negotiate as its predecessor. And SALT has obviously been the most successful arms control exercise to date. The Vienna force-reduction talks, the negotiations on a comprehensive test ban (CTB), and recent U.S.-Soviet attempts to regulate naval forces in the Indian Ocean and to control conventional arms transfers have made little or no progress.

But while some observers may be disappointed with the pace of arms control, others are distressed with its lack of impact on overall East-West relations. Ten years ago, SALT and other negotiating processes were viewed not only as instruments for controling military forces, but also as foundation blocks for building a "structure of peace" among the superpowers and their allies. Accordingly, SALT I was described as part of a wider process of U.S.-Soviet détente that promised to reduce competition in a number of arenas, including regional conflicts in the Third

World. Soviet actions during the 1973 war in the Middle East, Moscow's intervention in conflicts in Angola and the Horn of Africa, and, most recently, its invasion of Afghanistan have all but demolished the notion that arms control and détente are synonymous. Instead, the contentious idea that arms control is more necessary in times of superpower stress has risen to take its place.

U.S.-Soviet tensions clearly are responsible, in part, for the controversy that surrounds arms control. But thoughtful and substantive criticism is now being directed toward arms control itself. One reason that arms control is in crisis is that, as Raymond Aron recently pointed out, SALT and other negotiating enterprises have "accompanied and concealed" a tremendous expansion of Soviet military power during the last decade. For example, whatever SALT has achieved, it has not succeeded in stopping the Soviet Union in the last decade from deploying some 1,000 new land- and sea-based missile launchers or from increasing its number of deliverable warheads threefold. More important, there is now a consensus that regardless of SALT II, the Soviet Union has been able to acquire a sufficient number of accurate, high-yield warheads to threaten the bulk of U.S. land-based missiles. What this means for strategic stability, Moscow's risk-taking propensities, and U.S. political resolve is a matter of debate, but there can be little doubt that the creeping vulnerability of the *Minuteman* force will raise perplexing problems for defense planners during the next decade.

The growth of Soviet capabilities elsewhere will create other challenges for U.S. defense policy. In Europe, the continuing modernization of Warsaw Pact ground and air forces threatens to neutralize any gains in Western capabilities that may arise out of NATO's (the North Atlantic Treaty Organization's) long-term defense improvement program. A much more troubling development, however, is the growth—in size and quality—of the Soviet long- and short-range theater nuclear arsenal. Militarily, missile systems like the SS-20 and SS-21, and the Su-19 aircraft not only represent a substantial improvement in existing Soviet capabilities, but could also provide the Soviet Union, for the first time, with a credible capability to suppress the Alliance's in-theater escalation potential. The political implications of this development for the Alliance thus go beyond a simple concern about an "imbalance" in one category of forces and raise questions about the continued credibility of the U.S. "extended" deterrent.

The growth of Soviet naval and projection capabilities is a third area of concern. Although less impressive than Soviet advances in strategic and theater nuclear capabilities, Soviet advances in the ability to project power into distant areas may constitute the most troublesome military challenge during the next decade. Continuing conflict in the Middle East and Persian Gulf, Southern Africa, and Southeast Asia is likely and future Russian planners may find that Soviet gains in strategic and theater nuclear capabilities provide an "umbrella" from under which to conduct regional operations. New airlift and sealift capabilities, meanwhile, will provide the Soviet Union with the means to carry out these operations.

What is so striking is that existing arms control processes seem almost irrelevant to these emerging problems. It is even more disturbing, however, that arms control not only seems insensitive to a new class of military concerns, but may also reduce the ability of the United States and its allies to respond to these problems through unilateral military initiatives. For example, the 1972 SALT interim agreement on offensive missiles did little, if anything, to slow the Soviet Union down in attaining a capacity to threaten the *Minuteman* force through the deployment of the SS-18 and SS-19 intercontinental ballistic missile systems (ICBMs). Yet, for better or worse, the companion ABM (anti-ballistic missile) Treaty did foreclose a promising option for solving this problem: the deployment of hard-site ballistic missile defenses. Although both the Ford and the Carter administrations sought to curb the growth of Soviet ICBM capabilities in follow-on negotiations, the SALT II Treaty again fails to protect the *Minuteman* force from becoming vulnerable to preemptive attack.

As with the ABM Treaty, the SALT II accord seems to have already complicated unilateral U.S. efforts to come to grips with the problem by imposing constraints on the deployment of a mobile ICBM force. For a start, the Protocol attached to the treaty prohibits the deployment of mobile land-based launchers and air-to-surface ballistic missiles through 1981—a wholly theoretical constraint. A more practical constraint is the incompatibility of various mobile-missile basing modes with the verification requirements of the new treaty. The Carter administration ruled out the most secure (and least expensive) land-based mode—the multiple protective shelter or "shell game" system—on the ground that it would pose severe monitoring difficulties for future arms control regimes. Regardless of whether this assessment is correct, the administration initiated another approach to basing the new MX—the so-called "race track," a horizontal shelter system—that will be more costly, require more land, and is likely to arouse greater local opposition. All of these considerations could delay deployment of a survivable land-based missile or, possibly, cancel the systems altogether.

SALT's almost pernicious impact on *Minuteman* vulnerability is mirrored, in some respects, by its consequences for the changing nuclear balance in the European theater. As in the case of central strategic forces, the new treaty does little to arrest the growth of Soviet medium-range capabilities directed against Western Europe. In some ways, the accord actually seems to exacerbate the increasing problems confronting the Alliance in responding to the SS-20, the *Backfire* bomber, and other systems. Although the Carter administration insisted that the inclusion of sea- and ground-launched cruise missiles limitations in SALT II would not prejudice the ability of the United States to exploit such systems in theater nuclear roles after 1981, the political costs of protecting those systems from further limitation in any SALT III negotiation are likely to be high.

The mutual and balanced force reduction (MBFR) exercise in Vienna, meanwhile, is not only failing to help solve nuclear problems in Central Europe, but a negotiating outcome there could also conflict with Alliance efforts to stabilize the conventional balance in the region. The outcome that the West hopes to achieve in the negotiations—"parity" in man-power levels—seems increasingly irrelevant to the challenge of defending Central Europe from the type of "Blitzkrieg" that NATO confronts. Moreover, it is also possible that an MBFR agreement could hinder cur-rent efforts to improve NATO readiness and staying power, such as building up European reserves and augmenting U.S. reinforcements.

The negotiations on limiting Soviet and U.S. naval forces in the Indian Ocean and regional arms transfers were only underway for a short period of time before they were shelved by the Carter administration. Nevertheless, some of the same problems that beset SALT and MBFR talks surfaced again in these two negotiating enterprises. In areas around the Indian Ocean, greater regional conflict, together with the growing dependence of the West on oil from the Persian Gulf, have forged a strong argument for augmenting U.S. naval and air presence there. Yet an Indian Ocean accord that "stabilized" the presence of superpower navies in the region (and also neglected to control forces around the Indian Ocean littoral) would clearly hamper any serious U.S. effort to plan and prepare for contingencies in the region. The same is probably true of any accord controling arms transfers. The fall of the Shah of Iran demonstrated the limits to which U.S. arms sales can be used as a sur-rogate for American military power, but in an era when direct military intervention remains an unpopular option for projecting force, arms sales—as the Egyptian-Israeli peace process underscores—continue to be an especially important military and diplomatic instrument. When the United States lacks the interest and the ability to use surrogates in regional conflicts, agreements that limit U.S. access to local allies are likely to have particularly adverse consequences.

In sum, the problem with existing arms control exercises is not that they are merely failing to respond to the challenges to U.S. security that are likely to be dominating security planning in the 1980s. As we shall see below, it has been a mistake to believe that negotiations by themselves can cope with these problems. The bigger problem is that, in many instances, arms control seems increasingly to impede efforts to cope with these challenges through other means.

What Arms Control Can Do

It has now become commonplace for analysts and government officials to argue, as did Leslie H. Gelb, former director of the Bureau of Politico-Military Affairs, recently, that "as a result of specialization of narrow mandate, people all too often focus exclusively either on military programs or on arms control while losing sight of the other. Yet neither new forces nor arms control agreements are an end in itself. They are only means to an end, which is to ensure national security." But recognizing that a sort of analytical and bureaucratic "decoupling" between arms control and defense planning has occurred is only the first step toward finding a solution to the problem Gelb described. The second, more difficult step is to recognize that the conflicts and inconsistencies that plague arms control and defense planning flow, in the main, from misconceptions about what negotiations can accomplish. Thus, while it is now an article of faith that arms control cannot serve as a substitute for an adequate defense posture, U.S. negotiating strategy and conduct in many areas has assumed that this *is* the case. Indeed, some of the basic beliefs that underpin U.S. thinking about arms control seem to rule out the possibility of achieving greater compatibility between negotiating policy and military strategy.

The Functions of Arms Control

A central fallacy of the existing approach to arms control is the belief that the primary function of negotiations is to alleviate sources of military instability. Probably the most conspicuous aspect of the SALT enterprise is the absence of any shared consensus between the two sides over the role and utility of long-range nuclear weapons—in particular, the meaning of "strategic stability." And without such a consensus, negotiators have failed to work out solutions to such problems as ICBM vulnerability. In March 1977, for example, the Carter administration tabled a proposal that, from the U.S. perspective, would have restructured both sides' arsenals along more stable lines: the most threatening (and vulnerable) component of both sides' forces—land-based

ICBMs—would have been de-emphasized while each would have been free to build up its more secure sea-based and bomber forces.

Although some U.S. officials argued that Moscow's rejection of the so-called "comprehensive proposal" simply reflected a lack of imagination, there were sound strategic reasons for turning the American action down. For a start, given technological and geographical reasons, the idea of placing greater reliance on sea-launched ballistic missiles (SLBMs) and bombers undoubtedly appeared unattractive to Soviet planners. More important, from a doctrinal perspective, the Soviets probably viewed the growing vulnerability of U.S. ICBMs as a stabilizing rather than a dangerous development. What the March 1977 episode, along with the experience at MBFR, reveals is that lacking a consensus among negotiators over what "stability" constitutes, the most likely outcomes of arms control are agreements like the SALT II Treaty—accords that ratify rather than restructure prevailing trends in the military balance. This is surely why the Vienna talks have so far failed to produce an accord; while there are good reasons for the West to insist on manpower parity in the center region, the Soviet Union possesses equally strong incentives for maintaining its existing position of superiority.

The foregoing should not be interpreted to suggest that arms control outcomes do not have a military impact. Agreements, such as the 1972 ABM Treaty, can of course have a major impact on the plans of both sides. But, as in the case of the ABM Treaty, it is probably a mistake to view new agreements as part of a process of doctrinal convergence. The hypothesis that Moscow, by accepting severe restrictions on ABM deployment, agreed, in effect, to a system of "nuclear mutual vulnerability" must be judged against its continuing efforts in the area of air defenses, civil defense, antisubmarine warfare, and antisatellite systems. A much more plausible explanation for Moscow's decision to enter into the treaty is that with the U.S. *Safeguard* system ready to undergo deployment, the Soviet Union made a hardheaded decision to close off competition in ABMs. Again, the lesson is not that arms control outcomes reflect a narrowing of strategic beliefs, but that nations can sometimes reach agreement for very different reasons.

Arms Control and Military Change

A second fallacy that proceeds from the notion of arms control as a solution to defense problems is the idea that military programs that threaten existing negotiations somehow endanger deterrence. As suggested above, the most common result of arms control is not enhanced stability but the registration of reality; agreements are often controversial because, more than anything else, they spotlight military deficiencies. But when looking at the impact of military programs on arms control negotiations, there is a common tendency to confuse means and ends. Weapons that for one reason or another pose threats to existing negotiations are viewed as threatening stability when, in fact, the impact of their deployment might be just the opposite. An example is the U.S. cruise missile program. It is easy to understand why the cruise missile complicated efforts to complete the SALT II Treaty. The relatively small size of the missile posed challenges to verification, and its utility in both strategic and theater roles (armed with nuclear and conventional warheads) created daunting problems of categorization. The irony, of course, is that although cruise missiles posed a threat to SALT, their deployment in large numbers would be more likely to strengthen than to weaken deterrence. While cruise missiles are clearly second-strike strategic weapons, their ability to offer more durable basing modes at land and sea and their possible marriage to a new family of conventional munitions would certainly be desirable in theater roles. They might even raise the nuclear "threshold."

There can be little doubt that what some people refer to as the "qualitative arms race" can, at times, create military problems. New weapons technologies can increase first-strike incentives and produce such unwanted side effects as collateral damage. In the longer term, they can also force wrenching changes in prevailing patterns of military thought, as laser and charged-particle defensive systems might necessitate within a decade or more from now. At the same time, technological superiority continues to be an official goal of U.S. defense policy. Had the SALT process been underway in the early 1960s, the Soviet Union, together with many arms control proponents in the United States, would have probably maintained that the deployment of *Polaris* nuclear powered ballistic missile submarines (SSBNs) created verification difficulties and also represented another destabilizing round of the "qualitative arms race." SLBMs did represent a a new departure in military technology, but in an era of growing ICBM vulnerability, their deployment can hardly be viewed as anything but a beneficial development. If arms control is not a substitute for unilateral defense initiatives, then the political price of negotiating the fielding of new systems must be measured against the security benefits that will be gained from their deployment.

Disaggregating the Military Balance

The cruise missile case is also useful in highlighting the tendency of negotiations to distort, simplify, and most important, compartmentalize military reality. As the acronym implies, the SALT process uses as its central organizing principle the idea that there is a distinct class of U.S. and Soviet forces known as "strategic weapons." Although that description of the state of technology was generally accurate during the 1960s, a new class of more accurate and flexible systems, such as the cruise missile, is making the time-honored distinction between "strategic" and "general purpose" forces obsolete. Moreover, new munitions, such as fuel-air explosives and enhanced radiation weapons, are blurring distinctions between nuclear and conventional weapons.

As a result, the preoccupation of the SALT process with the "homeland-to-homeland" nuclear balance between the two superpowers has made it increasingly difficult to cope with weapons technologies that are relevant in both "central strategic" and regional military contingencies. SALT outcomes that limit these systems are unattractive because they foreclose options for upgrading theater defenses. At the same time, agreements that exclude these systems are equally unattractive, because, as the controversy over the *Backfire* at SALT II illustrated, neither side likes the idea of allowing the other to increase its intercontinental-range arsenal under the guise of expanding its theater forces. Because the United States has nuclear commitments to the defense of Western Europe, the notion of a "homeland-to-homeland" balance fostered by SALT has never been terribly attractive. During a period in which the systems limited by the process were not directly relevant to the defense of the theater, bilateral agreements were bearable. But in a period when it no longer is possible to compartmentalize the U.S.-Soviet strategic balance, new SALT agreements seem certain to challenge the military and political cohesion of the Western alliance.

If SALT points out the problems of trying to limit a functional category of arms, such as strategic weapons, the MBFR exercise underlines the dangers of geographical compartmentalization. Since the talks got underway in 1973, analysts have complained about the geographical asymmetries inherent in efforts to limit forces in an artificially bounded chunk of Central Europe. Some critics have worried, for example, that if any agreement covering U.S. and Soviet forces were reached, the United States would be forced to withdraw forces beyond the Atlantic while the Soviet Union would only have to move its forces back into the Western Military District. Most Western governments, however, have viewed this as an acceptable price to pay in order to achieve some semblance of manpower parity in the center region.

In a similar way, military reality was also distorted by the artificial geographical boundaries of the short-lived Indian Ocean negotiations. Discussing naval forces at sea without reference to shifting capabilities on land can probably only work against the West. For the foreseeable future, carrier-based aircraft will probably provide the only immediate air power that the United States will be able to bring to bear within the region. In the most critical areas on the Indian Ocean littoral and the Persian Gulf, Soviet land-based air could be decisive.

A more basic question is whether the attempt to freeze the existing naval balance at some rough level of "parity" is even a desirable goal in applying arms control to the Indian Ocean. In both SALT and MBFR, parity can be justified as a negotiating outcome, because both the United States and the Soviet Union possess roughly similar interests in guaranteeing their own security and that of their respective allies in Europe. However, the stakes for the two sides in the Indian Ocean, and more particularly the Persian Gulf and the Middle East, seem quite disparate. Although closer to the Soviet Union, the Gulf is far more important to the West. Arguably, then, the United States might need to maintain superior forces in the region.

It is also questionable whether equality is a desirable goal in approaching any negotiations on conventional arms transfers. As both political and military instruments, arms transfers confer influence in peacetime and, on occasion, leverage in time of conflict. Although the United States and the Soviet Union are commonly lumped together as the "two superpowers," they obviously differ in their ability to use military supply relationships to their own advantage. In such regions as Latin America, where the United States has long enjoyed greater access, the proposal for putting the superpowers on equal footing as regards arms sales seems to make particularly little sense.

The Bureaucratic Factor

Although the fallacies outlined above primarily stem from a conceptual tendency to make arms control an end in itself, they have been strongly reinforced by bureaucratic behavior. For example, while few analysts believe that the U.S.-Soviet balance in central strategic forces should be viewed in isolation from other aspects of the East-West military balance, it is almost inevitable that officials deeply immersed in the day-to-day complexities of SALT have paid little attention to the wider implications of negotiating outcomes. Thus, until European governments began to anxiously question the implications for Alliance security of cruise missile constraints at SALT, the Carter administration had not seriously considered how the negotiating process had begun to "spill over" into the realm of theater nuclear forces. Similarly, the administration was also late in recognizing the psychological and military problems posed for Europe by the SS-20—probably because the weapon had not emerged as a factor in either SALT or MBFR.

The tendency to seek parity in negotiations, even when parity might be an inappropriate goal, can also be explained in bureaucratic terms because diplomats are naturally attracted to proposals that appear equitable; that is, proposals that have a chance of being accepted. Finally, it is also understandable that officials responsible for arms control have a natural aversion to new weapons technologies—particularly to systems that appear to threaten central organizing concepts, such as the cruise missile at SALT, or pose verification problems, like the MX. Whatever case can be made for such weapons on strategic grounds, they make negotiations more difficult and, in the minds of negotiators, this is a much weightier consideration.

These factors help explain why, in a bureaucratic sense, the establishment of an arms control process is in some ways more important than whether the process produces an agreement. To begin with, the creation of an arms control process allows new participants to shape policy in the area under discussion. In the absence of arms control, decisions over military posture and weapons development and deployment are dominated by the Defense Department, with the armed services possessing a large voice in most matters. But once a "defense problem" is transformed into an "arms control issue," questions like the future of U.S. naval forces in the Indian Ocean also become the concern of the State Department and the ACDA. Indeed, both the State Department and ACDA have a vested interest in proliferating arms control negotiations, if only to maximize their impact on defense policy.

Just as there are strong bureaucratic incentives to begin negotiations, there are also payoffs to be gained from continuing them. Some years back, political scientists noted that in major weapons system procurement programs, military organizations often lost sight of the original military rationale for new systems and that "getting the job done" became the measure of bureaucratic success. Thus, even though the supersonic B-70 bomber was obsolete compared to Soviet high-altitude surface-to-air missiles (SAMSs) by the time it was ready for deployment, the organizational and personal stakes involved in the B-70 program made it almost impossible to turn the program off. In such a way, it was argued, developing inertia to weapons procurement was difficult to resist. By the same token, there has also been a bureaucratic inertia with regard to arms control when the goal of achieving agreement has supplanted an earlier strategic objective. A basic rationale plunging into the MBFR exercise in the early 1970s, for example, was to dampen enthusiasm in the Senate for unilateral withdrawal of U.S. troops from Europe. That rationale has ceased to exist, but the MBFR dynamic continues.

These factors are useful in explaining why arms control can sometimes become a bureaucratic end in itself, but they do not shed much light on how negotiations become decoupled from defense planning in the first place. At the heart of the matter are deep-seated differences of view over such basic questions as the utility of military force, the severity of the Soviet military threat, and the nature of U.S.-Soviet arms competition. On one end of the spectrum, there are those who argue that military force is of declining relevance in the post–Cold War era, that the Soviet Union is beset with all sorts of domestic problems and new foreign threats, such as China, and that the arms race is essentially a mechanistic game of "monkey-see, monkey-do." On the other end of the spectrum, observers argue that the utility of force has not declined, but the willingness of the United States to use force has been diminished. The Soviet Union is depicted as a stronger, increasingly more assertive power and the arms race is said, in fact, not to be a race at all, but a much more complex phenomenon in which both sides are running at different speeds and for different reasons. There is no way that government can resolve these differences, but what is surprising is how the structure of the national security establishment seems to widen them. Not only are arms control and defense planning functions currently fragmented throughout the government, but the nature of the interagency process seems more designed to create differences than to reach consensus.

In part, the existence of the ACDA is responsible for this state of affairs. Having no responsibility for either threat assessment or force planning, but possessing strong vested interests in negotiations, ACDA has little reason to get involved in the difficult trade-offs between arms control and unilateral military flexibility. This was not always the case. When it was created in 1961, the agency was seen as an instrument for bringing arms control issues to the attention of the national security establishment. But ACDA may have become a victim of its own success, or more precisely, the success of arms control. As arms control has moved from being a diplomatic experiment to a central fixture of U.S. foreign policy, ACDA's role has been displaced by arms control units within the Pentagon, the State Department, and the National Security Council. In order to justify its existence, therefore, the agency has had to become ever more doctrinaire in its adherence to the primacy of arms control. This not only has created unnecessary bureaucratic frictions, but has also, in many cases, curiously reduced the influence of the agency. The innovation of arms control impact statements has further accelerated the agency's estrangement from the defense planning community, because the process actually encourages the agency to adopt a different perspective on weapons issues than the Defense Department. The fact that ACDA and the Defense Department report to different committees on Capitol Hill and possess different congressional constituencies only serves to deepen this split.

In the Pentagon itself, other divisions are at work. It is no coincidence (as the Soviets are fond of saying) that the rise of arms control as a central policy objective accompanied the expansion of civilian control in the Pentagon. The so-called "McNamara Revolution" of the 1960s not only brought managerial reforms to defense management, but also a new sympathy for negotiated military restraint. Understandably, the military services viewed arms control as part of a larger threat to their traditional prerogatives. And they were correct in doing so. By framing military issues as arms control problems, civilian-dominated organizations, such as the Office of International Security Affairs, were able to gain considerable influence at the expense of the Joint Chiefs of Staff. Thus, like ACDA in the wider interagency process, the armed services, along with the Joint Chiefs, were gradually pushed to adopt extreme positions on arms control. As in the budgetary process, their views gradually lost credibility and they came to be seen as obstacles to agreement. In the process, the professional military has inevitably come to view arms control as a threat rather than an opportunity.

Finding a New Balance

The central argument of this chapter has been that arms control and defense planning are out of kilter largely because misunderstandings about what can be achieved in negotiations have been reinforced by bureaucratic behavior. There are some ways that these problems might be solved.

Scaling Down Ambitions

The central reality of arms control is that only rarely do negotiated outcomes address pressing military concerns. To reiterate, arms control is primarily useful for registering and codifying an existing balance of forces. This can be a useful outcome. At SALT, the belief that U.S. and Soviet strategic forces are roughly equivalent (at least in size) is probably critical to the maintenance of détente, however tenuous. In the same way, an MBFR agreement that provided for equal manpower ceilings (assuming the use of a mutually acceptable data base) would also create a condition of "optical parity" that would surely enhance political confidence in both Eastern and Western Europe. Moreover, arms control agreements can create a degree of predictability that is useful both politically and militarily. In criticizing arms control, it is easy to lose sight of the uncertainty that plagued political leaders and military planners during the first half of the 1960s. In the early part of the decade the tendency to exaggerate Soviet strategic programs led the United States to rush ahead with programs that by 1965 seemed unnecessary. However, American overreaction in the early 1960s probably fostered a tendency in the latter half of the decade to underestimate Soviet strategic ambitions, an even more dangerous development. Whatever else SALT II does, it will enable political and military authorities to agree on the character of the strategic environment in the mid-1980s.

But "optical parity" and predictability are not the same things as the maintenance of deterrence. In strategic forces, the maintenance of credible deterrence requires the deployment of U.S. land-based systems in a more survivable basing mode and, more controversial, an enhanced ability to threaten hard targets in the Soviet Union. In the European theater, deterrence also requires more survivable nuclear forces. It is possible that many options for bolstering deterrence in these areas could complicate future arms control efforts. There is no obvious solution to this dilemma. Some observers, despite the lessons of SALT II, seem interested in shaping a new set of grandiose goals for a new round of negotiations. In the view of this writer, that would be a major mistake. Asking too much from SALT III not only runs the risk of raising expectations that will surely be disappointed, but also places a national security burden on SALT that it cannot bear.

If there is a solution, it probably lies in asking arms control to do less instead of more. Thus, at SALT III, the United States should not seek severe quantitative reductions or tighter qualitative constraints. An accord that would provide both sides with some flexibility for dealing unilaterally with their separately perceived military problems might not only be more negotiable but also, probably, more conducive to overall stability. Scaling down ambitions for arms control will not totally eliminate the very real tensions between efforts to achieve "optical parity" at SALT and unilateral efforts to strengthen deterrence. But the first step toward wisdom in this area is to recognize that such tensions exist.

Using Arms Control to Bolster Deterrence

While negotiations alone are unlikely to produce solutions to military problems, arms control, in conjunction with U.S. defense initiatives, can offer some promising approaches to coping with new Soviet challenges. Probably the strongest military argument that can be made for SALT II is that by putting a ceiling on Soviet missile warheads, the agreement could potentially enhance the survivability of the MX (if the ceiling were extended beyond 1985). Without a limit on warhead fractionation, the argument goes, the Soviet Union could counter any deceptive basing system for a mobile missile by massively expanding its warhead inventory. There may be other ways that arms control outcomes could work synergistically with unilateral defense decisions. For example, a SALT III limitation on Soviet air defenses, particularly around hard targets, would ensure the continuing effectiveness of cruise missiles. At the same time, it would probably be a mistake to allow U.S. forces to become overly dependent on arms control constraints accepted by the Soviet Union. Although Moscow has agreed to warhead fractionation limits at SALT, the MX will not undergo deployment until after the treaty is due to run out. Thus, as SALT negotiations continue, the Soviets could either refuse to agree to further limits on fractionation or, more likely, exact a steep price in concessions elsewhere and demand major concessions in other areas as a price for enabling the United States to proceed with the MX.

The main way in which defense programs and arms control can interact positively is by enhancing U.S. negotiating leverage. As the ABM case suggests, weapons programs can provide incentives for the Soviet Union to consider negotiating outcomes that do more than simply ratify prevailing strategic trends. It has been suggested, for example, that Carter's MX decision could force the Soviet Union, for the first time, to think seriously about the merit of severe constraints on MIRVed (multiple independently targetable reentry vehicles) ICBMs. Yet, "bargaining chip" negotiating strategies must be approached with caution. In the ABM case, the United States possessed a system that was technologically vastly superior to what Moscow had and, equally important, its deployment lay right around the corner. These conditions are absent in the MX case. First, with the MX only now undergoing full-scale development, it is unrealistic to expect the system to provide the U.S. side with much negotiating leverage in the immediate future. Second, the system's hard-target capability will not be qualitatively different than Soviet systems undergoing deployment at the same time. Thus, it is probably unrealistic to expect that the Soviet Union would react to the threat of MX deployment by agreeing to a scheme for de-emphasizing land-based ICBMs. It would be a much more painful response to the MX if the Soviet Union were to find a more survivable basing mode for its own ICBMs.

Political problems also can arise from the inappropriate use of "bargaining chips." This is perhaps most clearly illustrated in the current effort by NATO to agree on a plan for modernizing long-range theater nuclear forces. Because of the sensitivity of nuclear deployment issues in various European states, governments are attracted to the idea of coupling an Alliance decision to proceed with the deployment of a new, long-range system with an arms control offer to the East. While this strategy might allow the Alliance to overcome domestic opposition in West Germany and Holland to modernizing U.S. nuclear forces in Central Europe, in the longer run, it could backfire. The problem is that it is hard to see why, at this stage, Moscow would be interested in any arms control proposal aimed at limiting long-range theater forces. Just as the MX, with an initial operating capability (IOC) of 1986, is unlikely to arrest Moscow's current deployment of the SS-18, an extended-range *Pershing*, with an IOC in the early 1980s, is unlikely to coerce Moscow into dismantling its existing SS-20s. At most, if the Alliance proceeds with the deployment of several hundred medium-range systems during the next few years, it is conceivable that Moscow would accept some upper limits on the size of its long-range theater forces. But even this outcome may not be possible. By hoping (and in some cases, pretending) that there is a negotiating solution to the SS-20 problem, when in all reality there is not, the Alliance runs the risk of being criticized for using arms control as a "fig leaf" to justify new military programs.

Refocusing, Restructuring, and Stopping
Arms Control

While it has become conventional wisdom that arms control considerations should be taken into account in shaping defense policy and programs, it is interesting that so little thought is given to how existing negotiations should be adapted to changing the military realities. Although a second SALT treaty has finally been completed, the principal problems that dragged out the talks, such as verification, Soviet ICBM preponderance, and the "gray area" weapons, loom as even bigger obstacles in SALT III. Thus, even if the United States entered the negotiations with fairly modest goals, SALT III could quickly become bogged down. In such circumstances, it would seem worth exploring whether a more piecemeal approach to SALT III—one that attempts to address one issue at a time—makes more sense than seeking a more "comprehensive" arrangement that tries to deal with several issues simultaneously. In a more sequential approach to SALT III, negotiators might first grapple with theater nuclear concerns, such as the status of cruise missiles, in the Protocol, while deferring discussion on "deep cuts" in central forces to a later phase of the talks.

It might also be profitable to change existing approaches at MBFR. Given the character of the Warsaw Pact threat, arms control outcomes that constrain the use, rather than the size, of military forces in Central Europe would be very useful. This, of course, is the essential function of "confidence building measures" ("associated measures" in MBFR parlance). Negotiated limits on force deployment and maneuver have only recently come under serious study, but if associated measures do offer a real possibility of complicating Soviet surprise attack options while enhancing tactical warning, then this is an avenue worth pursuing in Vienna.

In the future, MBFR may not be the best place to negotiate arms control in Europe. The French proposal for an arms control forum reaching "from the Atlantic to the Urals" makes far more strategic sense than continuing to do business in Vienna, especially if equipment limits, instead of manpower or confidence-building measures, are going to be the focus for negotiations.

The possibility of revising existing arms control arrangements to bring them more into line with emerging military realities should not be overlooked. Revision of the ABM Treaty to facilitate the deployment of hard-site missile defenses is an especially interesting option. So far, it has received little serious consideration out of a fear that tampering with the 1972 treaty could lead to an unraveling of the entire agreement. But the deployment of hard-site defenses might not only enhance the survivability of multiple-launch point ICBM basing systems; it also might even rule out the need for deceptive basing modes altogether by giving fixed silos a new lease on life.

Finally, while some negotiations might be usefully rechanneled and replaced, others should probably be abandoned for good. Controling American and Soviet naval deployments in the Indian Ocean, for example, is an effete idea. Not only is the concept of a "naval balance" in the region analytically unsound, but the goal of the negotiations—to freeze U.S. and Soviet naval forces at their existing levels—is most likely incompatible with growing U.S. security concerns in the region. At the very time that the region is taking on greater importance to the West, the Iranian revolution, radical currents in Arab politics, and local suspicions have made naval forces probably the only reliable way for the United States to project power into the area. When the United States has finally sorted out what it needs to be able to do in the region and has implemented these steps, then it might be useful to take another look at arms control.

Shaking Up the Bureaucracy

From the standpoint of organization structure and process, the goal of harnessing arms control to defense planning is hindered in two ways.

First, parochialism in negotiating perspectives makes it almost impossible to come up with any comprehensive strategy for arms control. Second, bureaucratic frictions and disconnections often make it difficult to mesh negotiating objectives with defense planning goals. In other words, means need to be found for increasing communication among arms controllers and between arms controllers and defense planners.

To begin with, ways must be found to minimize the bureaucratic polarization between arms controllers and defense planners. In retrospect, the creation of the ACDA may have been a mistake. By its very existence and role in the interagency process, the agency reinforces the idea that negotiations offer an alternative path to international security. Although it would be counter productive at this point to attempt to disband the agency or to incorporate it into the State Department, some marginal changes could bring the agency back into the mainstream of the policy process. For symbolic reasons, it is probably wise to insist that directors of the agency be civilians, but perhaps ACDA's charter could be amended to require that the deputy director be a serving military officer. Such a change might work two ways: it would bring an operational military perspective to senior levels of the agency and it would also give military officers a deeper insight into arms control.

Indeed, one of the most conspicuous failures of the present system is its failure to elicit and profit from high-level military participation. In striking contrast to the Soviet pattern, U.S. arms control has become a mostly civilian enterprise, viewed with suspicion and sometimes open hostility by the military services. This is the fault of both uniformed officers and their civilian counterparts. Rather than concerning itself with the broad policy implications of negotiations, the military establishment is overly preoccupied with how arms control will affect specific hardware programs. Yet, the parochial concerns of the military are often justified by the way arms controllers use negotiations to gain leverage over military force planning and weapons decisions. There is no easy solution to this problem, but it is clear that the Joint Chiefs of Staff and senior elements of the armed services must be given a larger role in arms control planning and the negotiations themselves. This not only means giving the armed services a larger advisory capacity, but greater responsibility in the actual conduct of negotiations as well. Greater military responsibility for arms control would foster greater harmony between defense and arms control objectives and negotiating outcomes that might win greater support within the military establishment.

The role of the State Department also needs to be examined. Even more than ACDA, the proliferating number of new negotiations has worked to enhance the influence of the State Department on defense questions. This has led to a significant expansion in the number of State Department officials focusing on military problems, particularly in the Bureau of Politico-Military Affairs. There has always been a notorious shortage of skilled defense professionals within the foreign service, so an increased competence within the State Department in this area is a healthy development. But the role of the department and, in particular, the Bureau of Politico-Military Affairs, should be kept in perspective. In the 1960s, there was legitimate concern that the Pentagon's Office of International Security Affairs was becoming a "little State Department." Now the State Department's Bureau of Politico-Military Affairs seems to be evolving into a "little Defense Department." The bureau does have an important role to play in assessing the political implications of proposed defense policies and programs. But it risks compromising this function by becoming a competitive center for defense analysis.

While some of these steps might help to break down a few of the barriers that have grown up within the bureaucracy, the tendency to compartmentalize different aspects of the arms control process will remain a serious problem. Conceptually, it is appealing to think about formulating a comprehensive arms control strategy that will be aimed at ensuring that negotiating goals in different settings remain coherent and compatible. But even if it were possible to formulate such a strategy, it would probably be too vague to be of much use. Instead of a "grand design" for arms control, it would be much more useful to institute a continuous system of monitoring existing negotiating processes. The system would examine a number of important questions: the relevance of existing U.S. arms control goals to changing military circumstances; the effect of various negotiating outcomes on planned and future American forces; the implications of negotiating outcomes for other arms control efforts; and finally, apparent changes in Soviet arms control policy. Of course, all of these questions are randomly examined in different parts of the government. But a high-level security planning office, perhaps situated in the National Security Council, that could centralize and coordinate the monitoring process might be able to produce new and far more useful variants of the Arms Control Impact Statement: not analyses of the narrow impact of new weapons on negotiations, but studies of the impact of arms control on American security.

Rediscovering Defense Policy

It is too easy to blame the defense policy dilemmas now confronting the United States on an unblinking enthusiasm for arms control alone. In fact, one reason that arms control has become such a dominant factor in national security planning is that in many areas, negotiations have proceeded in a defense policy vacuum. Arms control, in other words, has often become a surrogate to thinking about defense problems. It is easy to see why this has happened. Unlike before, today there is no general doctrine, such as "containment," around which to organize defense policy. Nor do military planners have the luxury of strategic superiority with which to avoid difficult choices. Instead, in an era of unprecedented Soviet military growth, the United States, still recovering from the shock of Vietnam, is profoundly uncertain over the meaning of the Soviet buildup and how to respond to it. Arms control, by promising to cope with the Soviet challenge while also restraining the United States from making an unnecessary military response, has seemed to offer an opportunity to escape from a divisive and enervating debate over defense policy.

But if the thesis of this chapter is correct—that arms control, in the final analysis, is mostly useful in only defining military problems—then negotiations cannot be used as a crutch. For arms control to play a useful role, U.S. goals in such areas as strategic doctrine, theater nuclear and conventional forces, as well as maritime and projection capabilities, must be outlined with far greater precision than they have been before.

One of the most difficult issues that must be addressed is the impact of growing Soviet strategic counterforce capabilities on the credibility of deterrence in the 1980s. While the so-called "Schlesinger Doctrine" of flexible strategic options aroused intense controversy a few years ago, today it is an accepted part of U.S. nuclear strategy. But beyond this, it has become difficult to discuss, in concrete terms, what the prevailing U.S. strategy for nuclear targeting is. For example, how far down the road will the Carter administration's concept of a "countervailing strategy" take the United States in matching the Soviet Union's warfighting approach to strategic deployment and employment? In the MX decision and other actions, such as recognizing the contribution that civil defense can make to strategic stability, the Carter administration seemed to toy with what could become a radical shift in deterrence strategy. But so far, the far-reaching implications of any such a shift have escaped real debate.

The relationship between strategic balance and U.S. deterrence doctrine for European security is another area which has escaped close scrutiny in recent years. What special demands does the requirement of "extended" deterrence place on strategic force design? The answer to this question may be important to the future of theater forces. In an era of strategic parity, it is questionable whether theater forces can any longer be considered as escalatory instruments. Escalation control and battle management obviously become more attractive, and these goals should thus be weighed heavily in decisions on the sizing and design of theater forces. At present, the NATO Alliance is still caught up in difficult and complex consultations over the deployment of a few hundred long-range systems that would be able to reach the Soviet homeland. While immensely important, the long-range tactical nuclear forces (TNF) issue should not be allowed to obscure the fact that the Alliance confronts a Soviet program for modernizing theater nuclear forces across the board. Again, lacking any overall consensus on the role of theater nuclear forces, if an effort is made to take a comprehensive look at the adequacy of NATO's existing posture—examining such controversial issues as whether "combined" nuclear and conventional options are now necessary to maintain deterrence—the most important implications of the Soviet actions are likely to be missed.

Basic issues could also be ignored in the area of conventional forces. The Alliance is engaged on a long-term defense improvement program, but that effort is proceeding with minimum discussion over NATO strategy. Although suggestions for radically transforming the Alliance along the lines suggested by Steven Canby and other critics are in many cases politically unfeasible, it is clear that NATO's existing adherence to linear and firepower-dominated concepts of defense need to be reexamined.

Finally, despite years of analysis, the great debate over whether sea control or projection should take precedence in naval force design is still unresolved. Although the growth of Soviet maritime power has made the sea control mission seem a more pressing requirement than ever before, resource constraints, the concurrent growth in Soviet projection capabilities, and political instability in the Southern Hemisphere have also made "strategic access" an equally important concern. The problem of course, is that even if these doctrinal issues are resolved, some basic force structure questions will have to be addressed, such as the familiar question of whether large-ship, small-fleet navies are more desirable than small-ship, large-fleet ones. In the area of projection, meanwhile, other problems need to be addressed, particularly whether the most important contingencies in the Persian Gulf and elsewhere are likely to be ones in which small, rapidly deployed forces will be decisive or whether larger, more slowly available forces with greater staying power will be crucial.

At present, these questions are being resolved on an expedient, piecemeal basis. Unless more coherent, long-term plans linking military purposes and force structure and sizing are adopted, arms control inevitably will be forced to take on a burden it is unsuited to bear. In the end, national security, along with arms control, will suffer.

2
Banning Nuclear Testing

Peter C. Hughes
William Schneider, Jr.

Introduction

Like many presidents before him, early in his administration Jimmy Carter expressed the hope of achieving a total cessation of nuclear weapons testing as a prelude to eliminating nuclear weapons altogether. Thus, despite, major disagreements within the U.S. government,[1] and without a formal position on what would constitute acceptable terms, in 1977 the United States revived the Geneva-based multilateral Comprehensive Nuclear Test Ban Treaty (CTBT) negotiations, with the United States, the Soviet Union, and Great Britain participating.[2] Serious differences among the participants in Geneva and equally ardent differences among members of the U.S. defense and arms control community concerning procedures for facilitating the detection, identification, location, and verification of unauthorized nuclear tests proved to be primary stumbling blocks in the negotiations. The election of Margaret Thatcher as prime minister in Britain in 1979 resulted in a more autonomous, activist, and critical posture in the negotiations than that espoused by her predecessor. These factors in conjunction with the 1980 presidential elections and along with the controversy that would have surrounded any comprehensive nuclear test ban treaty ruled out an agreement during the Carter administration. Nonetheless, the debate concerning the merits of a CTBT for U.S. national security interests persists in technical circles and remains a policy issue for the U.S. government in the 1980s.

The U.S. negotiating posture itself sheds light on what is fact and what is opinion in the debate. To preserve the option of resuming nuclear testing in the event of a significant problem in the U.S. nuclear weapons stockpile, the Carter administration proposed an agreement of only three- to five-year's duration. The administration also planned to announce upon the signing of any treaty the intent to resume nuclear weapons testing upon the expiration of that treaty unless studies showed that test resumption was not required. To broaden support for its efforts, the administration also proposed that any treaty extension would require Senate ratification. Further, in an effort to keep the U.S. nuclear weapons scientific community occupied and up to date in case of a Soviet breakout, the administration proposed that nuclear experiments, possibly with yields of up to 100 pounds, would be permitted under the CTBT. Additionally, the U.S. scientific community would be asked to study and assess the impact of any treaty on national defense capabilities and requirements, and to determine whether the United States should continue with the terms of a new CTBT negotiated when the existing agreement expired or return to the conditions of the pre-CTBT environment or accept some modified form of a CTBT agreement. Recognizing that no distinction could be made between nuclear experiments for peaceful purposes versus experiments for military purposes, the administration also insisted that a CTBT contain a moratorium on all PNEs, or peaceful nuclear explosions. Verification procedures were to include an international seismic data exchange, and the deployment of national seismic stations (NSS) on the territories of the participating nations. The NSS would transmit in real-time continuous and authenticated data, and, as proposed, would include safeguards oriented toward minimizing tampering and interference with the information flow. Under the U.S. proposal, on-site inspection (OSI) procedures would be negotiated, but non-mandatory. Areas outside of the regions where the NSS would be located would have suitable low-conductivity media (e.g., salt cavities) that could provide sufficient decoupling for low-yield devices (under three kilotons of nuclear yield) to assure that the Soviets could maintain an undetectable nuclear test program. The only high-confidence means of assuring compliance would be to have the right to make on-site radio-chemical inspections where a detonation is suspected. Such a compliance verification scheme would necessarily cover the entire United States and the Soviet Union. This represents a degree of intrusive inspection for which the Soviets have little enthusiasm.

Given the complexity and technical nature of the subject matter, it would not be surprising if the CTBT negotiations failed to generate the public attention that other arms control talks, particularly SALT, have. Yet, within the narrow community of nuclear weapons specialists, few issues generate such strident controversy. Advocates of a CTBT view it as perhaps the most imporant, substantive, and symbolic of all arms control acts. It represents, in the words of Isaiah, the opportunity to beat swords into plowshares, and spears into pruning hooks—it embodies the hope of returning the nuclear genie to its bottle. Underlying the advocacy by many CTBT proponents are critical and controversial assumptions concerning the role and purpose of U.S. nuclear weapons in the contemporary geopolitical environment, with profound implications for U.S. national security policies and alliance relationships. These issues, while often obfuscated, can be recognized in the debate that has divided the defense and arms control communities over a CTBT.

The rationale underlying the Carter administration's decision in 1976 to pursue a limited duration, three- to five-year CTBT has been documented in various public forums, including congressional hearings. In March 1978, in hearings before the House Armed Services Committee, a primary objective attributed to CTBT by administration witnesses was the positive effects such an agreement would have on the nuclear Non-Proliferation Treaty (NPT). According to Admiral Thomas Davis (Ret.) of the ACDA:

> The contributions of a comprehensive test ban to non-proliferation are major. . . . By applying equally to nuclear weapons states and non-nuclear weapons states, it would not have the discriminatory aspects of the Non-Proliferation Treaty that are to some extent responsible for important states not joining. . . . While it cannot be guaranteed that important potential proliferators will become parties, public statements . . . indicate a good likelihood that India will join, and we consider it likely that others will join also.[3]

Testifying in August 1978 before the House Armed Services Committee, Davis also contended that a major benefit accruing from a CTBT would be the constraints imposed on the modernization of Soviet strategic nuclear forces. He stated: "It is widely recognized that the United States currently enjoys an advantage over the Soviet Union in nuclear weapons design. A mutual cessation would essentially freeze nuclear weapons technology at current levels, and would, therefore, preserve the advantage."[4]

Also testifying in August 1978, Leslie Gelb, then director of the State Department's Bureau of Politico-Military Affairs, stated that a CTBT in conjunction with "future successes in SALT" would be central to containing the "U.S.-Soviet nuclear competition." Moreover, addressing a fundamental issue raised by CTBT critics, Mr. Gelb observed that although concerns regarding adequate verification existed:

> The common characteristic with all these agreements (such as SALT and a CTBT) we have negotiated (or are negotiating) is that they are not dependent upon any attempt to bring about an unrealistic level of trust between

the United States and the Soviet Union. These agreements are all based on
the simple fact that we and the Soviets on occasion recognize the com-
monality of interests in restraining the nuclear arms race in a careful, step-
by-step manner.

Equally important, the provisions of these treaties can be adequately
verified by effective national technical means, means which we already
possess. The treaties have in effect followed the pace of technical advance-
ment.[5]

If these assertions were not in dispute, opposition to a CTBT would be
significantly less pronounced. But as this chapter hopes to underscore,
the merits of a CTBT involve questions of judgment—judgment about
the opportunities and risks a CTBT would entail.

The denigration of risk, and assertion of benefit, made by CTBT proponents is at the heart of the controversy. Critics have been unable to
identify any high-payoff benefits that could accrue to acquiescence in the
terms of a CTBT; yet they assert that a proposed accord would involve a
considerable catalog of costs and risks. While some of the issues are, as
Leslie Gelb acknowledged in his testimony before the House Committee
on Armed Services, a matter of judgment, many of the issues are simply
technical controversies that, too often, have been addressed in a conclu-
sionary rather than analytic manner.

Questions relating to the benefits of a CTBT, particularly the consequences of such an agreement for non-proliferation objectives and its effect on the U.S.-Soviet arms competition, rely heavily on judgmental
factors since little empirical evidence is available to support or refute
competing arguments. However, a more reliable body of evidence exists
with respect to the effects of a CTBT regime on the current and projected
U.S. nuclear weapons inventory. From this body of evidence, it is hoped
that conclusions can be drawn about the consequences of a CTBT regime
for the U.S. national security posture.[6]

CTBT and Non-Proliferation

As discussed above, a primary argument for seeking a CTBT is that it
would build new support for the 1968 Nuclear Non-Proliferation
Treaty—in other words, that nations not already possessing nuclear
weapons would become signatories to the NPT and hence would be less
likely to acquire such weapons. It is suggested that some would-be
nuclear nations, such as India, Argentina, and Brazil, have refused to
sign the NPT because it is discriminatory, requiring non-nuclear
weapons states to forswear nuclear weapons while U.S. and Soviet

weapons stockpiles continue to grow and improve. The failure of the nuclear weapons states to fulfill their obligations under Article VI of the NPT—"to pursue negotiations in good faith on effective measures relating to cessation of the nuclear arms race at an early date and to nuclear disarmament"—is cited as another reason why some non-nuclear states refuse to accept the NPT.

But would a CTBT of limited duration, with the option to resume nuclear weapons testing, be likely to have much impact on any nation's decision to become a signatory to the NPT? Might it, in fact, have an adverse impact, particularly if the CTBT participants were to resume nucelar weapons testing? The answers to these questions are unclear, but it is clear that not all of the discriminatory aspects of the NPT would be removed if a limited number of nations signed a CTBT. The nuclear superpowers would still retain their nuclear weapons, and that is precisely what non-nuclear nations claim is discriminatory. Moreover, other nations possessing nuclear weapons, such as China and France, have made it clear that they will have no part of a CTBT. France is concerned about the growing conventional and theater nuclear capabilities of the Soviet Union and the Warsaw Pact on the European continent as well as a shift in the U.S.-Soviet strategic balance that has threatened the credibility of the U.S. nuclear umbrella over Europe. China, meanwhile, sees its position in no less ambiguous terms than France. It fears Soviet "hegemonism" and doubts that the United States has the determination and will to counter Soviet activism. In any event, as China seeks to become a major industrial power, it is likely to improve its military posture and pursue the capability to support national interests that will become increasingly global in scale.

At the same time, less ambitious or less developed nations are also more likely to be influenced by the external threats they perceive, and, in particular, local and regional power balances, than by the "weight of world opinion" on the acquisition of nuclear weapons. A global *tour d'horizon* indicates that some 30 nations could be capable of detonating a nuclear device in a period of 1 to 10 years after the decision is made. Many of these nations, particularly in the Middle East, exist in particularly precarious political and military environments. South Africa sees itself increasingly isolated internationally. South Korea has been reminded (ironically, by the Carter administration) that it probably cannot rely indefinitely on U.S. protection. Pakistan now not only sees a threat from its neighbor, India, but also faces a Soviet-occupied neighbor in Afghanistan. Pakistan, in fact, has still declined to ratify not only the Non-Proliferation Treaty but also the limited (nuclear) Test Ban Treaty of 1963. In Latin America, Soviet military presence is increasing, and

Cuban involvement in Third World affairs is becoming more open and aggressive. Brazil, outside the full force of the Latin American nuclear-free zone, has not signed the Non-Proliferation Treaty, and sees little reason to do so.

Speaking of the effects of a CTBT on U.S. nuclear non-proliferation objectives, Dr. Fred Charles Ikle, the former director of the ACDA, observed:

> A great many nations are now or soon will be able to build nuclear bombs. Yet, only a few countries have done so. The primary reason for this abstention is the confidence these countries have in existing security arrangements. . . . Which countries have been rumored in the last few years to have developed their own nuclear weapons? It is largely the countries that are outside an alliance system, or that feel insecure about our military guarantees. . . . If a nuclear test ban conveyed a one-sided military disadvantage on the United States, some nations now depending on our guarantees might actually move toward a nuclear capability of their own.[7]

While the effects of a CTBT on the Non-Proliferation Treaty might be debatable, there is little doubt that a treaty would not affect the spread of the technical capability to make nuclear weapons, or prevent countries from acquiring such weapons. As noted in testimony by the then Acting Assistant Secretary of Energy for Defense Programs in the Department of Energy, Dr. Donald Kerr, in 1978:

> CTBT has no direct effect on the proliferation of nuclear weapons. Testing is not essential for designing and building the simple first generation fission devices that a would-be proliferator is likely to want at the beginning of a nuclear weapons program. He needs only the special nuclear material and the knowledge and skills to assemble the device to be highly confident that it will work. . . . Most if not all of the nations which have built nuclear explosives detonated them on the first try. From this technical standpoint it is my opinion that what a proliferator would be sacrificing by signing a CTBT would be, essentially, whatever "prestige" or warning value he might see in carrying out a public explosion. He would not be depriving himself of the capability to develop nuclear weapons should he see them as essential to his national security or military ambitions.[8]

To the extent that signatories to a CTBT and/or the NPT were driven to the covert acquisition of nuclear weapons, there could indeed be a lack of "warning"—or deterrent—value, as mentioned by Dr. Kerr. Under such circumstances a CTBT could then, in fact, undermine rather than enhance the stability of local and regional power balances if it led to miscalculation on the part of would-be adversaries.

The Issue of Stockpile Reliability

While critics of a CTBT view its political objectives as exaggerated, and even poorly conceived and ill-defined, more central to the debate is the question of the impact such an agreement would have on U.S. military capabilities, and the evolving character of the U.S.-Soviet strategic balance. The issue in this debate centers on whether nuclear tests are necessary to retain confidence in the reliability of nuclear weapons.

Nuclear weapons are fabricated from chemically-active materials that deteriorate in unexpected and unpredictable ways. Proponents of a CTBT argue that so-called "proof-testing," conducting nuclear tests to check the nuclear weapons stockpile and to identify and/or correct problems, is not part of the present U.S. nuclear weapons maintenance program, and that, consequently, a ban on nuclear testing would have no impact on nuclear weapons reliability. In recent congressional testimony, nuclear weapons experts for the Department of Energy and the Defense Nuclear Agency did acknowledge that "proof-testing" had been rare. But they also stated that the philosophy and policy for U.S. nuclear weapons stockpile maintenance has been to incorporate stockpile reliability tests into the ongoing development test program: an extensive stockpile sampling program is undertaken and questions or problems that arise from this program are resolved by adding experiments to already planned tests. Donald Kerr, in 1978, said:

> The fact that we rarely conduct proof tests—that is, specific individual tests of a weapon pulled from the stockpile—is sometimes cited as evidence that testing is not necessary to maintain confidence in the reliability of the stockpile. This claim is false. We use the continuing testing program to confirm the design choices made in stockpile weapons; we reuse the tested technology of weapons in the stockpile in designing new weapons systems; if we encounter a stockpile problem, we may "proof" test its solution by adding an experiment to a test that is part of the continuing program. In effect, "proof" testing is built into the very philosophy on which our program is based.[9]

With a complete test ban, neither proof tests nor development tests would be permitted; therefore, the longer the period without testing, the greater the likelihood of a problem arising due to the unexpected and unpredictable aging process. Left uncorrected, aging problems can result not only in the loss of the reliability of a single warhead, but the complete malfunction of a large number of nuclear warheads, as reportedly happened during the U.S.-Soviet test ban moratorium of 1958–1961.

When one recognizes that there are four basic launch vehicles, the *Minuteman* II and III ICBMs, and the *Poseidon* and *Polaris* SLBMs, the consequences if even only one weapon design was to fail are evident. Congressional testimony indicates that there have been about 40 nuclear tests conducted with nuclear weapons within the stockpile, of which some 12 in the last 30 years were required "to make various weapons work, to make them safe to manufacture or handle, or to correct problems due to the aging of nuclear components."[10] If there were no nuclear tests, then confidence in the reliability of U.S. nuclear weapons would decrease, and their deterrence value *vis-à-vis* potential adversaries (particularly the Soviet Union) would be diminished. This, in turn, could lead to declining confidence in the U.S. nuclear umbrella for U.S. allies (not least for NATO). The same situation would apply to U.S. theater nuclear forces, the importance of which has increased with the growth of Soviet systems in Europe. The loss of confidence could occur for two reasons: on one level, if problems were detected, but could not be fixed without testing, and on another level, if the allies were to fear that some problems might not be detected without testing.

If U.S. strategic nuclear capabilities were superior, the failure in one strategic weapons system would not have the significance that it does today, when Soviet strategic capabilities have begun to exceed those of the United States. Now the United States finds itself in the position of having to respond to a broad spectrum of Soviet initiatives. Without the ability to conduct nuclear testing, the United States would, then, essentially be unable to adapt existing, or to introduce new, weapons designs to the stockpile, and U.S. strategic and theater nuclear force modernization programs for the 1980s would thus be impeded. Programs that could be affected by a CTBT include, among others, the maneuverable reentry vehicle (MARV), the *Trident* II SLBM, the advanced supersonic air-launched missile (ASALM), possibly the MX ICBM, and future warhead retrofits for the *Poseidon, Trident* I, and the MMIII missiles. Future theater nuclear force modernization programs that could also be affected include cruise missiles and any medium-range ballistic missile (MRBM). Naval plans for a nuclear-armed *Harpoon*, and tactical missile systems generally, would be affected, as would nuclear vulnerability-survivability tests for U.S. and allied military forces.[11]

There are numerous motives to introduce new nuclear weapons into the stockpile beyond the need to accommodate new nuclear delivery systems such as advanced cruise or ballistic missiles. One important objective of nuclear weapon design is to improve the safety with which the weapons can be handled and stored. One important innovation in recent years has been the development of an insensitive high-explosive that is resistant to the thermal and mechanical stress that would cause more energetic and sensitive high-explosives to detonate. This is particularly important in theater nuclear weapons, where the tactical environment of fire and high-velocity fragments could cause a nuclear weapon to detonate accidentally. Under some circumstances, significant design changes would be required as insensitive high-explosives have only two-thirds the chemical energy of conventional explosives. These design changes require that the weapon be tested.

In many cases, major design changes are necessary to reduce the ability of unauthorized personnel to tamper with a nuclear weapon. This will induce a requirement for testing the weapon to assure that any modification to selected nuclear weapon components has not degraded weapon performance or reliability. Safety and security modifications do not alter the performance characteristics of the weapon, but they do reduce the risk of accidental or unauthorized detonation. Such modifications are clearly in the public interest, but they may be precluded in important cases by a CTBT.

For more than a decade, U.S. policy has attempted, as an arms control measure, to limit the production of special nuclear material (SNM) appropriate for nuclear weapons, although the Soviets have not yet reciprocated. In the face of mounting requirements for more numerous (though generally of lesser explosive energy) weapons for the strategic and theater forces, a considerable strain has been placed on the policy of limiting SNM production. It has been feasible to renounce this policy only because (1) the retirement of older weapons has allowed the SNM contained in them to be recovered for use in new weapon production, and (2) new designs have used SNM more efficiently. Adoption of new SNM-efficient designs would also be precluded by a CTBT since such designs require testing. If a CTBT were an operative constraint, then older SNM-inefficient designs would have to be used, inducing a shortage of such materials. According to Department of Energy testimony:

A shortage of SNM could restrict the deployment of some delivery systems below otherwise optimum numbers. These possible consequences could create concerns of first rank which would require difficult and extensive compensatory deployments, or could produce significant reductions to our deterrent capabilities. . . . Not all yields could be provided and specific configurations could require major delivery system changes.[12]

The remanufacture of older designs has problems of its own. To meet planned weapon production levels, the United States would have to abandon its policy of abstention from SNM production. Even if adequate inventories were available, remanufacture is more difficult than many suspect. Nuclear weapons are mechanically, electrically, and chemically complex devices. Their manufacture employs exotic materials in a highly toxic environment (e.g., gold corrodes in the interior of a nuclear weapon). Weapon components are machined to extremely close tolerances using special "one-of-a-kind" techniques in their manufacture. Most of the weapons currently in the U.S. inventory were manufactured prior to the promulgation of Federal safety and environmental regulations contained in the Occupational Safety and Health Act (OSHA) and several statutes administered by the Environmental Protection Agency (EPA). Remanufacture of existing weapons would require an exemption from those statutes. Even if an exemption were obtained, remanufacture would be extremely costly because many of the materials and processes used to manufacture weapons in the 1950s and 1960s are no longer commercially available, and it would be necessary to start a low-volume production line.

Inevitably, some "shortcuts" would have to be taken simply to remanufacture older weapons if the United States were unable to develop and test new ones. The knowledge about what can be used during the manufacturing process as substitutes for unavailable materials or processes is in the hands of only a few dozen senior scientists and engineers in the nuclear weapons complex. This knowledge reflects more than three decades of "hands-on" experience with the development and testing process for nuclear weapons. In an environment where testing is prohibited, it would be unfeasible to replenish this critical cadre. This situation led the Department of Energy to state, in a letter to Chairman Melvin Price of the House Committee on the Armed Services:"Design experts from the DOE laboratories believe that current and planned U.S. nuclear weapons cannot be indefinitely maintained or remanufactured without nuclear tests."[13]

The Problem Of Asymmetry

Were a CTBT to affect both the United States and the Soviets equally, then it could have a positive impact on the strategic nuclear balance. Indeed, this is an underlying objective, briefly alluded to in the introduction, of many CTBT proponents. However, a CTBT that permitted no nuclear testing would probably not be verifiable, and the ability to test below the threshold level of verification would permit the Soviets both to maintain confidence in the reliability of existing weapons, and, possibly, develop and adapt new warhead designs for their weapons systems. Asked bluntly in congressional testimony whether it would be possible for the Soviets to maintain stockpile reliability under a nuclear test ban agreement permitting no nuclear testing, in other words, "could [the Soviets] test at levels that would be sufficient to maintain the reliability of their stockpile, but which could elude U.S. national technical means of verification," Admiral R. R. Monroe, the director of the Defense Nuclear Agency, responded in 1978: "Yes, I believe it would be possible for the Soviet Union to maintain stockpile reliability under a CTBT. . . . it should be possible for the Soviet Union to accomplish, undetected, any nuclear testing that might be required to maintain the reliability of their stockpile."[14]

In the same vein, commenting on whether the United States could adequately verify Soviet compliance with a complete nuclear test ban, William J. Perry, the Defense Department's Under Secretary of Defense for Research and Engineering in his FY 1979 report wrote:

> Current political initiatives toward a complete ban on nuclear testing have focused attention on a number of deficiencies in test identification and yield verification capability which do not appear capable of solutions in the near term. Two of the more critical problems are the wide uncertainty in current seismic yields and the limited ability to discriminate between earthquakes and underground explosions in the low kiloton energy range.[15]

The level of Soviet nuclear testing that could escape U.S. national technical means of verification is widely cited as being in the 5- to 10-kiloton range. As presented in a 1978 House Armed Services Committee Report:

> In order to retain the capability, including the scientific expertise, to continue to certify the reliability of U.S. nuclear weapons, and to obtain information with respect to weapons effects and survivability, it will be necessary to continue weapons testing at yields between 5 and 10 kilotons. Yields within that range are close to the threshold below which the probability of verifying—that is, proving—whether a detected seismic event was a clandestine nuclear test.[16]

In congressional testimony, however, witnesses from the government's technical and defense community asserted that the Soviet Union could conduct tests of higher yield than 5 to 10 kilotons, "with every expectation that these would either evade detection entirely or leave the United States unable to prove whether an 'ambiguous event' was a test or an earthquake," particularly were the Soviets to conduct their nuclear tests in seismically active areas. The result of such tests, as Dr. Robert R. Fossum, the director of the Defense Advanced Research Projects Agency, explained, would be that "we would expect to record a number measured in several score natural events each year, earthquakes, which we would not be able to say with assurance were not [nuclear test] explosions. And if we did detect an explosion, it would be mixed in among that [earthquake] population. So from a seismic standpoint, you are faced with a difficult problem of trying to pick one of those events and claim a violation."[17] So-called decoupling tests, tests conducted in large, underground cavities that existed or could be created in nondetectable fashion, would reduce the signal that is emitted from an explosion.

The magnitude of the problem of detecting, identifying, locating, and verifying a nuclear test is significant, particularly when it is noted that every year there are some 100,000 seismic events worldwide at magnitude 3, 10,000 at magnitude 4, and 1,000 at magnitude 5 (magnitude 4 and 5 corresponding to 5- to 10-kiloton nuclear tests in alluvium). As explained by Mr. Seymour Schwiller, a staff member to the House Armed Services Committee, "we may detect up to 100,000 events annually. If it turns out that only two or three per year are important clandestine tests, and we can't prove they are tests, not earthquakes, we are in deep trouble."[18] Thus, even if the United States could deploy substantially more seismic detector stations on Soviet territory than the Soviets would permit (the U.S. scientific community has recommended about 30), experts estimate that some 20 to 100 explosions (i.e., annual seismic events, equal to a 5-kiloton explosion, or higher, if masked) could still take place without being identified. For the United States to abrogate a CTBT, it would need to prove a clearly discernable Soviet violation, affecting the supreme national interest. Yet, given the uncertainties associated with determining violations, the United States is more likely to protest or express concern with little, if any, substantive consequence. Because of the ambiguities surrounding CTBT verification, an environment of greater mistrust could develop. Such mistrust would adversely affect wider aspects of U.S.-Soviet relations.

The notion that a CTBT would have an asymmetrical effect on Soviet and U.S. nuclear weapons can also be applied to the characteristics of the weapons themselves. The United States has emphasized technically sophisticated solutions to nuclear weapons design because U.S. missiles are of significantly less payload than their Soviet counterpart. Operating under severe volumetric and weight limitations, the U.S. nuclear weapons design establishment has been forced to adopt designs that have a smaller margin for degradation than would be the case if the United States could enjoy the same luxurious volumetric and weight limitations as the Soviet designers. Hence, if both sides complied fully under a CTBT, U.S. weapons would more likely suffer from environmental degradation than their Soviet counterparts. This could lead to an asymmetric loss of confidence in the reliability of U.S. weapons, undermining deterrence.[19]

The Scientific Infrastructure

How would a CTBT affect what Admiral Thomas Davis called the Soviet Union's "superior infrastructure of nuclear manufacturing and testing personnel"? It would probably be easier for a closed, authoritarian society, such as the Soviet Union, to retain the infrastructure and expertise for nuclear weapons development than an open society where scientists would be likely attracted to more challenging positions in industry. Certainly the Soviet abrogation of the 1958–1961 test moratorium both took the United States by surprise and found it unprepared. Moreover, given the significant lead-time required for test preparation (six to eight months for a typical U.S. test), it was clear that the Soviets, who conducted approximately 20 tests during the first month following their "break out" of the constraints of the moratorium, had been preparing for the tests well in advance. In the first two years after 1961, the Soviets conducted more tests above one megaton (300 megatons in total) than the United States had in its entire history. As a result, the United States lost its nuclear technology lead, with American experts differing only over whether the Soviets had achieved parity or had actually moved ahead.

Thus, while it is unlikely that we will learn much in detail about the Soviet state-of-the-art in nuclear weapons design, it should be noted that our technological advantage in delivery systems design—including associated developments such as precision guidance, small, light-weight propulsion systems, and high energy-density fuels—is dependent upon an advanced nuclear weapons design complex. The introduction of the advanced cruise missile would not have been feasible if the nuclear weapons complex had been unable to provide a nuclear warhead with a yield-to-weight ratio sufficient to enable the cruise missile to deliver a payload of sufficient yield to destroy its target. If the United States is to retain its technological lead (as an alternative to the proliferation of less capable systems in larger numbers), it must retain a nuclear weapons design and production effort compatible with such an objective. This cannot be done in the absence of testing.

Thus, it is questionable whether, in fact, a CTBT—even in conjunction with a SALT II Treaty—would curb Soviet weapons expansion. Not only does the United States have the experience of the 1958–1961 test ban moratorium, but also that of SALT I. In retrospect, it is evident that whatever political benefits the SALT I agreements may have entailed, the agreements did not put a "cap on the arms race." Indeed, as noted by the chairman of the Joint Chiefs of Staff, General David C. Jones, the "greater increase" in Soviet military capability "has occurred since the signing of SALT I, and we don't see evidence of slackening effort on their part."[20] Moreover, as the CIA recently argued:

> A SALT II agreement along the lines currently being envisioned would not in itself significantly alter [the CIA] projection of Soviet defense spending. Such an agreement would probably reduce the rate of growth of total Soviet defense spending by only about 0.2 of a percentage point per year. The resulting savings would amount to less than 1.5 percent of total defense spending projected through the early 1980s in the absence of an agreement.[21]

Thus, under a CTBT, even with SALT II constraints, a concerted Soviet defense effort is likely to continue, and possibly be directed into new channels. Moreover, given the existing asymmetries in the U.S.-Soviet force structure—not least in the area of strategic weapons—and differences in policies and military doctrines underlying the employment plans for these weapons, the deterrence and stability that the United States has been seeking by restraining its weapons deployment programs and arms control policies has not been reciprocated by the Soviets. The question facing the United States, then, is no longer how to avoid initiatives that might continue or accelerate the arms competition, but how to interpret and respond to a wide range of potential Soviet initiatives.

Conclusions

Cutting through the maze of arguments, several factual technical observations can be made:

First, nuclear weapons testing is necessary for the United States to retain confidence in the reliability of its nuclear weapons stockpile, and to adapt or develop new nuclear weapons systems.

Second, a three-year CTBT, as proposed by the Carter administration, might or might not affect the U.S. nuclear weapons stockpile, but reliability problems could develop at any time and might or might not be detected if testing is not permitted.

Third, the longer a test ban continues, the greater the uncertainty about the reliability of U.S. nuclear weapons.

Fourth, even with the proposed verification safeguards, clandestine Soviet testing would be possible. Accepting the proposed CTBT would, therefore, mean accepting some risk.

Fifth, clandestine Soviet nuclear testing would have military consequences that could affect U.S. national security objectives, including the credibility of the strategic nuclear deterrent and theater nuclear forces.

Sixth, a CTBT would have only minimal effect on the proliferation of nuclear weapons technology to other nations.

Given these conclusions, it is clear that the proposed CTBT is not consistent with the basic tenets of arms control policy as an element of U.S. national security policy, defined to mean that an arms control agreement should be equitable, verifiable, contribute to strategic stability, and preclude a break-out threat. The benefits of a CTBT would essentially be political—to add momentum to the Non-Proliferation Treaty with the hope that such an agreement would reduce the risk of nuclear spread—and symbolic—as a gesture toward reducing or eliminating nuclear weapons. With respect to the former objective, as the preceding discussion has illustrated, there is no *prima facie* evidence to support this hope, and it can be suggested that a resumption of nuclear testing by the superpowers would be harmful to non-proliferation. More importantly, ill-conceived and improperly defined arms control agreements can themselves serve as catalysts to instability and conflict. The inherent danger of a CTBT is that, as the reliability of the U.S. nuclear forces declines, precisely those forces we seek to contain could be set in motion. This danger can be illustrated by returning to a question introduced at the outset of this discussion.

Some proponents of a CTBT believe such an agreement would not significantly impact U.S. nuclear weapons capabilities, yet other proponents advocate the CTBT for precisely that reason; in other words, as a result of a CTBT, new nuclear weapons would be unavailable and confidence would be lost in the reliability of existing ones. In essence, the latter proponents want to "denuclearize" U.S. national security policy. While the merits of strategic nuclear deterrence might be debated, it is clear that strategic nuclear weapons have acted to inhibit any major conflicts, and have served as tools with diplomatic, political, and military leverage. Some proponents of a CTBT hope that the resultant lack of confidence in the reliability of nuclear weapons could reduce the risk of the first use of such weapons. But to the extent that the United States would unilaterally lose confidence in the reliability of its own nuclear weapons, the balance of forces would also be affected, with adverse consequences for U.S. foreign policy and national security interests. Moreover, to the extent that the credibility of the U.S. security umbrella is undermined, it could erode allied and Third World confidence and cause more nuclear weapons proliferation. Moreover, "extended" deterrence has always been an element of U.S. national security policy. Indeed, the threat of using nuclear weapons to defend Western Europe, even in response to a conventional threat, has been both an implicit and explicit component of U.S. policy. This policy is particularly critical in the face of Soviet theater nuclear advantages and the existing U.S.-Soviet strategic balance that already has raised questions about the credibility of the U.S. "nuclear umbrella" over Western Europe.

Meaningful arms control has often proven elusive. More often, imprudent arms control agreements have undermined the stability they sought to achieve. To avoid this inherent risk of the arms control process, arms control must remain but one element of U.S. national security policy, tied to the nation's defense requirements and linked to its verification capabilities. In this context, U.S. ratification of the 1974 Threshold Test Ban Treaty would represent a more gradual, but consistent, step in the arms control process. Similarly, test ban efforts must remain integrally related to other U.S. arms control efforts, and in particular, the strategic arms control process.

Finally, while technology is often viewed as the source of modern man's most severe problems, that is so only if we fail to remain its master and, instead, become its slave. When properly exploited and developed, technology—even in the field of weaponry—can and should contribute to deterrence and stability. As the Bible says, Adam, once tempted to eat the forbidden fruit, could not undo his act. So is the dilemma of modern man. Like Prometheus, twentieth-century man may have to learn that fire, once possessed, can no longer be returned to the gods. This recognition can lead to its proper development and control.

Notes

1. For a discussion see: Richard Burt, "President Overrides Advisors," *International Herald Tribune*, 27 May 1978; and Robin L. Beard, "The Proposed Comprehensive Test Ban Treaty: Issues and Controversies," *Congressional Record*, pp. E 1960–1961.

2. Richard Burt, "U.S. Aides Split on Atom Test Ban," *New York Times*, 21 April 1978, p. 42. Also Rowland Evans and Robert Novak, "Test Ban: Bypassing the Chiefs," 26 May 1978; "Return of the Hawk," 12 June 1978; and "Test Ban Policy: Dealing the Pentagon Out," 20 April 1978 (all from the *Washington Post*).

3. See the House Armed Services Committee Hearings of 15 and 16 March 1978, "Current Negotiations on the Comprehensive Test Ban Treaty," p. 3. (Hereafter only referred to by title.)

4. See the House Armed Services Committee Hearings of 14 and 15 August 1978, "Effects of a Comprehensive Test Ban Treaty on United States National Security Interests," p. 132. (Hereafter only referred to by title.)

5. Ibid., p. 110.

6. A discussion can be found in the House Armed Services Committee Report of 13 October 1978, accompanying the Hearings: "Effects of a Comprehensive Test Ban on United States National Security Interests." See also Donald G. Brennan, "A Comprehensive Test Ban: Everybody or Nobody," *International Security*, Spring, 1976, vol. 1, no. 1, pp. 92–117; and Donald R. Westervelt, "Candor, Compromise, and the Comprehensive Test Ban," *Strategic Review*, Fall, 1977, vol. 5, no. 4, pp. 33–44.

7. "Effects of a Comprehensive Test Ban Treaty on United States National Security Interests," pp. 136–137.

8. Ibid., pp. 8–9.

9. Ibid., p. 29.

10. Ibid.

11. Ibid., p. 21.

12. "Current Negotiations on the Comprehensive Test Ban Treaty," p. 96.

13. Ibid., p. 95.

14. Ibid., p. 59.

15. The Honorable William J. Perry, The FY 1979 Department of Defense Program for Research, Development, and Acquisition, 1978, pp. viii–39/40.

16. Report accompanying "Effects of a Comprehensive Test Ban Treaty on United States National Security," p. 9. See also the Beard statement referred to in note 1. Beard points out that nuclear testing in the three to ten kiloton range is verifiable, and that despite efforts to classify the fact it is a matter of public record. A useful document to review contains the hearings published by the Joint Committee on Atomic Energy entitled: "Status of Current Technology to Identify Seismic Events as Natural as Man Made," 27–28 October 1971.

17. "Current Negotiations on the Comprehensive Test Ban Treaty," p. 45.

18. "Current Negotiations on the Comprehensive Test Ban Treaty," p. 72.

19. "Effects of a Comprehensive Test Ban Treaty on United States National Security Interests," p. 36.

20. For a more detailed discussion see: Peter Hughes, "SALT and the Emerging Strategic Threat," *Air Force Magazine*, March 1979, p. 49.

21. Ibid., pp. 51–52.

3
Force Reductions and Security in Europe

Robert A. Gessert

In late 1980, the seventh anniversary of the start of formal negotiations between NATO and the Warsaw Pact on "Mutual Reduction of Forces and Armaments and Associated Measures in Central Europe" (which opened in Vienna on 30 October 1973) presented little cause for commemoration or celebration. In fact, a year or more before, there seemed to be an emerging consensus among more serious students and advocates of arms control that these negotiations—commonly called mutual and balanced force reduction (MBFR) talks in the West—had all but ground to a halt and offered little hope of contributing "to a more stable relationship and to the strengthening of peace and security in Europe," which is their formal goal. But the Soviet invasion of Afghanistan in December 1979 put the whole issue of MBFR—along with other aspects of détente—into almost total disarray.

This chapter, first, briefly reviews the background of the Vienna talks; second, examines the main developments of the talks; third, assesses present and future alternatives to MBFR from a Western point of view; and finally, presents some reflections on the general relation of arms control and military policy and planning from this perspective. The question that haunts this whole discussion is "Is MBFR an idea whose time has gone?"

The Early Attempts

If one had to identify a single post–World War II decade that has shaped all thinking about arms control and military policy and planning in general and the West's approach to MBFR in particular, it would be hard to select a better decade than that of 10 November 1958 through 5 November 1968. That decade opened with the Surprise Attack Conference (SAC) between East and West (10 November to 7 December) and closed with the election of Richard Nixon to the U.S. presidency. From an arms control perspective, this decade could not unappreciatively be designated the William C. Foster decade, since he headed the U.S. delegation to SAC in 1958 and the U.S. Arms Control and Disarmament Agency (ACDA) from its beginning in 1961 to the end of the Johnson administration.

As Robin Ranger has pointed out in a recent essay on MBFR, the SAC could especially be taken as the starting point for the West's approach to arms control—as a means toward security in Europe. Ranger noted that the West viewed SAC as "a meeting of experts to discuss technical/military problems in respect of systems of observations and inspection designed to reduce the danger of surprise attack," while the Soviet Union had "sought discussion of a selection of political proposals, for the most part not susceptible of technical assessment." The West's proposals—shaped by luminaries such as George Kistiakowsky, Jerome C. Wiesner, and Albert Wohlstetter as well as William Foster— amounted to a "complex series of what would now be called confidence-building measures (CBM), providing mutual reassurance that neither side was planning a surprise attack, concentrating on measures affecting strategic delivery systems (because of the Gaither Committee Report of 1957) but including: 'concentration of ground forces or their logistic support; increases of transport capabilities, the movement of missiles or other warhead delivery vehicles; changes in scale and scope of maneuvers; increases of personnel.'"[1]

The decade that opened with the failure of the SAC of 1958 did include the negotiation of such multilateral agreements as the Antarctic Treaty of 1959, the Limited Test Ban Treaty of 1963, the Outer Space Treaty of 1967, the Treaty Prohibiting Nuclear Weapons in Latin America of 1967, and the Nuclear Non-Proliferation Treaty of 1968. It also saw the opening in 1961 of the continuing forum in Geneva of the Eighteen Nation Disarmament Committee, later to become in 1969 the Conference of the Committee on Disarmament and now, simply the 40-member Committee on Disarmament.

Of more immediate concern, this seminal decade also encompassed in 1967–1968 a flurry of activity within NATO to propose a discussion with the Warsaw Pact of mutual force reductions in Europe. NATO had ended 1967 with the adoption of the long-awaited Harmel Report on "The Future Tasks of the Alliance" with its focus on the two themes of détente and defense. The year 1967 had also marked the completion of the move of NATO headquarters from Paris to Brussels, the separation of French forces from participation in the integrated military command structure, and the adoption of MC (Military Committee) 14/3 on the "Overall Strategic Concept for the Defense of the NATO Area." NATO's call, at the end of its ministers' meeting in Reykjavik in June 1968, for initiation of a "process leading to mutual force reductions" was, of course temporarily derailed by the entry of five Soviet divisions into Czechoslovakia in August of that year.

The decade, 1958–1968, was seminal for post–World War II arms control theory as well as practice. Indeed, one could make a not unconvincing case that we have been living ever since on the intellectual capital generated in that period. During this decade, a virtual consensus emerged over the idea that arms control and military policy and planning were two sides of the same national security coin. This was, perhaps, best exemplified in the writings of Thomas Schelling. His writings, at least as much as any other's, led to the classical formulation that—in the more recent and skeptical words of Christoph Bertram—"the traditional objectives of East–West arms control have been three: to reduce the likelihood of war by increasing stability; to reduce the damage of war if war does break out; and to reduce the economic cost of preparing for war."[2]

This classical formulation of the objectives of arms control probably enabled as well as reflected the intellectual activity and near consensus of the 1958–1968 decade. The first two objectives were clearly objectives of the West's military policy and planning. Under the influence of Defense Secretary Robert McNamara, the third objective also became an objective of military policy and planning. This convergence of arms control and military objectives doubtless lent arms control a certain realism and "respectability" in defense circles and kept it from becoming the preserve of idealists, antimilitarists, and "disarmers." On the other hand, it may have contributed to the present sense of malaise by apparently "papering over" real conflicts that have always existed among idealists and realists; the divergence of public expectations and actual accomplishment; complex and divergent interests among allied partners to any negotiation; and the dichotomy between the West's "technical/military" approach to arms control and the East's "political" approach.

The first serious treatment of MBFR within NATO circles in 1967–1968 is symptomatic of this malaise and the conflicts of interests, complexities of motivations and goals, and divergence of approaches that appeared to be covered over by arms control theory.

By 1967 many studies had been conducted to analyze the prospects for and political-military implications of various arms control measures for the European environment. The U.S. Army's former "think tank," the Research Analysis Corporation (RAC), for example, had examined U.S.

and Soviet versions of general and complete disarmament (GCD) applied
to Central Europe, different types of disengagement (a persistent Soviet
proposal), varieties of Rapacki and Gomulka proposals for a nuclear-free
or a nuclear-freeze zone, and even radically asymmetric types of proposals that included placing infrastructure limitations on Soviet buildup
capability in the Warsaw Pact area combined with force reductions. Virtually none of these and other such studies held out any significant hope
of achieving reductions in the likelihood of war, in the damage that
would result from war, or in the cost of preparation for war. In fact,
many such studies concluded that most force reduction measures that
seemed susceptible to negotiation with the Warsaw Pact would likely
worsen NATO's security in Central Europe rather than improve it; they
might also increase U.S. costs—especially of preparing for war—by requiring extensive dual basing of equipment, greater lift capacity, and
costly maintenance of strategic reserves in the continental United States
(CONUS). If nothing else, the desirability of mutual force reductions
from Central Europe always foundered on the geographic asymmetry of
the two alliance structures. U.S. and Canadian forces "reduced"—that is,
removed—from Europe would have to recross 3,000 miles of ocean in the
event of a buildup crisis or war, while Soviet forces would have to
traverse only several hundred miles of interior lines of communication.

Despite such almost universally gloomy predictions about the putative
security benefits of MBFR in Central Europe, the NATO allies—led by
Britain and West Germany—began pressing in 1967 not only to formulate a NATO position on MBFR, but also to propose discussion and/or
negotiations with the Warsaw pact. The reasons for this were clearly
political rather than military. The predominant motivation—
acceded to by Washington, although it dragged its feet—was to forestall
further pressure from the U.S. Congress (especially the Senate) to reduce
U.S. forces stationed in Europe as expressed in the Mansfield Resolu-
tions. The Johnson administration bowed to this pressure partly because
it feared unilateral U.S. withdrawals could lead to more substantial
reductions by the European allies and to a general unravelling of
NATO's conventional force structure.

In 1968, another "compelling" reason that NATO formulated and proposed approaches to MBFR for NATO-Warsaw pact discussions and
negotiation was to counter mounting pressure from the Eastern bloc to
call a European security conference (ESC). The idea was that an ESC
might diminish if not dismantle the post–World War II alliance structures, confirm and legitimize the Soviet Union's hegemony in Eastern
Europe, recognize the more-or-less permanent division of Germany, and
significantly reduce the role of the United States in Western Europe. The

Western allies were more or less united in opposing such an ESC at that time, unless they could extract significant concessions from the Soviet Union indicating its willingness to withdraw a portion of its forces from East Germany, Hungary, and Poland. This was especially important to West Germany, whose embryonic *Ostpolitik* was beginning to take shape under the Grand Coalition of Chancellor Kiesinger and Foreign Minister Brandt. The invasion of Czechoslovakia on 20–21 August 1968 brought further immediate consideration of either MBFR or the ESC to an abrupt halt.

Other motivations besides the transitory political ones gave some impetus to the 1967–1968 MBFR discussions and deliberations within NATO. A momentum for arms control had been building, and the argument was made that it is better to discuss than to fight. An initiative to reduce the dangers in the confrontation of ground forces was thoroughly consistent with the Harmel Report's emphasis on détente as well as defense. Multilateral, inter-alliance discussions on MBFR would at least "test the water" with the other side. Many who argued this way felt that small initial steps were better than large schemes to reduce forces substantially or to alter or establish parity in forces. Some favored concentrating on those force elements on either side that gave the other greatest cause for alarm, such as Warsaw Pact tanks and NATO strike aircraft. Others argued for even more modest but confidence-building measures such as advance notification of large-scale troop maneuvers and exchange of observers.

Despite the setback of Czechoslovakia, Richard Nixon's accession to the presidency in January 1969 opened, in his words, "an era of negotiation" with the Soviet Union. Virtually simultaneously with the formal opening in Vienna in April 1970 of negotiations between the U.S. and the USSR on strategic arms limitations, the NATO allies again stepped up pressure to develop a common position on MBFR and to look toward reproposing discussions with the Warsaw Pact. New studies were ordered within and on contract to the U.S. government (including NSSM-92) to assess the political and military implications of MBFR and to determine the best approach that would contribute to stability and security in Europe.

It should surprise no one that the outcome of the 1970 studies was little different from that of studies conducted between, say, 1962 and 1968. Little stability or security benefit for the West could be found in withdrawing U.S. forces by 3,000 ocean miles compared to withdrawing Soviet forces by 500 to 600 interior miles. Similarly, no security benefit would appear to accrue to the West from reducing effective West German forces in the same proportion as far less effective East German forces. Only if the West could induce the East to accept significantly asymmetric force reductions did there seem to be any hope of finding a direct security benefit to MBFR.

Nonetheless, domestic pressures continued in the United States and in other allied states to reduce the security burden in Europe, and MBFR seemed to respond to and to counter such pressures. Also, Eastern pressure to call an ESC had mounted during the "era of negotiation" and seemed to have found a more responsive chord in the new SPD (Social Democratic Party) government in West Germany under Willy Brandt's leadership and his new *Ostpolitik*. With very little consensus on the best approach to MBFR, the geographic area to be covered, the types of forces to be included, or the method of reduction, NATO again issued a "Declaration on Mutual and Balanced Force Reductions" at its ministerial meeting in Rome in May 1970 and requested Italy to transmit this Declaration to "all interested governments." The Warsaw Pact responded quickly in June 1970, stating that reduction of "foreign troops in Europe" might be discussed in a special organ to be created by an ESC.[3]

Bonn's *Ostpolitik* reached something of a high-water mark in August of that year with the signing of a Non-Aggression Treaty in Moscow between West Germany and the Soviet Union. With President Nixon pledging that, if the European allies followed suit, the United States would "maintain and improve their forces in Europe and not reduce them except in context of reciprocal East-West action,"[4] MBFR seemed to have clearly reinforcing motives of forestalling domestic pressures to reduce and to continue a real process of East-West détente. There were, to be sure, many in the West who felt that NATO should not rush into MBFR talks without having "its own act together," and the study of Allied Defense 1970 (AD70) had shown how badly this was needed from a military point of view. They were only partly assuaged by the argument that MBFR might provide an occasion for this if the allies could be convinced of the importance of entering talks on MBFR from a position of strength. MBFR had begun to develop a momentum of its own.

The West's momentum toward MBFR received an unexpected impetus from Soviet General Secretary Brezhnev on 14 May 1971 when he dropped his insistence that "reduction of foreign troops" be considered only in a special organ of an ESC and invited the West "'to taste the wine' and begin exploratory negotiations on the reduction of military forces and armaments in Europe."[5]

Other events in 1971 and 1972 rapidly accelerated the momentum of MBFR. These included the signing of the first stage of the Four Power Agreement on Berlin in September 1971; a joint communiqué by

Chancellor Brandt and General Secretary Brezhnev in Moscow later that month announcing that they had exchanged views on reduction of armed forces and armaments in Europe; and repeated expressions of interest by Brezhnev in Yugoslavia in September and in Warsaw in December of 1971. The signing of the Interim Agreement on SALT in May 1972 was followed almost immediately by a mutual endorsement of "the goal of ensuring stability and security in Europe through reciprocal reduction of armed forces" by Nixon and Brezhnev. On 31 May 1972 the NATO ministers agreed to join in preparatory talks on a Conference on Security and Cooperation in Europe (CSCE), instead of the narrower ESC that the Soviet Union had hoped for, and again proposed multilateral discussion of MBFR. SALT II Negotiations opened in Geneva on 21 November and preparatory talks on a CSCE opened in Helsinki the following day. The "era of negotiation" was in high gear and on 31 January 1973 representatives of 12 NATO countries and 7 Warsaw Pact countries met in Vienna to begin exploratory talks on mutual force reductions.

The Vienna Negotiations

By the time formal negotiations began on 30 October 1973, East and West had agreed that the area for reduction would include, on the Western side, the territories of West Germany and the Benelux countries and, on the Eastern side, the territories of East Germany, Poland, and Czechoslovakia. Corresponding to this area, known in the West as the NATO guidelines area (NGA), the direct participants in the talks would be the states on either side with forces stationed in the area. Thus, in the West, Canada, Britain and the United States are direct participants along with the four states encompassed by the NGA. In the East, the Soviet Union is a direct participant along with the three whose area is included. Other states of each alliance (except France, who chose to remain outside the MBFR negotiations, and Iceland and Portugal) are participants with "special status." Little else was agreed to by the time the talks started except vague general statements about the goal of the talks and that the scope and timing of specific reduction arrangements would "in all respects and at every point conform to the principle of undiminished security for each party."

Although the West had been proposing such talks a full four years before the East agreed, it was the East that presented the opening formal proposal. In brief, it is well known that the East's proposal called for "symmetric" reductions of ground forces in three phases. In the first phase, each side would reduce by a total of 20,000 troops: the United States and the Soviet Union, 10,000 each; West Germany and East

Germany, 5,000 each; and other direct participants, a total of 5,000 among them. Thereafter, reductions would be by equal percentages applied to all direct participants individually: a 5 percent reduction in the second phase and a 10 percent reduction in the third phase. Reductions would be by entire units, including the conventional and nuclear weapons associated with them. Units designated for reduction within the states indigenous to the NGA would be disbanded.

The West's initial proposal—tabled two weeks later—was quite different. Reductions would be carried out in two phases. The first phase would deal with U.S. and Soviet ground forces only and called for a 15 percent reduction for each. For the United States this meant about 29,000 troops, and, for the Soviet Union, about 68,000. The West's proposal stipulated that the 68,000 amounted to a tank army and should be accompanied by a reduction of 1,700 tanks. The second phase of reduction was characterized, not by the numbers or percentages to be reduced, but by the end result of the reduction: about 700,000 ground force personnel remaining within the NGA for each side. The West also stipulated that reductions would have to be accompanied by specific measures to verify compliance and ensure that withdrawn forces would not be used to build up forces on the flanks.

It was clear from the outset that such divergences in approach would be difficult to reconcile. An apparent impasse quickly developed over the premises and goals of the negotiations. The West's position proceeded from the premise that an imbalance or disparity of forces had long existed within the NGA and that, in addition to reducing existing forces, the MBFR forum should be used to correct or significantly redress this disparity. The negotiating goal was parity at a lower level—about 700,000 ground force personnel on each side. The East proceeded from the premise that the existing "correlation of forces" had preserved the peace for over two decades and should be continued, albeit at proportionately reduced levels. Moreover, the East—always concerned about West German manpower—insisted on individual country force ceilings against the West's notion of collective alliance ceilings with flexibility for adjusting balances among country force levels.

Although the West's position appeared to be aiming at achieving a "military balance" in the NGA, it was evident that the nature of its proposal was responsive to some of the intra-alliance and domestic political considerations that had played such a key role in the West's proposing the negotiations. To be sure, at face value the West's proposal called for reductions that were clearly asymmetrical: in the first phase, the Soviet Union would reduce by about two and a half times as much as the United States; in the second phase, to achieve the desired parity, the Warsaw

Pact as a whole would have to reduce by about 225,000 more men compared with about 77,000 on the NATO side—almost a three to one ratio. With little reason to believe that NATO's bargaining strength could induce the Pact to accept such disparity in reduction, the West's position seemed calculated to educate the public and to gain acceptance of the notion that there should be a "floor" to NATO ground force reduction (700,000 men) even more than a ceiling.

The West's opening position clearly reflected its ambiguous motives for wanting MBFR in the West as well as its lack of a real consensus about arms control and military policy and planning in this area. Several months before the talks formally opened, John Yochelson pointed out many of the dilemmas faced by the West in its search for an approach to MBFR in the light of conflicting, if not irreconcilable, domestic and intraalliance interests in the subject. Still unprepared after about six years of sporadically analyzing, discussing, and proposing MBFR talks, the West was forced to "put up or shut up." Yochelson discussed three broad strategies for the imminent MBFR talks that he saw in the Washington community during early 1973 when the West was finally forced to face up to concrete negotiations. In his words, these strategies were:

1. The Quick Fix, designed to secure limited manpower reductions rapidly without sinking into a morass of technical detail;
2. The Ever Present Balance, intended to maintain a stable security equilibrium through comprehensive negotiations;
3. The Protracted Parley, aimed at engaging in a long-run dialogue to build confidence and gradually ease the hold of the Soviet Union within the Eastern bloc.[6]

Yochelson noted that each of these approaches envisaged MBFR as a response to a different primary problem: the first was conceived chiefly to quiet domestic demands for reduction, the second to keep military scales precisely balanced, and the third to forge new political relationships. After describing the background, justification, and possible form of each of these "alternative" strategies in different terms, Yochelson acknowledged that "real" policy could partake of all of them. In fact, this aspect of his assessment and prediction was remarkably accurate. Responding to different—and often conflicting—problems and interests simultaneously, the West's negotiating position has seemed fully satisfactory to almost no one who hoped for either quick or clear results. Nevertheless, the MBFR talks did, in the wings or in the background, keep conflicting Western interests in some balance and did maintain a real dialogue with the East relatively free from acrimony and intransigence.

These are modest achievements, but achievements nonetheless not to be dismissed with impatience.

Movement from the initial negotiating positions of each side was slow indeed. After a two-year impasse, the West attempted to break the deadlock with a new offer in December 1975. This was the "Option III" proposal, so-called because it was the third of three possible proposals the U.S. had tabled within NATO. Option III added to the West's initial position an offer to remove 1,000 nuclear warheads plus 54 nuclear-capable F-4 aircraft and 36 *Pershing* missile launchers. The West also agreed to include air force manpower and proposed a combined ceiling of 900,000 on air and ground forces after reduction plus the separate ceiling of 700,000 on ground forces manpower. This "sweetener" was tabled as a "one-time offer," dependent on concessions from the East.

The Option III offer seemed dubious at the time and remained so until it was effectively replaced by the new NATO position introduced in December 1979, simultaneously with the decision to improve NATO's long-range theater nuclear force (LRTNF) posture. On the one hand, it was known that the United States was considering withdrawing some of its more aging and vulnerable nuclear warheads from Europe anyway. Was this just another attempt by the West "to get something for nothing"? Or was it only a reasonable "bargaining chip" approach to arms control? On the other hand, removing 54 nuclear-capable F-4s and 36 *Pershings* would not be totally insignificant, and this approach seemed to respond to NATO considerations in the late 1960s that suggested that mutual force reductions should trade those capabilities which seemed most troublesome or offensive to the other side. NATO has always been worried about the Warsaw Pact's armored threat, and the Pact has always protested NATO's forward basing of U.S. nuclear systems and German hands on nuclear delivery vehicles. If the Soviets would remove a tank army and 1,700 tanks from East Germany in exchange for 90 NATO nuclear delivery vehicles and 1,000 aging (and maybe useless) warheads, wouldn't this be a good bargain?

The difficulty with the Option III proposal was that it was made at a time when Western Europe was confronting a theater nuclear threat as real and ominous as the conventional armored threat. While it might be wise militarily to replace aging and vulnerable systems with new and improved theater nuclear systems, in the highly political environment of arms control negotiations the offer to exchange "some" nuclear systems for "some" conventional systems can quickly lose the qualifier "some." If the 1,000 nuclear warheads were obsolete or so dangerously vulnerable that they needed to be removed or replaced anyway, it would seem far better to announce that decision without linking it with ongoing negotiations or diplomatic moves.

Nonetheless, the East's response to the West's offer of December 1975 was to modifiy its initial proposal in February 1976. Although advertised as "major concessions" to the West, the East's modifications seemed disappointing at best. The "major modification" was to accept the West's proposal for two-phased reductions rather than three. In addition, the East specified which weapons systems should be included in reductions. More importantly, the East had also begun to yield to the West's insistence that the ultimate goal of reduction should be to establish approximate numerical parity in manpower within the NGA. This shift converted an original disagreement in principle into a "numbers game" with the East maintaining that approximate parity in manpower numbers already existed within the NGA.

Between 1976 and 1978 virtually no movement took place in either side's negotiating position, and the MBFR talks seemed completely stalled in a data deadlock. With the advent of the Carter administration, a set of new U.S. initiatives—to move simultaneously on NATO force modernization and on arms control—were suggested. In April 1978, the West dropped its insistence that the proposed first-phase Soviet reduction of 68,000 men and 1,700 tanks be taken in the form of a tank army: the Soviets would be free to take this reduction as they chose. Also, to remove the suspicion that the United States was only interested in a first phase, the West agreed to make the first-phase reduction contingent on a firm commitment by all direct participants to the second-phase reductions.

With the data deadlock still unresolved, the East responded to the West's April initiative with its own modifications to the proposals in June 1978. The principal concessions to the West accepted the goal of a common ceiling of 900,000 men for ground and air forces and a sub ceiling of 700,000 for ground forces in the NGA and offered some flexibility in the treatment of national sub ceilings. The East also "conceded" to accept the principle of trading U.S. tactical nuclear weapons in exchange for Soviet tanks. Instead of the 1,700 Soviet tank reduction the West had initially proposed for the first phase, the East proposed 1,000 tanks in the light of the subsequent Option III offer.

From June 1978 until October 1979, the MBFR talks seemed stalled again. NATO, of course, had other preoccupations and did not seem to mind very much that MBFR was on a back burner. In stark contrast to the political situation in 1967–1969 when the fear of substantial unilateral U.S. reductions loomed large and in 1971–1973 when the "era of negotiation" opened up, after 1975 (when General Haig became SACEUR) NATO was increasingly concerned with more critical developments. The problems stemmed from the growing military imbalance in Central Europe, evolving out of what General Haig dubbed NATO's "decade of neglect;" the Warsaw Pact's steady modernization and strengthening of its conventional forces in Eastern Europe; and, since 1976–1977 when the first SS-20s were introduced, the Pact's long-range theater nuclear buildup.

NATO's long-term defense program (LTDP) was conceived in 1977 and launched at the summit meeting of May 1978. The shaky commitment of all states to increase defense spending annually by 3 percent after inflation, the burst of interest in armaments collaboration and other aspects of NATO "RSI" (rationalization, standardization, and interoperability), and, finally, NATO's own long-range theater nuclear force improvement proposed by the High Level Group (HLG) and created along with the LTDP were NATO's preoccupations from early 1977 through almost all of 1979. Interestingly—almost ironically, in view of the cumbersome history of MBFR negotiations—the latter appears to have galvanized Brezhnev to make new MBFR-type moves in his speech in East Berlin on 6 October 1979, commemorating the thirtieth anniversary of the founding of the German Democratic Republic. Brezhnev's remarks threw the West into some new confusion about how to advance on the two lanes of détente and defense and in what forums.

MBFR Alternatives

By the middle of 1979, the Vienna negotiations on MBFR had been widely criticized in the West from a variety of points of view on diplomacy, arms control, and military policy and planning. To some, the negotiations appeared to have outlived their usefulness in dealing with domestic pressures within the United States and other NATO countries for reducing forces and cutting defense spending. To others, who had seen in the negotiations an opportunity to advance détente and to relieve the tensions of military confrontation in Central Europe, the haggling over ceilings, sub ceilings, and other data seemed to have mired the proceedings in hopeless tedium. Those who looked forward to improving stability and security in Central Europe through the making of rational bargains with the other side found both West and East guilty of having missed an important opportunity for progress.

Leslie Gelb, for example, writing in mid-1979 about NATO's position in the negotiations asserted that:

> Even if the Warsaw Pact accepted such an agreement, there is no certainty that it would do much for European military stability. But it is clear that there is no end in sight for this six-year-old marathon with so many nations negotiating over so many complex issues. Meanwhile, MBFR is blocking needed efforts to get down to some more realistic arms control in Europe.

Perhaps the best approach would be to end MBFR with a successful whimper—a token withdrawal of 20,000 Soviet troops and 10,000 U.S. troops from Central Europe.[7]

Other analysts, such as Jeffrey Record and Stephen Canby, had also earlier criticized the West's approach to MBFR for its preoccupation with aggregate levels of manpower.[8] They saw force structure, doctrine, and posture as the principal determinants of military balance and saw the numbers preoccupation as self-deluding and self-defeating. Thus, by the end of the decade, there was almost a chorus of criticism of the Vienna talks in general and the West's negotiating position in particular.

Much of this criticism is hard to quarrel with and could be summarized in roughly the following way:

1. The West entered the MBFR talks primarily for political reasons—domestic, intra-alliance, and inter-alliance—without a coherent view of how those talks could contribute to real stability and security in Europe.

2. The West's negotiating position reflected at best a desire for simplicity in negotiation, an approach aimed at reducing the cost of maintaining forces, and a desire for the symbols rather than the substance of détente.

3. The West's security would not be materially improved if the East accepted its proposals, which focused on an inappropriate measure of military capability (gross manpower), could not adequately account for the geographic asymmetry, and compounded the problem (with Option III) by offering to trade a critically needed component of NATO's deterrent posture (tactical nuclear weapons) for minor reductions in Pact offensive strength.

4. In its preoccupation with numerical parity, the West was missing the opportunity to deal with the dangers of surprise attack within the NGA—dangers that are the real sources of instability and insecurity for NATO. The talks should have focused on the "Associated Measures" mentioned in the formal title of the talks in order to find mutually acceptable confidence-building measures.

5. In view of the Final Act of the CSCE in Helsinki in 1975, the French proposal for an All-European Disarmament Conference tabled at the UN Special Session on Disarmament in 1978, and the signing of SALT II in 1979, the time seemed overdue for a rethinking and a possible restructuring of the West's approach to, and the preferred forum for, MBFR.

Given such criticism, is there anything to be said for the MBFR negotiations as they were conducted at Vienna between 1973 and 1980? While the foregoing criticisms are valid, there are four reasons for urging caution about altering courses in MBFR too abruptly or shifting to another forum such as SALT III or the CSCE to seek stability and security in Europe:

1. While the original political motivations for entering the MBFR talks may have been inadequate or wrong and, in any case, now appear to be obsolete, there are some strong political reasons for continuing in the Vienna forum and for maintaining continuity with the positions the West has taken. Sometimes it is better to "cut one's losses" than to prolong discussions that have outlived their usefulness. Nonetheless, a new U.S. initiative to shift the West's MBFR position abruptly or to halt it appear likely to be more disturbing to intra- and inter-alliance relations than is worthwhile. There is now little confidence in either European capitals or in Moscow about the constancy or predictability of U.S. leadership in defense or in détente. SALT II and its ratification by the Senate was critically important to many Europeans, not because of the substance of that treaty, but because they saw it as a test of U.S. leadership in détente and arms control. With or without SALT II, there is still a strong desire, particularly among the social democratic parties of Europe, for some measure of success in the MBFR talks in Vienna. Recent Soviet declarations, while obviously aimed at derailing NATO's theater nuclear force improvement, have abetted this desire.

2. If MBFR could be denuclearized—as, for example, Stanley Sloan had strongly urged[9]—there seems to be significant value in sustaining a forum that concentrates on conventional force and armament levels. After the long, complicated negotiation of SALT II, it seems that a SALT III type of forum would be more appropriate for dealing with the most urgent issues of stability and security in Europe by tackling the "gray area" problem. The Vienna MBFR forum is definitely not the place to deal with this problem. On the other hand, SALT III could become hopelessly complicated if it took on conventional levels as well as nuclear ones. In Europe, the conventional and nuclear levels and postures are, to be sure, inextricably linked; the West's arms control policy must be coherent enough to encompass that linkage. But this does not mean they should be negotiated in the same forum. In fact, it suggests they should be negotiated in separate forums as long as they are negotiated from a coherent posture. Maintaining separate forums for conventional and nuclear negotiations requires patience in the West as well as coherence in policy—both admittedly difficult—and a resistance to the temptation to use obsolete capabilities (as in the Option III proposal) as "bargaining chips" or negotiating ploys. Separate, but implicitly linked, forums can provide opportunities for reinforcing leverage if the West has a coherent

negotiating strategy. The December 1979 decision by NATO to propose the removal of 1,000 aging nuclear warheads in response to Soviet calls for a freeze in TNF deployment was a step in the right direction toward freeing the Vienna forum from nuclear negotiations.

3. While it is important to focus, in the conventional area, on the real elements of instability in Europe—that is, on dangers of surprise attack deriving from Soviet force structure, doctrine, and posture—as compared with mere numbers of tanks and manpower, it does not follow that MBFR should be dropped in favor of an All-European Disarmament Conference or greater emphasis on Basket One of the CSCE. The argument is similar to that about SALT III: there is value in separate and narrowly defined negotiating forums, even though the issues are clearly linked. In this case, however, there is overlap as well as linkage. There is no reason that needed CBMs cannot be negotiated in both forums. The few CBM that did come out of CSCE could clearly be strengthened in Vienna. The West's position in MBFR should be to welcome and endorse these and to try in Vienna more clearly to "associate" them with force reductions. The Vienna talks should not lose sight of—any more than they should build false expectations about—force reductions and substitute CBMs for them. On the other hand, there is not much hope that CSCE, with 35 disparate members, can profitably tackle force reductions. The MBFR talks are the only feasible forum in which CBMs and force reductions can be directly associated with one another.

4. By its very nature, arms control in general—and, perhaps, MBFR in particular—is susceptible of extreme optimism and extreme pessimism. An optimist has been described as one who believes that this is the best of all possible worlds. The pessimist is one who fears the optimist may be right. As far as the MBFR talks are concerned, this writer comes close to being a pessimist. Negotiated conventional force reductions to reduce the cost and burden of security in Europe is a goal—however distant—worth keeping alive, if we do not invest extravagant expectations and expend energy and wisdom that would be better applied to defense improvements. Between the dangers of expecting too much and expecting too little of any particular set of negotiations, it is preferable to err on the side of expecting too little without abandoning all expectation. MBFR is a difficult problem and not the West's most urgent one. Indeed, negotiating a balanced, fair, and convincing MBFR agreement that in itself would assure stability and security in Europe makes the problem of negotiating a balanced, fair, and convincing SALT agreement look simple. It would be a mistake to build expectations that MBFR—or its al-

ternatives in CSCE or SALT III—can directly contribute to achieving security in Europe. At most, we should expect MBFR to reinforce security achieved by other means and trim our negotiating goals and forums to that expectation.

Concluding Observations

The greatest threat to creative and realistic arms control thinking in the West is the impatience and cynicism born of extravagant expectations and extravagant disappointments. It would be tempting, in retrospect, to lay too much of the blame for this on the intellectual capital as well as the enthusiasm generated in the seminal decade of 1958–1968, especially about the convergence of arms control and military planning. There is some possibility now that disillusionment will hasten a premature end to negotiations and to the intellectual capital that ushered them in. It may reflect nothing more than this writer's predilection to be out of step with the times, but in the 1960s there was a danger of our rushing into negotiations, and now the danger seems to be our rushing out of them.

This is not the place for an examination of different schools of thought on the relationship of arms control and military policy and planning or for an analysis of historical change and continuity. It is the place, however, to emphasize again that—as symbolized in the classical formulation of arms control objectives—the late 1960s left us with an intellectual consensus that implied a strong convergence between arms control and military policy and planning. This convergence also suggested that there could or should be a similar convergence of arms control and military policy and planning for our adversaries (and our allies) and that this duality of convergence makes negotiation of agreements possible and promising. At the popular level, this phenomenon also has built great expectations about the "era of negotiation."

Clearly the duality of convergence of arms control and military policy and planning between adversaries was not as great as hoped for. Whereas in the West the presumed convergence of arms control and military policy and planning has led us to believe and behave as if arms control could serve as a substitute for military power, or at least certain aspects of it, in achieving security, the East apparently regards arms control as a way to augment military power. Put differently, Eastern and Western positions on arms control have not changed much since the Surprise Attack Conference of 1958: the West looks to arms control to help solve technical/military problems; the East regards arms control as a political means of supplementing military policy and planning.

The West should probably never have regarded negotiated arms control as more than a modest, albeit important, way to discipline and confirm prudent military policy and planning as a part of overall national (and alliance) security policy. But what should we expect for the immediate and longer-range future? The Soviet Union-Warsaw Pact will continue to try to stalemate the United States and other Western powers at the strategic nuclear level, to maintain a distinctly favorable advantage in conventional and theater nuclear forces on the European continent, and to increase its ability to project forces elsewhere in the world, particularly into the vital Persian Gulf area. The United States and NATO, having effectively accepted strategic nuclear parity, will seek to maintain Alliance deterrence and defense capabilities in Europe, but only with difficulty and distraction, and will be very hard pressed to match or counter the Soviet Union's growing ability to project military power elsewhere. The Soviet Union will promote arms control measures and negotiations for propaganda purposes, when it is militarily convenient as in SALT, and insofar as it does not limit Soviet freedom to project or exert military power and influence when the Soviet Union feels it has an advantage. European NATO will continue to seek arms control measures and negotiations as an alternative to military buildup to match Soviet power. That is, the Alliance will continue to see arms control as a preferred alternative to, and not a supplement to, military power.

Within the past five or six years, U.S. and NATO military planners have focused attention on shoring up theater deterrence and defense, particularly in the conventional area. The steady qualitative modernization and quantitative expansion of Soviet-Warsaw Pact conventional forces are now widely recognized and regarded as providing capabilities far beyond anything needed for internal security or for defense against NATO. Under political and economic pressure, however, European members of NATO have also continued to seek signs of détente in the MBFR negotiations, and have been willing to make significant concessions to the Warsaw Pact's negotiating posture, as the strongly preferred approach to European security. European NATO has also endorsed— with some uneasiness about the "gray areas"—the negotiations that led to the SALT II agreement, for similar reasons. Rather than expressing great dissatisfaction with the progress of MBFR or seeking an alternative forum for it, the United States should let the Vienna talks continue, both to contain and to remain open to European concerns for progress in this area, but with due limitations on their scope and on their emphasis.

With this continued concern to move simultaneously on defense and détente, NATO has to a large extent merely been "hoping for the best."

There remains little real consensus in NATO on the most critical defense needs to ensure stability and security in Europe and the proper balance among strategic nuclear, theater and tactical nuclear, and conventional forces in ensuring stability and security. For some time now, the most critical need in NATO has been to improve and rationalize the theater nuclear posture. This came to a head in December 1979, but was not resolved in the fragile decision to link nuclear modernization with a new arms control offer. In the long run, the TNF decision far overshadows the Vienna exercise in importance to security in Europe, and its maintenance should affect all deliberations about the future of MBFR. Divergent U.S. and European reactions to the Soviet invasion of Afghanistan, which closely followed the NATO decision, have only underlined the lack of a coherent arms control and security policy in the West.

The fragility of the TNF decision demonstrates that NATO will soon have to confront and possibly reinterpret or revise its "overall strategic concept"—including a rational and credible concept for the use of theater nuclear forces—to deal with current realities: the Soviet Union will continue to try to neutralize NATO's theater nuclear posture, to maintain at least strategic equivalence with the United States, to modernize its conventional forces, and to achieve a capability for using them outside the NATO area. It is far more important that MBFR be seen in this context. New initiatives should not be taken to get MBFR "back on the track" or on "a new track" until there is much greater clarity on what that "track" is.

Notes

1. Robin Ranger, "An Alternative Future for MBFR: A European Arms-Control Conference," *Survival*, July-August 1979, pp. 165–66.

2. Christoph Bertram, *The Future of Arms Control, Part II: Arms Control and Technological Change: Elements of A New Approach*, Adelphi Paper No. 146, London, The International Institute for Strategic Studies, Summer 1978, p. 6.

3. U.S. Congress, Senate, Committee on Foreign Relations, *Prospects for the Vienna Force Reduction Talks*, prepared by the Foreign Affairs and National Defense Division, Congressional Research Service, Library of Congress, Committee print, Washington, D.C., August 1978, p. 29.

4. NATO Information Service, *NATO Facts and Figures*, Brussels, January 1976, p. 283.

5. U.S. Congress, *Prospects for the Vienna Force Reduction Talks*, p. 30.

6. John Yochelson, "MBFR: The Search for an American Approach," *Orbis*, vol. 17, no. 1, Spring 1973, p. 30.

7. Leslie Gelb, "The Future of Arms Control (1) A Glass Half Full," *Foreign Policy*, no. 36, Fall 1979, p. 30.

8. Jeffrey Record, "MBFR: Little Progress but Disquieting Trends," *Strategic Review*, Summer 1978, and Stephen Canby, "Mutual Force Reductions: A Military Perspective," *International Security*, Winter 1978.

9. Stanley R. Sloan, "New Directions for MBFR," *The Washington Quarterly*, vol. 2, no. 2, Spring 1979.

4
Arms Control and Defense Planning in Soviet Strategic Policy

Benjamin S. Lambeth

Introduction

One of the central themes in the classic U.S. strategic literature of the 1960s held that arms control and defense planning ought to be treated as complementary approaches to the enhancement of nuclear deterrence.[1] What set this notion apart from prior concepts of "disarmament" was its rejection of appeals for force reductions as desirable ends in themselves and its insistence that arms control be pursued as an integral component of broader national security policy. Although it hinged critically on the untested assumption of joint superpower commitment to a shared conception of strategic stability, this outlook nonetheless marked a major advance in U.S. thinking about nuclear matters through its characterization of arms control and strategy as opposite sides of the same coin.

In the years since that initial groundswell of arms control theorizing, the actual experience of the United States has been mixed. During the early negotiations leading to SALT I, the American side generally conducted itself with notable singularity of purpose. The Soviet Union, after all, was still busily engaged in a major buildup of its own strategic forces, and the prevailing hope was that a freeze on offensive force expansion and ABM deployment by both sides once the Soviet Union attained parity would provide the Soviets an incentive to eschew further deployments and help serve the larger cause of deterrence by locking the superpowers into a stable relationship of mutual vulnerability. So long as the logic of this approach was supported by reasonable hopes for Soviet

This is a revised version of a paper prepared for presentation at a colloquium on Arms Control and Defense Planning held at the Johns Hopkins School of Advanced International Studies, Washington, D.C., November 28, 1979.

compliance, U.S. SALT behavior remained congruent with the underlying goals of U.S. strategic policy.

With the more recent signs of Moscow's determination to continue pressing for strategic advantages in the qualitative arena and its reaffirmation that competitive instincts still outweigh the elements of cooperation in U.S.-Soviet strategic relations, however, an increasingly entrenched division has come to exist within the U.S. strategic community over the question whether solutions to U.S. security requirements over the coming decade ought to be pursued through continued efforts at SALT or through a reversion to primary reliance on unilateral measures. This bifurcation has been a direct outgrowth of the gradual breakdown in the national consensus on strategic policy engendered by the unyielding thrust of Soviet force modernization. It was starkly punctuated by the severe difficulties that blocked Senate ratification of the SALT II Treaty under the Carter administration. It has been exacerbated, moreover, by the relentless growth of an independent arms control subculture within and around the U.S. government as a result of the progressive institutionalization of SALT. Within this emergent constituency many individuals have acquired natural ideological or bureaucratic commitments to the uninterrupted pursuit of negotiated agreements with the Soviet Union, seemingly irrespective of their possible effect, one way or the other, on broader U.S. national security.

The measures of merit advanced by the theoretical arms control notions that originally inspired U.S. entry into SALT insisted that the ultimate value of an agreement lay in its prospect for reducing instabilities conducive to nuclear war or for minimizing the damage such a war would inflict should it nonetheless occur. However noble an experiment SALT I may have been in this regard, most observers on both sides of the strategic divide would agree that SALT II utterly failed to satisfy either criterion. On the contrary, the *Minuteman* vulnerability problem that now promises to be upon us by the mid-1980s constitutes a net *erosion* in the stability of the strategic balance that prevailed a decade ago. The proliferation of warheads permitted by the massive throw-weight capacity of the fourth-generation Soviet ICBMs now being deployed has every prospect of becoming a monument to the failure of SALT II to constrain the destructiveness of Soviet weapons as well.

Yet despite this record of questionable service to U.S. security, the arms control apparatus and its protagonists both in and out of government have continued their quest for SALT as though it enjoyed natural legitimacy. At best, for want of needed U.S. force improvements aimed at plugging the holes left uncovered by the various agreements achieved to date, SALT has become an exercise in strategic irrelevance. At worst, it has been conducive to what Albert Wohlstetter has caustically termed a "mad momentum of arms control" with a life of its own. In all events, the history of SALT attests to a strategic community working at significant conceptual and policy cross-purposes, either oblivious of or indifferent to the proposition that arms control ought to be a subordinate instrument of overall national security planning.[2]

In marked contrast to this division of the U.S. arms control and defense communities into ideologically opposed camps, the Soviet Union has consistently approached SALT as a unified actor with a well-developed sense of strategic purpose. The Soviets have never regarded arms control as an *alternative* to unilateral defense investments (as many U.S. SALT enthusiasts tend to have done) but rather have treated it as a direct adjunct of their national security planning, much in keeping with the original U.S. scholarly arguments noted above. The critical difference has been in the ultimate goals sought by Soviet planners. The U.S. case for linking arms control to force development was intended to provide the basis for a coordinated approach to deterrence stability through negotiated self-denying ordinances aimed at proscribing weapons deployments that might give either side a credible first-strike capability. The Soviet case appears to have been motivated by a self-interested desire to bring U.S. force planning into an explicit negotiating context that might allow Soviet planners to impose constraints on U.S. strategic programs, while at the same time exacting American acceptance of countervailing Soviet programs and pursuing whatever margin of strategic advantage the traffic of SALT and détente might allow. In this sense, Moscow's arms control policy has not only been consonant with Soviet defense planning but indeed has constituted an integral part of it, aimed at helping achieve—to the maximum extent possible—Soviet strategic goals cheaply through negotiation rather than through the more costly avenue of unrestrained arms competition.

Any effort to get at the detailed planning assumptions and organizational workings of Soviet arms control decision making will meet with formidable obstacles posed by Soviet secrecy and societal closure. Moreover, much of what we do know about Soviet SALT processes and objectives has already been discussed at length in the Western analytical literature. Accordingly, the remarks that follow will neither pretend to offer the final word on Soviet arms control motivations nor attempt to reconstruct in any detail the history and purposes of Soviet participation in SALT. Rather, I will simply try to advance a considered view of how Soviet arms control involvement should be understood, with particular emphasis on the important differences between the Soviet approach and that of the United States. I will briefly examine the role assigned to arms control in the overall Soviet concept of national security, review some specific examples suggested by the apparent linkage between Soviet ICBM modernization programs and SALT negotiating positions, and finally highlight those features of the Soviet SALT policymaking context that most clearly illustrate the close integration of arms control and force planning in Soviet defense deliberations.

Arms Control in Soviet Strategic Thinking

During the formative years of the postwar era when the United States was clearly the predominant nuclear power, the Soviet Union made almost a national industry of generating multiple negotiatory schemes couched in the language of "general and complete disarmament." Despite the intensity of their diplomatic campaigning, however, the Soviets conspicuously refrained from coupling these exhortations with tangible gestures of self-restraint that might indicate any real commitment to arms control beneath their declaratory rhetoric. Instead, their calls for "disarmament" typically featured comprehensive proposals of a sort they knew in advance would prove unacceptable to the United States, thus allowing them to project an image of reasonableness and devotion to "peace" without having to make any substantial sacrifices in the process. At this level of discourse, Soviet negotiatory posturing was merely a component of Moscow's larger foreign propaganda effort rather than a reflection of serious willingness to undertake reciprocal measures of self-denial in strategic force deployment. Whatever thoughts the Soviet leaders may have privately harbored concerning the long-term utility of genuine arms control measures remained subordinated to the more immediate needs of catching up with the United States in aggregate strategic nuclear power.[3]

With the advent of SALT, however, Soviet arms control behavior became dramatically transformed from hollow diplomatic drum-beating at the United Nations to a serious pursuit of bilateral negotiations aimed at achieving realistic agreements whose terms might ultimately serve Soviet security interests. The most telling indication of this emergent Soviet seriousness of intent was the transferral of responsibility for formulating Soviet arms control proposals from the Ministry of Foreign Affairs (the traditional repository of earlier Soviet "disarmament" activity) to those defense-related organizations directly concerned with Soviet force-structure development. By this time, as a result of its vigorous military buildup first set in motion following the Cuban missile disaster of 1962, the Soviet Union had finally achieved a posture of acknowledged parity with the United States and could accordingly begin thinking about the potential benefits an arms control dialogue might offer in helping to preserve that hard-won achievement. Although the Soviets entered SALT with more diffidence than enthusiasm and had little expectation at the outset that it would ultimately become the centerpiece of U.S.-Soviet diplomatic relations, the tentative expression by Foreign Minister Gromyko in June 1968 that the Soviet Union was now ready for an "exchange of opinion" on mutual restrictions in strategic offensive and defensive arms nonetheless marked a major watershed in Soviet thinking about arms control.[4]

The Soviet acceptance of SALT as an appropriate instrument for helping manage the superpower competition, on the other hand, in no way constituted either a testament to any broader change in fundamental Soviet security conceptions or evidence of Soviet convergence toward prevailing American notions about arms control. For Soviet planners, the very idea of "control" is anathema because of its implied relegation of Soviet security to imposed arrangements requiring conscious Soviet self-denial and reliance on the uncertain prospect of reciprocal enemy "good behavior." This reluctance to countenance such restraints is a natural outgrowth of the Soviet Union's rejection of such Western concepts as "stability," "mutual deterrence," and "essential equivalence," which envisage a preservation of the status quo and call for each side to accept an autonomous "system" of superpower interaction allegedly self-equilibrating in nature, yet grounded on assumptions of adversarial rationality and forbearance.[5] This intellectual outlook largely accounts for the emphasis placed by Soviet military doctrine on the importance of maintaining a capability for fighting a nuclear war in the event deterrence fails and substantially explains the massive efforts the Soviets have undertaken over the past decade to expand and modernize their strategic and general-purpose forces.

More important, this outlook also provides the context in which Soviet SALT behavior should be understood. Like their U.S. counterparts, the Soviets appreciate the unmitigated horrors a nuclear war would unleash and unquestioningly accept the necessity of ensuring deterrence as their first order of strategic business. Their notion of how this goal ought to be pursued, however, is notably different from that which has, at least until recently, rested at the heart of accepted Western strategic theory. This divergent Soviet view entails, among other things, an abiding belief in the unreliability of deterrence, a related conviction that some recognizable form of victory in nuclear war is theoretically attainable if the proper weapons and strategies are maintained, and a consequent stress on the indispensability of large offensive forces, continued investment in active and passive defenses, and adherence to a concept of warfare that expressly accommodates the option of preempting.

From the beginning of SALT, this conception of the nuclear predicament and its force-posture imperatives has had a major impact on Soviet strategic programs and has been largely responsible for the repeated disappointments the United States has encountered in its efforts to draw the Soviets into a common language of strategic discourse. It has been the principal factor behind the Soviet Union's singular failure to date to offer any SALT initiative with the principal intent of enhancing strategic "stability." It also explains the Soviet Union's refusal to abide by any agreement that essentially formalizes Soviet strategic vulnerabilities or coopts Soviet participation in solving the unilateral security problems of the United States. On the first count, Moscow's rejection of "mutual assured destruction" substantially accounts for the extensive Soviet civil defense effort, the parallel Soviet pursuit of active defenses against U.S. bombers and cruise missiles, and advanced R&D on ballistic missile defense. On the second count, the Soviet repudiation of "stability" through mutual exposure to nuclear devastation explains Moscow's cultivated indifference to the growing problem of *Minuteman* survivability and the Soviet leadership's determination to seek as much in the way of unilateral force advantages as Soviet resources, SALT constraints, and U.S. tolerance will permit. Against the possible objection that these Soviet preferences merely reflect the parochial self-interests of the uniformed services, it should be recalled that no less a "moderate" than the late Premier Kosygin was moved to tell President Johnson at the Glassboro summit in 1967 that a ban on ballistic missile defenses was, in Henry Kissinger's words, "the most absurd proposition he had ever heard."[6] For a whole variety of historical and cultural reasons, belief in the necessity of defending the homeland with every means available is deeply rooted in the Soviet political-military psyche. The idea that nuclear weapons have somehow rendered international security a "community responsibility" requiring cooperative restraints on the part of both superpowers is simply counter to the long-established patterns of Soviet strategic thought.

The net effect on SALT created by this Soviet propensity to rely on unilateral initiatives rather than on negotiated measures for assuring Soviet security has been a clear Soviet determination to use arms control in support of Soviet strategic goals. Seen from this perspective, SALT has proven for the Soviets to be a lucrative means for seeking to impose constraints on *American* exploitation of military technology while providing a context for continuing the development and operational application of *Soviet* military technology with the express blessings of the United States, as reflected in the formal language of whatever agreements that Soviet negotiating finesse can help bring about. For Soviet planners, SALT has not been an exercise in "arms control" at all. Instead, to bend the idiom of Clausewitz somewhat, it has been a continuation of strategy by other means.

Moscow's acceptance of the ABM treaty is a representative case in point. Although that gesture was widely interpreted by Westerners at the time as tacit proof that the Soviet Union had finally assimilated the wisdom of U.S. "stability" theory and acknowledged the inexorability of mutual vulnerability as the only solution to the nuclear security dilemma, it is far more likely that the Soviets saw the technically superior U.S. *Safeguard* ABM as a threat to the emerging Soviet fourth-generation ICBM force and were driven to sacrifice their own marginal *Galosh* ABM as a necessary price for defusing that threat until Soviet technology could produce a more effective ballistic missile defense. In sharp contrast to U.S. orthodoxy, Soviet military doctrine has shown no sign over the years of having abandoned its traditional emphasis on the importance of strategic defense in modern warfare. In consonance with this doctrinal preference, the Soviet defense community has continued to conduct vigorous and well-funded development and test activities in BMD technology with unrelenting determination throughout the period of the treaty.

This self-serving exploitation of SALT for unilateral gain has been less a product of calculated Soviet malevolence than simply a natural extension of Soviet strategic logic. Soviet leaders, both civilian and military, recognize the uncertainties of deterrence, refuse to count on it even as they try their best to preserve it, and regard as their principal responsibility of national stewardship the maintenance of credible military capabilities for vouchsafing Soviet survival in the event of its catastrophic failure. Soviet military doctrine, in turn, considers nuclear victory to be technically feasible and offers explicit conceptual and hardware solutions for achieving it should circumstances permit no alternative. As a consequence, Soviet defense policy seeks the maintenance of a plausible war-fighting capability and demands vigorous Soviet efforts to deny the enemy a similar capability. Unlike the United States, the Soviet Union has no intellectual tradition that treats arms control and stability as alternatives to unilateral force enhancement. Its national security principals regard SALT as but one of a broad variety of methods for assuring a strategic posture capable of achieving Soviet wartime political-military objectives should lesser options for maintaining Soviet survival prove unavailing. In these circumstances, it is not surprising that Soviet spokesmen should display such umbrage at Western intimations that their apparent obstinacy at SALT reflects an affront to the "spirit" of arms control. Their failure to show obeisance to this "spirit" is less an example of Machiavellian double-dealing than an indication that the premises and motivations behind U.S. participation in SALT have simply been fundamentally alien to the Soviet way of thinking about strategic affairs.

SALT and Soviet ICBM Modernization

Perhaps the clearest testament to the interdependency of Soviet arms control behavior and defense program implementation may be found in the way Soviet negotiators have exploited their so-called "informational asymmetry" advantage created by Soviet secrecy for seeking SALT agreements that would avoid significantly impeding Soviet ICBM modernization plans. During the initial SALT I discussions on offensive forces, the Soviet delegation adamantly refused to agree on a precise definition of what constituted a "heavy" ICBM and succeeded in producing a settlement that remained studiously vague regarding permissible volumetric expansion of SS-11 silos.[7] At the time SALT I was concluded, the Soviets had not yet begun flight-testing their SS-19, which was intended to replace the SS-11. U.S. intelligence thus has little basis for anticipating the dramatic improvement in payload capability which that system portended. Less than a year after the Soviets had secured their needed ambiguity in the SALT I accord, however, the demonstrated performance capabilities of the SS-19 revealed an effective throw-weight increase of between four and five times that of the SS-11, to the profound consternation of the U.S. defense community.[8]

As a result of the hard-target capability afforded by their MIRVed SS-19 inventory (with the additional support of their SS-18 force), the Soviets have, for all practical purposes, "legally" acquired through negotiating stratagem a credible counterforce option against *Minuteman.* This is precisely the sort of "destabilizing" posture that U.S. entry into SALT was intended to head off. Had the American side possessed the requisite information and foresight to insist on more restrictive missile and silo growth limitations, the SS-19 would have been ruled out as an acceptable Soviet alternative. Yet we know with hindsight that the SS-19 must have been in full-scale engineering development for some time before SALT I was concluded. It is thus a fair presumption that the Soviets intended it to be a central mainstay of their ICBM posture at least through the mid-1980s. Given the considerable momentum that had almost surely accumulated in the SS-19 program well before the 1972 Moscow summit and the evident Soviet determination to see the system attain large-scale deployment, it is interesting to speculate whether the Soviets might have so valued the promise of that weapon that they would have been prepared to let SALT I go by the boards altogether if it threatened, through U.S. insistence on more constraining language in the interim agreement, to stand in the way of SS-19 deployment. As matters turned out, however, the negotiating instructions given to the Soviet delegation so handily supported achievement of the SS-19 program's needed technological maneuvering room that conscious leadership contrivance, rather than coincidence, constitutes the only plausible explanation.

In general, the Soviet approach to SALT I seems to have been carefully orchestrated with the intent to secure U.S. consent to an agreement that would allow preexisting Soviet missile modernization programs to achieve the objectives that were intended by Soviet planners in any event. To be sure, the numerical restriction on ICBM silos and SLBM tubes did place a ceiling on the permissible size of the Soviet launcher inventory and, for all we know, may have forced the Soviets to settle for a somewhat more modest construction effort than they might have been inclined to pursue in the absence of SALT. There seems little question, however, that the Soviet leaders were fully determined from the outset not to allow SALT to get in the way of their highly valued qualitative force improvements. This commitment to tailoring their SALT proposals and bargaining strategies to directly support their ongoing strategic postural improvements rather than to serve any broader quest for "stability" (which would have required significant material concessions) was emphatically underscored by their careful insistence on ambiguity in the terms governing allowable SS-11 silo modification. It was further reflected in their adamant refusal to countenance the MIRV deployment ban originally proposed by the United States during the initial negotiating rounds of SALT I and their equally persistent demand for an advantage in SSBN numbers on what was later revealed, through intercontinental-range flight testing of the SS-N-8 SLBM, to have been completely spurious and disingenuous grounds of "adverse geographical asymmetries."[9]

For that matter, the Soviets never consented to any limitation on actual *missile* numbers but rather to a limit on the total number of observable launch *facilities*. This left them free to continue producing and stockpiling a reserve inventory of boosters and warheads that might be drawn upon in crises to support either a silo-reload option or a supplementary ICBM force maintained in unhardened but concealed launch positions.[10] Although many U.S. intelligence officials consider this unlikely and claim possession of adequate verification techniques to detect any significant Soviet missile stockpiling effort, the fact remains that to this day we still have no confident knowledge of the size of the Soviet ICBM inventory.[11]

A final example worthy of note concerning the commanding role played by unilateral strategic interests in shaping Soviet SALT behavior was the categorical Soviet refusal even to entertain, let alone consider, the comprehensive proposal for ICBM reductions put forward by the Carter administration in March 1977. Even though this proposal included an avowed U.S. willingness to forego MX in return for a drawdown of deployed Soviet heavy SS-18 launchers, it was summarily rejected by the Soviet leadership on the ground that it would result in an unfair advantage for the United States. Although this "unfair advantage" would, at best, have merely given the U.S. side a somewhat more balanced Soviet ICBM threat to confront, the Soviets proved unprepared to pay the price of tangible cuts in their established base of strategic power in return for what they evidently regarded as little more than a tenuous U.S. promissory note. Whether the Soviets were genuinely offended by the surprise and publicity with which the U.S. administration sprung its proposal or simply felt that, if left alone, MX would ultimately die a natural death in the arena of U.S. domestic politics, the fact remains that they refused to allow any concession to the goal of a more moderated East-West arms competition to undo their substantial offensive force improvements, which they maintained had already been ratified by SALT I and the subsequent Vladivostok accords. If the comprehensive Carter proposal was indeed advanced, as some of its authors claimed after the fact, with the intent to "smoke the Russians out" and test their commitment to "real arms control," one can scarcely imagine a more definitive Soviet reply than the one it abruptly provoked.[12]

It should be noted before leaving this topic that the primacy of unilateral strategic program commitments in Soviet SALT policy suggested by the examples just presented does not mean that the Soviet defense-industrial complex operates as a hermetically sealed Leviathan totally unaffected by conflicting considerations emanating from Soviet interests in a continued relationship of détente with the West. On the contrary, there are several indications in the terms of SALT II that the Soviets fully appreciated the extent to which they successfully bamboozled the United States in SALT I, recognized the difficulties they would encounter in trying to get away with such sleight of hand again in the face of an adversary now forewarned and less malleable, and accordingly agreed to at least three concessions on further ICBM modernization of a sort that, in a liberal interpretation, could be seen as reflecting top-level political reversal of previously authorized and funded missile design activities. The first was the Soviet consent to cancel the SS-16 program, the second was Moscow's agreement to limit itself to a single follow-on ICBM beyond the current fourth generation, and the third was the ultimate Soviet expression of willingness, after much heel-dragging, to accept a "five percent rule" governing permissible growth or downsizing of its chosen follow-on system from the established baseline parameters of the SS-19.

On the first score, one could plausibly reply that the solid-propellant SS-16 had long been plagued with well-known developmental problems and that by agreeing to give it up, the Soviets offered little more than the gratuitous discarding of a weapon they probably had no intention of deploying in significant numbers in any event. In the case of the latter two examples, it would be hard to build a convincing argument that the Soviet missile design community escaped with its vested interests as intact as it apparently did after SALT I, even though demonstrated Soviet negotiating guile and residual uncertainty about what range of options the "five percent rule" still leaves open for the Soviets may ultimately prove to satisfy the bulk of intended Soviet fifth-generation ICBM improvements notwithstanding the constraints of SALT II.

All the same, there is little evidence that the Soviets have abandoned their abiding view of SALT as a diplomatic adjunct of their broader effort to acquire a strategic war-fighting capability, irrespective of whatever upsetting consequences this may have on the long-term pattern of Soviet-U.S. interaction. They have shown no sensitivity whatever to repeatedly articulated U.S. security concerns and plainly consider their emerging threat to *Minuteman* as *our* problem, despite its destabilizing potential and the possibility that it will drive the United States toward major offsetting measures we might genuinely prefer to avoid. They have further refrained from showing any interest in self-restraint along the lines of the abortive U.S. proposal to trade MX for their "heavy" ICBMs and have succeeded in gaining considerable indirect leverage over the MX basing mode by using the SALT I silo-limitation provision to force MX out of its earlier vertical-shelter arrangement and into the more expensive horizontal basing scheme.[13] Altogether, whatever one might be able to say about the various bureaucratic compromises that have left their mark on Soviet programs as a consequence of SALT, the Soviet Union has—in clear contrast to recent U.S. experience—remained thoroughly unafflicted by any gross inconsistency of strategic objectives or disruptive "left hand knoweth not" syndrome in its efforts to coordinate SALT with its broader force improvement plans.

The Institutional Setting
of Soviet Arms Control Planning

Probably the main reason for this close integration of Soviet SALT policy and defense planning is the fact that the key institutions and individuals responsible for these two areas of activity are all but indistinguishable from one another. It would require far more space than is available here to provide a full reconstruction of what we know about Soviet organizational arrangements and procedures for dealing with these interrelated matters.[14] Their most salient feature, however, is the clear predominance (if not outright monopoly) of military influence and presence in Soviet SALT decision making. As noted above, during the early years of the Cold War when East-West arms control activity was largely a matter of countervailing propaganda posturing without much underlying seriousness, the business of "disarmament" proposing was left to diplomats in the Foreign Ministry while the uniformed professionals went about dealing with the more pressing concerns of undergirding Soviet national security. Once the SALT dialogue that commenced in the late 1960s began to highlight the potential value of arms control for supporting Soviet strategic ambitions and channeling the arms competition in a direction more congenial to Soviet interests, however, authorities in the Defense Ministry, General Staff, and military-industrial apparatus moved into the breach as the key players in the SALT forum, relegating the formerly preeminent Foreign Ministry to a largely passive implementation role. Although the initial Soviet SALT delegation was nominally headed by a seasoned Foreign Ministry official, Vladimir Semenov, its overall composition was heavily weighted with representatives from the armed forces and defense-related ministries. Virtually all Western accounts of the turbulent history of SALT since those early beginnings leave little room for doubt that it was the latter who figured most prominently in shaping the character of Soviet negotiating style.

Unlike the American side, with its sizeable bureaucratic infrastructure expressly devoted to the pursuit of arms control, the Soviet Union has no readily-identifiable "arms control community" or SALT constituency apart from the armed forces and the military-related ministry and party officials primarily responsible for Soviet defense policy. Although civilian analysts in the various Soviet research institutes are occasionally called upon to generate background studies on such peripheral matters as American strategic perceptions and the impact of domestic influences on U.S. defense policy, they are expressly enjoined from submitting formal SALT proposals or otherwise participating in Soviet SALT policy deliberations and are almost completely cut off from the critical sources of data about Soviet strategic programs that would be required to support any such activity.[15] The same apparently applies even to government officials in the Foreign Ministry more directly involved in SALT matters, as best underscored by the now-classic case of General Ogarkov's admonition to the U.S. SALT I delegation to refrain from discussing the details of Soviet strategic forces in the presence of his civilian associates on the Soviet team for the reason that such information was "strictly the affair of the military."[16]

By all available indications, the Soviet defense community not only maintains a tightly-guarded monopoly of information regarding strategic plans and SALT options but also an exclusive role in the formulation of Soviet SALT negotiating positions. This primacy accorded to military interests in the Soviet SALT process was highlighted during the eleventh hour of negotiations over SALT I at the Moscow summit in 1972, when the Soviets interjected as their principal arbitrator the chairman of the Military-Industrial Commission, L. V. Smirnov, who Henry Kissinger described in his memoirs as "a personality new to all Americans present."[17] Through his responsibility as the principal overseer of Soviet military R&D and strategic programs, Smirnov is one of the most authoritative bureaucratic players in the development and modernization of Soviet strategic forces. His public surfacing in so critical a negotiatory role during SALT I was a revealing indication of his deep and driving influence (along with that of the Defense Ministry more generally) in shaping Soviet SALT proposals so as to accommodate collateral Soviet interests in the realm of advanced weapons development and deployment.

Aside from this close association, if not outright indivisibility, of Soviet arms control planners and defense decision makers, the Soviet national security community enjoys a degree of maneuvering freedom and immunity from disruptive internal influences far greater than that obtainable in the highly pluralistic U.S. system. There is no legislative body comparable to the U.S. Congress to place obstructions in the path of Soviet SALT planning or to voice special interests to which Soviet strategic policymakers must be responsive. There is no recognizable Soviet "arms control lobby" in any position to put forward influential SALT proposals that would threaten to cut against the grain of established Soviet military doctrine and policy. Finally, there is no significant "hawk/dove" dichotomy *within* the Soviet political-military-industrial nexus tasked with strategic responsibilities that might suggest any fundamental disagreement over the basic objectives and modalities of Soviet national security policy. Although there were some faint hints during the initial period of exploratory probings prior to the start of SALT I that could have been read as indicating somewhat less than unbridled military enthusiasm for what the Soviet Union might be getting itself into,[18] there has generally appeared in subsequent years to be a remarkable convergence of political and military views on the basic desiderata of Soviet military investment and the overall goals of Soviet security planning. Whether it constitutes a cause, a consequence, or both, this coalescence of Soviet SALT behavior with unilateral Soviet strategic interests has been steadfastly assured by the nearly total institutional integration of civilian and military viewpoints in such critical centers of decision making as the Defense Council, the Military-Industrial Commission, and indeed the Politburo itself.

To what extent SALT considerations are caught up in—and affected by—Soviet domestic politics is hard to say given the paucity of available information that might shed useful light on this question. It is highly unlikely, however, that Soviet SALT involvement is even remotely buffeted by the sort of wide-ranging institutional rivalries and conflicting political values that so heavily influence the course and character of U.S. strategic policymaking. However much Brezhnev may have staked his own political fortunes and those of his potential successors on the continued success of SALT and détente, he has almost certainly done so with a careful eye toward the abiding purpose of that commitment, namely, the enhancement of Soviet power. Neither he, nor any other principals of note in the Soviet hierarchy, are likely to have come to regard SALT either as a process with intrinsic value or as something the Soviet Union is necessarily obliged to pursue at the expense of continued force improvements deemed vital for underwriting Soviet military doctrine and global objectives.

Notes

1. This proposition received its first systematic treatment in the landmark symposium edited by Donald G. Brennan, *Arms Control, Disarmament, and National Security* (New York: George Braziller, 1961). Its most thorough development may be found in Thomas C. Schelling and Morton H. Halperin, *Strategy and Arms Control* (New York: Twentieth Century Fund, 1961).

2. This tendency first developed during the latter years of the Nixon/Ford incumbency and reached its pinnacle under the leadership of President Carter. Since the advent of the Reagan administration, however, there have been signs of a determined effort to put the defense and foreign-affairs components of the U.S. government back on a common track and to reintegrate the arms control process into its proper place in national security planning. In his recent confirmation hearings, the director-designate of the U.S. Arms Control and Disarmament

Agency, Eugene Rostow, expressly reflected this commitment in his assertion that "our ten years of experience with SALT I and SALT II have been painful and unsatisfactory. Our first task, therefore, is to reassess the role of arms limitation agreements in our foreign and defense policy." Michael Getler, "Rostow's Testimony Illustrates Reagan's Shift on Arms Control," *Washington Post*, June 24, 1981.

3. The earlier history of this period is well reviewed in John W. Spanier, *The Politics of Disarmament: A Study in Soviet-American Gamesmanship* (New York: Praeger, 1962). See also Alexander Dallin, *The Soviet Union and Disarmament* (New York: Praeger, 1965) and Thomas B. Larson, *Disarmament and Soviet Policy, 1964–1968* (Englewood Cliffs, N.J.: Prentice-Hall, 1968).

4. Report by Foreign Minister A. A. Gromyko, "On the International Situation and the Foreign Policy of the Soviet Union," *Pravda*, June 28, 1968.

5. The most commonly-cited expression of this Soviet doctrinal orientation is the following comment made by the late Major General Nikolai Talenskii in justification of Soviet efforts in ballistic missile defense during the mid-1960s: "When the security of a state is based only on mutual deterrence with the aid of powerful nuclear rockets, it is directly dependent on the good will and designs of the other side, which is a highly subjective and indefinite factor. . . . It would hardly be in the interests of any peaceloving state to forgo the creation of its own effective means of defense against nuclear-rocket aggression and make its security dependent only on deterrence, that is, on whether the other side will refrain from attacking." "Antimissile Systems and Disarmament," in John Erickson, ed., *The Military-Technical Revolution* (New York: Praeger, 1966), pp. 225–227.

6. Henry A. Kissinger, *White House Years* (Boston: Little, Brown, 1980), p. 208.

7. The protocol to the interim agreement stipulated that silo expansion not exceed "10–15 percent of the present dimensions," but left undetermined whether that included both depth and diameter or only one or the other of these parameters. See *Arms Control and Disarmament Agreements* (Washington, D.C.: U.S. Arms Control and Disarmament Agency, June 1977), pp. 142–143.

8. Colin S. Gray, "Soviet Rocket Forces: Military Capability, Political Utility," *Air Force Magazine*, March 1978, p. 52.

9. As one may recall, the interim agreement granted the Soviets a roughly three-to-two numerical advantage in ballistic missile submarines, on the ground that the longer transit times required for Soviet SSBNs to reach their patrolling stations compared to those of the United States due to unfavorable geographic circumstances necessitated this margin of Soviet superiority in order to provide Moscow the capability to match the number of U.S. boats on operational deployment at any given time. The speciousness of this argument only became clear in the aftermath of the 1972 summit that produced the SALT I accords, when full-range testing of the SS-N-8 confirmed its capacity to cover most U.S. targets from Soviet territorial waters.

10. For further discussion, see Amrom Katz, *Verification and SALT: The State of the Art and the Art of the State* (Washington, D.C.: the Heritage Foundation, 1979), especially pp. 32–37.

11. A U.S. intelligence study published in 1979 reportedly claimed that the Soviet Union may have accumulated as many as a thousand ICBMs beyond the number formally accounted for in the SALT I agreements. See Henry S. Bradsher, "New Study Raises Soviet Missile Total," *New York Times*, April 12, 1971.

12. For a full review of the pertinent details on this episode, see Strobe Talbott, *Endgame: The Inside Story of SALT II* (New York: Harper and Row, 1979), pp. 38–67.

13. The U.S. Air Force presently maintains that the horizontal shelter scheme for MX has turned out to be operationally preferable to the abandoned vertical basing mode in any event because of its inherent advantage in supporting a dash redeployment of MX on assessment of imminent attack. The fact remains, however, that the original impetus behind the horizontal shelter arrangement stemmed from concern on the part of the Carter administration about the possible ambiguities the vertical silo configuration might have raised concerning MX compliance with SALT I and the subsequent Vladivostok accords.

14. The most thorough treatment of what is publicly known about these Soviet arrangements and procedures may be found in Thomas W. Wolfe, *The SALT Experience* (Cambridge: Ballinger, 1979), pp. 49–77.

15. For an insightful first-hand argument to this effect by a former Soviet researcher who headed the Disarmament Section of the Institute of World Economy and International Relations, USSR Academy of Sciences, see Igor S. Glagolev, "The Soviet Decision-making Process in Arms Control Negotiations," *Orbis*, Winter 1978, pp. 767–776.

16. John Newhouse, *Cold Dawn: The Story of SALT* (New York: Holt, Rinehart and Winston, 1973), p. 56.

17. Kissinger, *White House Years*, p. 1233.

18. As a case in point, one Soviet military commentator with well-established hardline credentials publicly argued only three months following Foreign Minister Gromyko's expression of willingness to open a SALT dialogue with the United States that "we cannot agree with the view that disarmament can be achieved as a result of peaceful negotiation of this acute and complex problem by the representatives of opposing social systems. . . . Under contemporary conditions, the primary task of the socialist countries is the strengthening of their armed forces, increasing their capabilities and their readiness." Colonel Ye. Rybkin, "A Critique of Bourgeois Concepts of War and Peace," *Kommunist Vooruzhenykh Sil*, No. 18 (September 1968), p. 90.

5
Theater Nuclear Forces and "Gray Area" Arms Control

Michael Higgins
Christopher J. Makins

Ever since the Soviets deployed substantial numbers of nuclear weapons oriented toward Europe in the 1960s, studies within the Alliance of where the advantage would lie in a theater nuclear war have been inconclusive. Many Europeans believe that if such a conflict favors either side, it probably favors the Warsaw Pact, whose armor advantage and shorter, more secure lines of communication would take on overriding significance in face of the enormous attrition of a nuclear war. More importantly, most Europeans believe that a "limited" nuclear exchange would leave Europe devastated, while sparing the United States and the Soviet Union. For these reasons, Europeans in general have resisted the concept of actually fighting and winning a nuclear war in Europe, preferring instead to rely on the threat of automatic escalation (coupling) to U.S. strategic forces to deter Soviet aggression. During the early days of American nuclear superiority, this strategy suited the United States as well. After the Soviets started to achieve a significant second-strike capability with their central strategic forces in the 1960s, however, this strategy began to lose its appeal to the United States and, for many Europeans, its credibility.

Not surprisingly, a succession of U.S. governments, starting with the Kennedy administration, has attempted to redirect NATO strategy toward a flexible response posture emphasizing conventional forces. For

This paper was originally written for presentation to the National Security Affairs Conference at the National Defense University in July, 1979. Although minor amendments have been made to refer to subsequent events, we decided not to revise it substantively to take account of those events—notably the December 12 Alliance decision on long-range TNF modernization and subsequent efforts to bring about East-West negotiations on long-range TNF. We believe that our original conclusions, by which we stand, are the more cogent for being presented in essentially their original form.

the Europeans, however, prolonged conventional war has little more appeal than nuclear war, especially since the cost of being prepared to fight a conventional war is prodigious, given the Soviet propensity for large active-duty military forces. And most significantly, many Europeans (especially the French) have seen U.S. attempts at shoring up conventional defense, and its emphasis on "battlefield" applications of nuclear weapons, as efforts to "decouple" the U.S. strategic forces from NATO defense.

Current NATO strategy reflects these strains over nuclear weapons doctrine. MC 14/3, the approved NATO defense strategy, is a compromise in which the Europeans accepted flexible response, with its requirement for initial conventional defense, while the United States reaffirmed its readiness to escalate to strategic nuclear war if necessary. Although both parties agreed that theater nuclear weapons would remain deployed in Europe as a vital link between conventional and strategic capabilities, the agreement has not reconciled their fundamentally different points of view. To most Europeans, theater nuclear weapons—with their potential for escalation—are directly linked with U.S. strategic forces; to the United States, however, these same theater weapons, with their potential for controlled application, offer the best hope of containing a nuclear war short of strategic exchange.

The purposeful ambiguity in employment doctrine has served to dampen conflict and division within the Alliance on nuclear issues. But it has also become a large impediment to effectively planning the application of nuclear weapons and, consequently, to the process of acquiring and deploying them. As a result, NATO has deployed an extensive assortment of systems and weapons in Europe with little apparent balance with respect to ranges, yields, and in-theater deployments. While this situation has historically been acceptable to most Europeans—indeed, some believe the lack of coherence in NATO deployments enhances deterrence because NATO responses are unpredictable—recent developments have combined to reduce European confidence in the deterrent value of theater nuclear forces.

The most striking of these developments is the erosion of confidence, both in U.S. leadership and its strategic umbrella, prompted in part when the Soviets secured the capability to threaten U.S. territory with their strategic forces, but more recently by other factors, including the polarization of debate within the United States over the adequacy of its strategic forces. This, in turn, has aggravated European concern about Soviet activities such as deployment of the SS-20 missile and the *Backfire* bomber. The upshot is that the traditional European dependence on the threat of nuclear escalation as the primary deterrent is becoming less and less comfortable, and Europeans as well as Americans have recognized a need to "do something" about nuclear forces in Europe. But doing something that makes sense both to Europeans and Americans requires some degree of consensus over the role of nuclear weapons in Alliance strategy. Employment doctrine ambiguity, although serving a useful function in the past, is no longer appropriate, in view of the need for decisions on theater nuclear force improvements and negotiating policies. While ambiguity once permitted the Alliance to avoid damaging disagreements, it has now become a potential source of divisiveness.

U.S. efforts during the 1970s and the recent NATO High Level Group deliberations have made the European Defense Ministry, armed forces, and defense scientist/researchers more aware of the need for clear concepts of how theater weapons would actually be used in conflict and what kinds of force improvements would be required to make their potential employment in different roles more "credible." But there has been little broader acceptance among political and other leaders or in public opinion of realistic roles and missions for theater nuclear forces in Europe. Yet politicians and the public must assimilate these issues if force posture decisions are to receive broadly based and durable support and if the allies are to avoid damaging disagreements as they move into negotiations.

European Theater Nuclear Forces in East-West Negotiation

The ambiguity of Alliance doctrine on the role of TNF has been paralleled in recent years by the uncoordinated way in which TNF have become involved in East-West negotiations. Four separate, though related, developments that have occurred should be briefly recalled in their order of appearance—forward-based systems (FBS) in SALT, Option III in MBFR, cruise missiles in the SALT II Protocol and the enhanced radiation weapon (ERW).

Despite all the diplomatic ballyhoo on the subject of FBS, the Alliance has never developed a consensus on the substance of the matter. Although the fate of SALT II is uncertain, the SALT II Statement of Principles, were it ever ratified, would commit the United States to "resolve" some of FBS issues in SALT III. In that case, the Alliance would have to broach the substance in one way or another and reinforce the need for a set of agreed Alliance policies on TNF.

Concerning Option III in MBFR, the offer of once-for-all, indivisible, non-reciprocal withdrawals of U.S. nuclear systems in exchange for Soviet tanks proved to be a mistake in the long run, even though it appeared to offer promise of progress in the negotiations at the time. It did not provide a key to unblock the negotiations; its non-reciprocal nature (which was a consequence of the asymmetrical allied position on tank withdrawals) was mocked by the Soviet TNF buildup; it became the target of Soviet bargaining efforts (in their proposals of May 1978, the Soviets offered to reduce fewer tanks in exchange for the same number of nuclear systems that were to be withdrawn in Option III); it became increasingly hard to view as a once-for-all injection of TNF into East-West negotiations since it had lain on the table for five years; and for a period it inhibited allied efforts to pursue, through the NPG, work on TNF modernization.

The handling of the cruise missile issue in relation to the SALT II Protocol showed how difficult such matters are to resolve in the Alliance. However, the European suspicions that the United States was willing to trade allied interests (however unclearly defined) for exclusively U.S. advantage in SALT was a fundamental problem—hard to overcome even with better consultations. As with Option III, and more strongly so over cruise missiles, the lack of any clear Alliance doctrine on the role of TNF permitted uncertainty and doubt about the significance of U.S. negotiating moves to grow.

Finally, the U.S. idea, which may or may not have been a serious one, of matching restraint in ERW deployment with Soviet restraint in SS-20 deployment emerged as a naive political gesture unrelated to any overall conception of negotiations about TNF or their role in Alliance strategy.

Some would draw from this historical mosaic and from other considerations the conclusion that the Alliance ought not to be in the business of negotiating about TNF at all. In this view, not only are negotiations more likely than not to lead to agreements that are disadvantageous to the West, but they are almost bound to have a dangerous demobilizing effect on Western political and public opinion. Thus the Alliance should simply decline to negotiate about FBS or theater-based cruise missiles in SALT, withdraw the ERW offer as Option III was withdrawn in December 1979, and ignore any consequent Soviet protests.

There are two types of arguments against this conclusion. First, it remains a distinct possibility—and an increasingly important one—that real security gains may be made from negotiations. To permit TNF deployments in Europe to evolve without a serious effort to negotiate beneficial, qualitative or quantitative restraints is unnecessarily risky for the Alliance. The questions—and perhaps more importantly, prejudices—at issue here are so far-reaching as to preclude thorough treatment in this chapter. Second, for numerous reasons of geography, history, and political psychology, several Western European countries attach great importance to trying to negotiate an improvement in East-West relations. One can argue about the permanence of this attitude without doubting its present political force. At the least, therefore, as recent Alliance discussions have shown, an effort to pursue a TNF negotiating policy alongside TNF modernization policies is essential if Western European support for modernization is to be gained.

This chapter accepts the premise, derived from recent experience, that in the foreseeable future negotiated agreements cannot be expected to lead to a militarily significant reduction in the threat that TNF poses for both the Western allies and the Warsaw Pact. The most that negotiations can achieve is a greater degree of predictability, and therefore stability, in the level of TNF deployments and possibly some moderation of the rate and nature of change in those deployments through qualitative restraints (e.g., on "new types," testing, etc.).

The fundamental question about negotiations, therefore, is how best to seek such benefits as they *can* confer. The four cases described earlier, and the inherent logic of the problem, suggest that there are two ways to progress with negotiations on TNF. The first approach would be to continue to deal with them piecemeal, with some issues falling into MBFR, some into SALT, others conceivably elsewhere, and thus some being dealt with multilaterally, some bilaterally and so on. Short-term political experience and negotiating inertia are powerful arguments for this approach. The second route would be to develop a more coherent and comprehensive approach to those negotiations. To choose between these two approaches, it is necessary to examine first, the military context and secondly, the political context of TNF in Western Europe.

The Military Context for Theater Nuclear Forces

The current purposeful ambiguity in NATO's TNF employment doctrine stems not so much from uncertainty about TNF capabilities, or disputes over which targets are most suitable for TNF, as from disagreement over which of the wide range of potential options offers the greatest deterrence, and, hence, for which options the force should be best suited in size and structure. The underpinnings for this disagreement and the backdrop against which it is played out can be found in current NATO and U.S. TNF employment policies, which are spelled out in a series of documents expanding on the basic flexible response concepts of MC 14/3.

These documents reveal that both Alliance and U.S. policies call for the full range of employment capabilities. But whereas the NATO-approved documents are concerned more with the political impact of initial NATO use against fixed targets and the linkage to the American strategic war plan, the Single Integrated Operating Plan (SIOP), U.S. policies concentrate more on the military results of controlled TNF application, retaliatory use and preplanning and on the impact of TNF on the conventional defense. This situation reflects two rather polarized concepts of TNF use. The first of these can be characterized as the "European" view and the second, the "American" view, although both concepts have strong advocates on both sides of the Atlantic. The two concepts offer rather different answers to the fundamental question of TNF deployment and TNF arms control.

The "European" concept sees TNF as essentially serving two functions: first, deterring aggression by implying almost automatic nuclear retaliation to any kind of aggression—nuclear or conventional; and secondly, in the event of war, giving a political signal of willingness and ability to escalate to the SIOP. For these roles, finely tuned systems and deployments are not necessary and might even give an aggressor the wrong impression. In this point of view, almost any concept of military advantage to be derived from TNF employment is dangerous, in that it implies a possibility of large-scale, limited nuclear war in the theater. Holders of this view might see a need for improved longer-range systems capable of penetrating into the Soviet Union as a political response to SS-20 deployments. But they would be unlikely to wholeheartedly support more general improvements in TNF warfighting capabilities.

The second, or "American," concept holds that the most effective deterrent derives from a credible capability to prevent an aggressor from achieving his military objectives, and that it would take a combination of strong conventional forces and theater nuclear forces that can be applied with precise effects to influence the course of a battle. Holders of this view would likewise support modernization of the longer-range systems because of the increasing vulnerability of aircraft in this role and a recognition that the *Poseidon* SLBM is unsuited to it in many cases. But they would also want parallel improvements across the whole range of TNF systems and their support to be sure that TNF can be controlled, can actually survive until used, and can do the desired amount of damage to military targets.

Neither of these concepts provides a suitable basis for allied TNF force posture and negotiating policy decisions. The "European" concept plays down or ignores the fact that even giving a political signal requires real operational capabilities that, at present, are highly suspect. For example, the Soviet nuclear forces and their command and control (C²) are configured and trained to preempt NATO nuclear attacks—that is, to react with a massive strike of their own *within* NATO's nuclear preparation and decision time. Given current NATO nuclear decision processes, C², and TNF vulnerabilities, it is not at all clear that NATO could execute a limited first strike "signal" even if it chose to. Moreover, the "European" concept presumes that while there is a political requirement for European participation in a general nuclear war, U.S. strategic forces can make up for any deficiencies in theater forces. Yet, with the growing vulnerability of the U.S. land-based missile forces, the proliferation of targets, and the SALT constraints on U.S. central systems, the ability of those systems to cover European military targets independent of theater forces is decreasing. And, in any event, U.S. central systems are mostly not well suited for several target types most relevant to Alliance defense (e.g., hardened command, control, and communications sites).

The "American" concept suffers from putting too much emphasis on limited nuclear warfighting, which is anathema to Europeans, and not enough emphasis on the political necessity to maintain the strongest possible link to the SIOP. For this reason, proposals such as the one to improve the security and survivability of TNF and their C^2 against Pact nuclear attacks—which, as suggested above, are almost certainly needed even to carry out the "European" concept—all too often indicate a willingness to consider a widespread nuclear exchange in Europe without escalation. Such proposals consequently fail to command general Alliance support.

It is, therefore, highly unlikely that NATO can agree on TNF employment in a strong and specific enough way to provide a durable basis for rational force posture and negotiating policy decisions using either of these popular concepts. What is needed both for military, and, as will be argued below, for political purposes in the Alliance is a renewed effort to find and elaborate on a concept that can attract a broader base of support among the allies. Such a concept would have to make the relationship of TNF to the SIOP, at one end of the spectrum, and to the conventional battle, at the other, more explicit. So far, although the Alliance has agreed to deploy 464 ground-launched cruise missiles and 108 *Pershing* II ballistic missiles in Western Europe between 1983 and 1985, it has failed to formulate a widely shared strategic rationale for these systems.

At the "Eurostrategic" end, U.S. central systems and longer-range theater systems must provide the major deterrent and the eventual response to massive Soviet threats against the European target base. Improvements in TNF command and control and in longer-range systems' pre-launch survivability and ability to penetrate defenses are important to this role.

At the combined arms end of the spectrum, TNF provide the principal deterrent to massive Soviet conventional attacks, unless the Alliance were to develop the ability to contain such attacks conventionally. But to be an effective deterrent, TNF must be demonstrably capable of halting a large-scale combined arms attack and preventing loss of territory. This requires an ability to locate and destroy military targets in the field and their support in the rear. Strategic forces are not designed nor configured for this purpose, but theater forces are. TNF forces of all ranges—not just battlefield systems—are required for this purpose. The large proportion of shorter-range TNF systems in the allied inventory is perhaps the greatest weakness of the present allied posture—both militarily and in terms of political opposition in Western Europe.

This argues for refurbishing the original conception of deterrence into a "seamless web" of capabilities across the whole spectrum of forces, if there is to be a basis for a new consensus within the Alliance. Western European allies have gradually come to accept that—despite their distaste for fighting a prolonged conventional war in Europe—overall deterrence is strengthened if the Alliance has stalwart conventional defenses. They might, therefore, eventually agree that overall deterrence would be enhanced by a more effective demonstrable capability to execute a broader range of options than the present theater nuclear forces provide.

The evolution of such a consensus would depend on several factors. First, it would be facilitated by successful development of a broader range of TNF selective employment plans (SEPs) that could, at the same time, effectively relate to political efforts to prevent further escalation and terminate hostilities. Secondly, a new consensus would obviously influence and be influenced by near-term, force-posture decisions at all levels, particularly concerning TNF. The nuclear-armed cruise missile perhaps provides the most interesting example of these points. Since it would have to be employed on a relatively large scale in order to penetrate even relatively small sets of targets, the cruise missile's suitability as a vehicle for conveying the desired political signals might be compromised in the eyes of many Western Europeans. That would justify the inclusion of a ballistic missile component such as *Pershing* II in any longer-range TNF modernization program. Force-posture decisions at the conventional and SIOP levels will also influence development of this consensus and subsequent TNF decisions. At the conventional level, force-posture decisions may help to develop such a consensus by maintaining the level of nuclear "threshold" (in short, the longer the need for nuclear decisions can be delayed, the more credible the capability to apply the TNF effectively). Decisions at the strategic level may help by maintaining European confidence in the U.S. nuclear guarantee and in its deterrent effect on the Soviet Union.

Within the "seamless web" doctrine, force-posture decisions for TNF should logically be based on the need to provide a demonstrable capability to counter threats to NATO territory, rather than the capability to signal intent to escalate and to participate in a general nuclear response. The latter capability will be contained in a theater nuclear force that is properly configured to support the land battle in Europe (including an in-theater capability to strike targets in the Soviet Union). Similarly, for negotiating purposes it is the tie between conventional forces and TNF that is crucial. The goals of negotiation must be designed to protect the Alliance's capability to configure its conventional and theater nuclear forces so as to complement each other. To take only one example, the threat of nuclear strikes forces an aggressor to disperse his forces and thereby alters the requirements for conventional defense. Safeguarding the link at the SIOP end of the spectrum is a less difficult negotiating posture; it is, in essence, an intra-Alliance problem of conceiving limited, deep-strike options that are politically acceptable and that deliver the desired signal. A TNF negotiating structure that focuses on how TNF contributes to U.S. SIOP forces at the expense of operationally decisive interaction among TNF and conventional forces risks damaging NATO's overall defense posture as negotiations unfold. Bilateral U.S.-Soviet negotiations on longer-range TNF, of the sort that the Soviets finally agreed to in the spring of 1980, and which clearly relate these systems to the U.S.-Soviet strategic equation rather than to the theater balance, would run precisely this risk.

Targeting asymmetries, and relative numbers and dispositions of forces on the two sides, also argue against isolating longer-range TNF for special arms control treatment. Although both sides aim at essentially the same kinds of military and military support targets with theater-oriented weapons, two very important differences must be noted in the relative capabilities of the two sides to attack these targets:

1. There are many more targets for TNF at all ranges on the Pact side than on the Western side, yet the Pact currently has many more theater-oriented weapons than the allies.
2. A large fraction of the Pact targets are in the Soviet Union and can only be covered by longer-range systems (>1,500km), while the comparable allied targets can be covered by Warsaw Pact systems of much shorter range (>600km).

Since the Soviets' prime objective in any negotiation about theater-oriented systems must be assumed to be to limit the number of allied systems capable of striking the Soviet Union, these targeting asymmetries appear to offer the Soviets a striking advantage if negotiations are confined to longer-range systems. Whereas the allied capability to attack Soviet targets depends exclusively on longer-range systems, the Soviets can mount essentially identical threats to Western European targets with long-, medium-, or even short-range systems. Moreover, these longer-range systems—dual-capable aircraft, *Pershing* IIs, and ground-launched cruise missiles (GLCMs)—are also the only allied systems capable of striking Pact military targets in the East European countries. The Soviets should be delighted with the prospect of limiting numbers and improvements in allied systems capable of striking the Soviet Union (and also targets deep in Eastern Europe)—a capability for which the West needs the greatest improvements, while only exposing a small fraction of their forces to negotiation and retaining the ability to target all of Western Europe.

By contrast, negotiated agreements should seem useful to the allies only if the agreements could potentially stabilize and make more predictable the entire TNF threat to Western Europe without leaving open legitimate paths by which the Soviets could circumvent the agreements' intent, as would be the case if only longer-range systems were limited. Further, the current Alliance posture is "bottom heavy" in its emphasis on battlefield systems, and that is where the allies are most likely to find any negotiating capital that they might have.

Some of these relationships are displayed graphically in the accompanying charts. Figure 5.1 compares Alliance and Pact theater-oriented nuclear forces with ranges greater than 600km. It shows that if allied systems on both sides and *Poseidon*—which is already covered in SALT—are excluded from negotiation, and if U.S. systems incapable of striking the Soviet Union (and comparable systems on the Soviet side) are likewise excluded, the negotiation would boil down to bargaining between a large and versatile mix of Soviet aircraft and longer-range missiles—each of which has a modernized version in process of deployment—versus U.S. dual-capable aircraft (every one of which is desperately needed for conventional defense) and U.S. drawing board missiles. Figure 5.2 shows how the aircraft and missile components change over time, illustrating that U.S.-Soviet freezes at current levels and limits on the introduction of new missile systems would probably have little impact on Soviet TNF—because of their current high levels and because their new generation missiles are already being deployed. The figure also shows that freezes and limits on new U.S. deployments would greatly impact the Alliance, which is just in the process of deciding what types and how many new missiles to deploy. (These considerations are magnified by the targeting asymmetries discussed earlier.)

Figure 5.1

Comparison of Alliance and Warsaw Pact Theater Nuclear Delivery Systems — 1978 (ranges ≥ 600km)

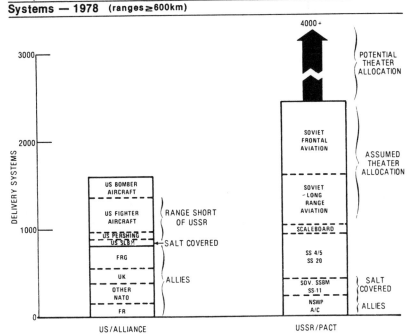

NOTE: NUMBERS DERIVED FROM PUBLICLY AVAILABLE DATA. PRIMARY SOURCES: THE MILITARY BALANCE 1978-1979 (IISS 1978), AND "ARMS CONTROL ENTERS THE GRAY AREA" BY METZGER AND DOTY IN INTERNATIONAL SECURITY VOL. 3 (WINTER 78-79).

One final point arises about negotiations. The classification of TNF delivery systems by range is inherently imprecise when it comes to aircraft or cruise missiles. The attempt to reach a satisfactory classification around a given range criterion is therefore certain to introduce an element of complication into the negotiation (and into corresponding force improvement programs) that would be extremely troublesome.

In sum, therefore, this consideration of the military context of TNF strongly suggests two conclusions:

1. An effort to refurbish the concept of the "seamless web" of deterrence as it applies to TNF is a vital prerequisite to a sound set of force-posture and negotiating policies. The links of TNF to U.S. SIOP forces and to conventional forces are of equal importance to the Alliance. But it is the relationship between TNF and conven-

Figure 5.2

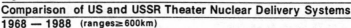

Comparison of US and USSR Theater Nuclear Delivery Systems
1968 — 1988 (ranges≥600km)

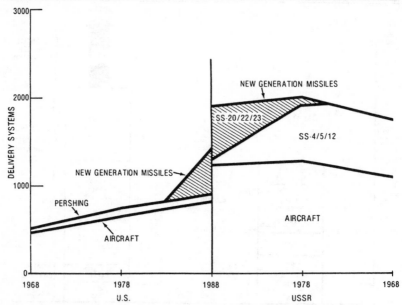

NOTE: NUMBERS DERIVED FROM PUBLICLY AVAILABLE DATA. PRIMARY SOURCES: THE MILITARY
BALANCE 1978-1979 (IISS 1978), AND "ARMS CONTROL ENTERS THE GRAY AREA" BY METZGER AND
DOTY IN INTERNATIONAL SECURITY VOL. 3 (WINTER 1978-79).

tional forces which must primarily determine TNF force-posture
decisions and negotiating strategies.

2. TNF of all ranges (with the possible exception of atomic demoli-
    tion munitions [ADMs] and very short-range systems) should be
    covered together in negotiations. This would reflect operational
    reality, avoid placing the Alliance at a crucial bargaining disad-
    vantage, and help ensure that Western European security, as well
    as the security of the Soviet homeland, gets proper attention in
    TNF negotiations.

European TNF in their Political Context

Three important sets of political issues arise in connection with European TNF policy—domestic politics in Western Europe, intra-Alliance
politics, and the East-West politics of the negotiating approach ad-
vocated here. These will be discussed in turn.

Western European Domestic Politics. The fundamental question here is whether Western European elites and publics can assimilate a coherent role for TNF in Alliance strategy and, if so, how that consensus can be facilitated. The narrower the base of support for Alliance TNF policies, the more prone those policies will be to erosion by political opposition, Soviet propaganda and diplomatic pressures, and any further decline in European confidence in U.S. reliability. By contrast, the greater the degree of assimilation that can be achieved, the stronger should be future allied cohesion and European confidence in the credibility of deterrence.

Some would argue that the spectre of the nuclear devastation of Western Europe is so formidable that no set of policies could gain widespread acceptance of TNF, unless it serves as the shortest of fuses to ignite the SIOP forces. If this is correct, then governments can either insist on modernizing TNF against irreconcilable political opposition or shrink from such decisions to avoid that opposition.

However, there is no particularly compelling reason to adopt this view. During the 1970s, Europeans progressively assimilated the idea of a serious conventional defense, and this has shown that a combination of growing Soviet threat, U.S. pressures for force improvement programs, good political management, and a visible and carefully worked-out negotiating effort (i.e., in the conventional force case, MBFR) can cause attitudes to shift outside the narrow circle of defense specialists. But it would take the greatest possible degree of mutual understanding and agreement about allied policies on force posture, on negotiating strategy, and on the relationship between the two for there to be such a shift of opinion about TNF.

First, the force posture. The divergence between the present posture and doctrine is too easy a target for those in Europe who are skeptical about the role of TNF. The danger now is that a policy to modernize longer-range TNF in isolation will be open to criticism in Europe because it does not also rationalize the shorter-range systems and the doctrine for their use. This point has been made frequently, notably in the Netherlands—where some moderates accept the case for modernizing longer-range TNF, but believe that selling the idea (notably the basing rationale) would be difficult if it seemed merely to expand the role of TNF in Alliance strategy. The same point is also valid to a greater or lesser extent in other Western European countries, including West Germany and Belgium.

The need for a comprehensive approach also arises in connection with negotiating policies. A partial approach to negotiations on TNF, whether concentrating on longer-range or on shorter-range systems, is open to obvious criticism because Soviet TNF can threaten Western Europe with systems of essentially any range. The concept apparently adopted by the Alliance in December 1979—concentrating only on longer-range systems and, in effect, principally on ground-launched missiles of longer range—is wide open to this criticism. The flaws inherent in such a partial approach would make it difficult for Alliance governments to defend that negotiating position publicly. Consequently, governments are also unlikely to wean their publics easily from an interest in negotiation, even in the quite conceivable event that no useful negotiated agreement seems to be "in the cards."

Finally, the relationship between force posture and negotiating policies also needs to be as coherent as possible. Ideally, this should be done by defining both the minimum deployment levels required on the Western side—even if allied negotiating goals were quickly achieved, and the additional options that would need to be implemented if they were not. While this may not be easy to do, it is desirable to make the attempt.

Perfect coherence in these various respects is not easy to attain. Failure to totally satisfy each of these requirements need not prevent greater assimilation of the TNF roled in the Alliance countries. But the more nearly that coherence can be attained, the greater the prospect of promoting such assimilation.

Intra-Alliance Politics. The two central issues are the implications of European concerns about the reliability of the U.S. strategic nuclear guarantee and the related question of what approaches, to TNF negotiations in particular, can best protect the cohesion of the Alliance into the middle and late 1980s.

The role of trans-Atlantic confidence, or the lack of it, in determining attitudes toward defense issues in Western Europe is as obvious as it is often hard to measure. All too frequently, as with the question of European—especially German—concern about the SS-20, the basic issues of European confidence in U.S. reliability are perceived, discussed, and "resolved" in terms of other issues. But failure to distinguish between the observed symptoms of concern and the true causes of the disease can make the chosen treatment largely ineffective.

There is no need in this chapter to discuss in detail why European confidence in the reliability of the U.S. strategic guarantee has declined in recent years. That it *has* declined is now generally accepted, although there is less agreement as to how far the previous level of confidence can be restored. That it could decline further is equally clear, given that the allies face potentially divisive issues both *within* the context of European security (SALT II ratification and SALT III) and *without* (energy, Middle East problems, economic and monetary issues).

In this situation, the Western European allies find themselves pulled in different directions on TNF posture questions. On the one hand, they are inclined to want reassurance from the United States in the form of actions that reaffirm the U.S. guarantee—both for themselves and for the Soviets. Thus, for example, many Germans have attached importance to basing new longer-range TNF in Western Europe on the ground—as a visible symbol of commitment—and at times too hastily dismissed arguments for sea-based systems, such as the sea-launched cruise missile (SLCM), on military and/or other grounds.

On the other hand, some Europeans, consciously or unconsciously, see the need for some insurance against increasing doubt about U.S. reliability. This concern explains the gradual (and not always very explicit) revival of interest in the importance of having TNF placed under the sole control of a European nation and, in particular, of a modernized British nuclear force.

The interests of future Alliance cohesion dictate that a two-pronged policy on TNF modernization be adopted to deal with this situation. First, the suitability of allied TNF to perform their assigned missions, rather than calculations about short-term political reassurance to West Germany, should primarily determine what kinds of systems are deployed, since the level of European confidence in allied TNF as a deterrent is likely ultimately to depend on this. If the characteristics of sea-based forces make them attractive as components of a new, longer-range TNF mix, then the United States should make the case for them on military and technical grounds and recognize that providing effective and lasting political reassurance to West Germany makes more sense than simply accepting current German perceptions of which TNF systems would best provide such reassurance.

Secondly, the major allies need to address, much more explicitly than ever, the issue of placing their TNF under the control of Western European countries as a contribution to allied deterrence. At present this essentially means some placement under British control since—despite continuing hints of shifts in certain French circles—the French are not ready to depart from Gaullist orthodoxy to the extent of discussing the placement of their forces under anyone else's control. However, discussion should at least consider developing some forces in Europe with minimal U.S. assistance (for example, cruise missiles and their launchers). The French might procure such forces for their own national purposes, but eventually they would contribute to a concerted TNF capability in British and French hands.

The United Kingdom, the United States, and West Germany hold the vital keys to this lock: The United Kingdom, because if the British—and especially the Conservatives—could overcome their persistent tendency to think that their nuclear forces are intended almost exclusively for British national purposes, they could initiate a dialogue, notably with West Germany, about how those forces could contribute to overall Alliance goals (and thus, in effect, help to alleviate German anxieties). The present British Government has indicated that it may be more open-minded on this subject than its predecessors, although it is too early to know what, if any, new policies will emerge. The United States, because its ability to influence the British in this direction remains considerable and because its cooperation would be required to implement any concrete proposals along this line. But deciding to use its influence in this matter would require the United States to undergo a painful process of reflection about the further dilution of its domination of Western nuclear policy. West Germany, because if it could make the importance it attaches to the potential theater role of its neighbors' nuclear forces more explicit, then the British, and perhaps the United States, might adopt a more imaginative approach. By contrast, the French are unlikely to make any direct contribution in this area. However, their concern with the potential consequences of German anxieties about U.S. credibility has been such that the French would probably be interested in, and in certain circumstances sympathetic to, any British efforts to take German requirements into account in their forthcoming force-posture decisions, just as they have been tacitly sympathetic to U.S. longer-range TNF modernization programs.

Intra-Alliance psychological and political pressures also influence the allies' attitudes toward TNF negotiations. These pressures have pushed the Alliance toward the line of least resistance in the short term, even at the risk of intensifying the longer-term problems of preserving Alliance cohesion.

In the United States, two factors have been striking. First, the experience—and bureaucracy—of SALT and the SALT-ocentric bias of U.S. policy on East-West problems has created a reluctance to modify the character of SALT and a desire to assimilate longer-range TNF problems into the SALT orbit. This reluctance has been reinforced by a disposition in some quarters to reassert the traditional pattern of U.S. dominance in the Alliance, if only to avoid the frustrations inherent in a more multilateral conduct of Alliance affairs. Some of the more dubious arguments for handling a negotiation on longer-range TNF bilaterally in SALT III appear to have derived from these predispositions. One such argument is that longer-range TNF must be handled separately from other TNF for negotiating purposes because it is desirable to avoid complexity and deal with those parts of the problem that lend themselves most readily to solution. Quite apart from other reasons why dealing only with longer-range TNF would actually be disadvantageous to the West and why an attempt to discriminate between longer-range TNF and others creates greater complexity, this argument flies in the face of the U.S. experience in SALT and MBFR. In both negotiations, complexity has for the most part become a necessity in order to achieve a sound negotiating posture on inherently complex issues. And while the Western European allies would certainly like to see further progress made toward stabilizing the central strategic balance through SALT III as soon as possible, that would arguably be more likely to occur if TNF issues were detached for treatment elsewhere than with what could well become a TNF albatross around the neck of SALT.

The major Western European countries are subject to different pressures, too, that dispose them to shy away from participation in any TNF negotiations and to favor dealing with longer-range TNF, if any at all, in a bilateral SALT III. The French case is the clearest. French opposition to having French nuclear forces limited by any agreement is total and will remain so as long as Gaullist doctrine about nuclear issues has a politically, if not intellectually, secure grip. There was no prospect of substantial change before the Presidential elections of 1981 and not much thereafter. The logic of these attitudes, however, is not overpowering. The French themselves insist (rightly) that their nuclear forces are central systems and that for this reason alone (with the possible and minor exception of *Pluton*) they should not be covered in any negotiation on TNF.

At the same time, the French concern with German anxieties about their security and the touching French efforts to revive flagging German confidence in the reliability of the U.S. nuclear umbrella are inconsistent with the fundamental tenet of Gaullist nuclear doctrine—that a nation will only use nuclear weapons in defense of its own national territory. This inconsistency appears to be making itself felt among some French intellectuals. But for the time being, the grip of orthodoxy and a basic skepticism about the feasibility of useful TNF negotiations is so strong that at least one answer that Gaullist doctrine would appear *not* to preclude—a TNF negotiation, including France, from which French nuclear forces would be excluded as central systems—is still not seriously considered. Yet such a negotiation, if successful, could help alleviate German anxieties by making the TNF balance more stable.

The German approach has been still less conclusive in logic, although equally powerful politically. Germans have been reticent to be directly involved in nuclear decision making (especially since the SPD wants to be free of responsibility in this area while party pressures are against enhancing the TNF role in Alliance strategy), and this inhibits direct

German involvement in any TNF negotiations. This attitude doubtless also owes something to West Germany's evident desire to play down its concern with U.S. reliability—a concern that surfaced in 1978 and apparently has more recently been superseded by a revived emphasis on the need for Alliance solidarity and confidence. In both these ways, the German attitude has been rooted in short-term expediency and ignored the fact that direct German participation alongside the United States in TNF negotiations would be likely (again on the MBFR model) to create greater understanding and cohesion, not the reverse. It should also presumably offer the SPD some domestic political dividend by showing that they have embarked actively on a new phase of détente. In fact, Schmidt's exploitation of the breakdown of most direct U.S.-Soviet discussion on such subjects enabled him to use his meeting with Brezhnev in June 1980 to facilitate resumption of U.S.-Soviet contacts on TNF arms limitation and thus earn some domestic political kudos.

The British case is less clear, only partly because the new government has not yet worked its way through the problem. British reluctance for its SLBMs to be covered in any TNF negotiation is understandable. But, as with the French forces, there is no reason why British forces should not be considered as central systems for treatment (if anywhere) in SALT. For the rest, the British desire not to become involved in TNF negotiations probably derives mostly from skepticism—all the stronger now that the Conservatives are in government—about the value of, and prospects for success in, such negotiations. This attitude is almost certainly mutable. Any sign that the United States—or West Germany—attaches importance to British participation could well bring about a change of heart.

It follows, then, that the Alliance is in a curious position. Having taken several initiatives to include TNF in negotiations (or virtually so)—such as Option III, the ERW "offer," the insistence on a negotiation track parallel to the December 1979 decision on GLCMs and the *Pershing* II—the major allies remain either skeptical about the value of these initiatives or inhibited from developing a coherent and comprehensive policy framework within which to set them. In particular, although the European allies have been the principal source of pressure for a negotiating policy on the longer-range TNF, they apparently lack the will or capability to participate extensively in or to undertake the analytical work essential to its development. Yet nothing in recent experience (notably with MBFR) justifies the conclusion that Western European governments, which have in recent years been increasingly inclined to form strong opinions of their own on these subjects, will necessarily be content simply to follow the U.S. lead in formulating negotiating positions.

In this atmosphere the lessons of SALT I and SALT II about the effects that bilateral dealings between the United States and the Soviet Union have—on issues affecting European security—are of decisive importance to allied cohesion. The history of the SALT decade's effect on the Alliance has been traced elsewhere, and two conclusions have clearly emerged from it. The first is that Western European suspicions about U.S. propensity to trade away European interests against purely U.S. ones are endemic and damaging—especially in the absence of any direct European experience with the negotiations or responsibility for formulating negotiating policies. The question is not how to eradicate, but how to control those suspicions. After all, the TNF issues are more important to Western European security in several ways than they are to that of the United States.

The second conclusion is that the inherent practical and bureaucratic obstacles to consultative procedures that satisfy Western European governments that the United States has taken their interests fully into account and adequately defended them in negotiation are such as to make the theoretical ways in which consultations could be improved largely irrelevant. Conceivably, some mechanisms in which European representatives were directly involved in U.S. policy-making deliberations and, in effect, given veto rights over U.S. negotiating positions where they directly concerned Western Europe could meet the need. But it is far from certain. And even arrangements of that kind would not automatically give Western European governments a feel for the dynamics of negotiation—or the sense of political responsibility—essential to making sound judgments on tactics. Thus, proceeding in this way would involve an unnecessarily high risk of allied dissatisfaction and unease as negotiations developed.

These conclusions suggest that any negotiations on TNF should be multilateral and that TNF should be defined to exclude British and French "strategic" forces that would be considered to be equivalent to U.S. and Soviet central systems. The United States would appear to be the only country with enough political room for maneuver and standing in the Alliance to be able to conclude such an initiative with any hope of success. And even if, as seems possible, Britain and West Germany could be persuaded to join, France would surely not do so. Since this is the case, it would be essential to try to work out some (rather informal) consultative mechanism in which the French would agree to participate so that their suggestions could be considered, and also some means of taking into account those French forces—such as *Pluton* and its successors—that could only with difficulty be called central strategic systems.

This conclusion may strike horror into the hearts of many for whom multilateral negotiations seem a wearying prospect. But, for all their problems, both MBFR and CSCE have been enormously successful in *Alliance* terms as sources of allied self-confidence and consensus on issues that, at the outset, seemed menacingly divisive. Participation *is* important and does help political elites and public opinion to assimilate the subjects being treated. The parallel with the SALT-related frictions is striking. If, as argued above, the concerns (notably about the SS-20) that have stimulated recent European interest in TNF negotiations are symptoms of a disease whose basic cause is a decline of confidence in the United States, a substantial way to treat that disease should be through procedures explicitly designed to restore that confidence—so far as it can be restored.

East-West Politics. The third set of political issues relates to the East-West dimension of the TNF negotiation problem. Is there any reason to suppose that the Soviet Union would agree to the negotiating approach recommended here?

The immediate Soviet reaction to a Western proposal to deal with TNF in the multilateral context proposed here would in all probability be adverse. They have a long-standing and self-interested view that SALT should cover all systems which can hit Soviet territory, but not others. And we have already discussed their obvious interest in dealing with longer-range TNF separately from other TNF. But the ultimate Soviet reaction cannot be predicted with confidence. As with SALT and MBFR, it may take an effort to persuade them to accept the idea, and that effort need not fail. Among other things, the West would have a fair amount of leverage in view of what would appear to be a strong Soviet desire to bring U.S. cruise missile programs in particular and FBS in general under negotiation. If this is so, then the West should be able to exercise considerable influence by standing firm on the position that either all TNF must be considered together in a multilateral forum or there should be no negotiations on any theater systems at all.

This approach would be all the stronger since the Western position would provide a substantially logical, cohesive forum for discussing all kinds of nuclear forces—central strategic and theater—according to criteria as cogent as any that the Soviets could advance. Similarly, although the Soviets might prefer to see British and French systems included in the theater balance, Western acknowledgment that those systems could be discussed in SALT at a proper time should give the Soviets a modest advance on the present position.

But the decisive argument in this connection is that it does not much matter if the Soviets reject the proposal, at least not immediately. For the critical facet of the policy is that by presenting a comprehensive and easily defensible approach to the whole range of TNF problems, the Alliance would be in a much stronger position to preserve its cohesion in the face of Soviet rejection (or indeed the stagnation of negotiations) than it would with the piecemeal approach that present policies seem to be taking. Thus the defensive strength of the proposal against Soviet propaganda campaigns and counter-proposals might well prove to be its most important characteristic.

Conclusion and Postscript

The argument of this chapter has been that in approaching the problems of TNF posture and negotiation, the allies' fundamental aims should be to protect the cohesion of the Alliance throughout the 1980s and promote greater assimilation by Western European societies of the role of TNF in Alliance strategy. By optimizing their policies and programs to meet these two aims, the allies would be more likely to achieve stable deterrence and a strong common defense than by policies that, however apparently decisive and impressive in the short-term, have tended over time to increase intra-Alliance frictions and domestic opposition to Alliance strategy. In this perspective, several different lines of argument converge on two main conclusions. The first is that TNF modernization should be approached across the whole range of TNF and with a view to producing a force posture that reflects a more coherent doctrine and takes into account both U.S. insistence on a clearer military rationale for TNF employment and the primary European interest in TNF as indicators of further escalation. The second conclusion is that TNF negotiating options, which should so far as possible be closely interlinked with the modernization process, should also cover essentially the whole range of systems in a multilateral negotiation and not involve piecemeal treatment of different subsets of TNF in different—and in part bilateral—negotiating contexts.

The deterioration of the East-West climate and the stalling of the U.S. SALT ratification process have made the prospects for successful TNF negotiations dimmer. At the same time, they have made the creation of a separate TNF negotiation, albeit bilateral, more likely if any progress flows from Chancellor Schmidt's meetings with President Brezhnev in

June 1980. The same developments have both facilitated the acceptance of the allied decision to deploy new longer-range TNF in the form of 464 GLCMs and 108 *Pershing* IIs starting in 1983—even though reservations persist in varying degrees in the Netherlands, Belgium, and West Germany—and confirmed the wisdom of having some arms limitation proposal on the table from the West. Without such a proposal, Western European opinion would undoubtedly have been more susceptible to spurious Soviet proposals in late 1979 and early 1980.

But neither the TNF modernization issue nor the arms limitation effort are yet out of the woods. Not only has longer-range TNF deployment yet to take place, but difficult decisions are looming on the modernization of middle- and shorter-range systems. And the difficult questions of the scope and nature of the arms limitation proposals that were left unresolved in December 1979 have yet to be faced, possibly in the heat of actual negotiations. Thus, while the December decision has served its purpose well thus far and has, in particular, bought valuable time for an attempt to deal with the more difficult outstanding questions, those questions will continue to press upon allied policymakers. For this reason, we believe that the underlying case made in this chapter for a more systematic attempt to set allied TNF policy into a broader context of nuclear employment concepts and negotiating objectives retains its full force.

6
Institutional Impediments

William L. Hyland

At this writing, the SALT II Treaty and Protocol are now moribund. A number of commentators are tolling the death knell for strategic arms control and perhaps for any arms control. In part this reflects disappointment with the terms of the new SALT agreements. Ironically, the case for the present agreement was summed up best by a presumptive opponent, the chairman of the Joint Chiefs of Staff, General David Jones, who commented that the SALT agreements were a "modest but useful" step. But there is also a broader disenchantment with the SALT "process."[1]

This disenchantment is taking various forms. First, there is the now standard reaction that takes the form of attacks against weapons systems such as the MX ICBM, which seem dictated by the new agreements; analysts invariably find alternative systems that are somehow more "stable," but unlikely to be built.[2] Second, there is the obsession with reductions; this is sponsored by both left and right as indicated in the near unanimous (13-2) vote of the Senate Foreign Relations Committee in support of a vaguely conceived reduction scheme for SALT III. Third, there are those who advocate a series of amendments that will supposedly magically transform a defective agreement into an acceptable one. Finally, there is the effort to build a tight linkage between SALT and a five-year defense projection, which, incidentally, points up the vague relationship that has existed until now between the SALT agreements and longer-term strategic planning.

This said, an obvious question is: how did this rather unhappy state of affairs come to pass? What happened to the elaborately conceived theories and ideas of the early 1960s about arms control and strategic stability? There are, of course, a number of elements that contributed to the present situation: turmoil in domestic politics, a shift in the balance between Congress and the Executive branch, deterioration of U.S.-Soviet relations, frustration over the slow pace and limited scope of arms control negotiations, a growing concern that the balance of strategic power is indeed shifting against the United States and, finally, a fear that in pursuing the arms control "process" we are somehow contributing to a national lethargy over genuine security concerns.

But there is another aspect; namely, that the theory and practice of arms control have become distorted by the confrontation with realities. It was argued persuasively in the early 1960s that arms control could be achieved because of several new factors including what was described as the "unity of strategy and arms control"—that is, the recognition among arms controllers that there would be continuing need for defense even under conditions of significant disarmament; the willingness of defense planners to take arms control options into account; and a mutual acceptance of the need to subordinate both defense and arms control to a wider concept of national security. Military planning without reference to arms control would thus be inadequate. Arms control would be strengthened by the participation of military planners. The traditional antagonists—the military and the arms controllers—would be drawn together by a common interest in achieving strategic stability.[3]

The organizational implication was to create over-arching bureaucratic mechanisms and institutions—initially known as executive committees, that would reconcile diverse interests and produce a framework for high-level decisions. The Arms Control and Disarmament Agency (ACDA) was created in this context. The initial success of the limited test ban negotiations seemed to bear promise of further progress. The result, however, has been at best a modest success, and in some significant respects, a resounding failure: (1) arms control considerations have competed with, rather than supplemented, a coherent military strategy (for example, a major new system—the MX—was designed in large part by SALT negotiating considerations); (2) major weapons systems have become part of the bargaining process, and increasingly deprived of a strong strategic rationale for their existence outside of a negotiating context; the potential NATO decision to accept 572 intermediate-range ballistic and cruise missiles involves, as an apparent precondition, a negotiating proposition in order to guarantee political support for eventual deployment in Europe, and (3) the two presumed partners, defense and arms control, have remained antagonistic, but in a bizarre sense—defense officials, including the uniformed military, consume much of their strength arguing over negotiating tactics, for which they are ill suited, while ACDA spends much of its energy combatting new weapons systems and designs, in part through the cumbersome process of Congressionally-mandated Arms Control Impact Statements.

In sum, arms control has become less of a component of national strategic military planning and more of an alternative; negotiating propositions have become an escape from the dilemmas of long-term programming. Stability is thus sought in marginal bargains about changes in some Soviet systems, rather than in the creation of an equilibrium through a combination of U.S. programs and negotiated arrangements. Arms control has thus become a diversion from strategy.

The Organizational Pattern

The problems of orchestrating defense policy and arms control were illustrated in the early years of the Nixon administration. Despite some back-channel maneuvering by the White House under Henry Kissinger, the major SALT and defense-policy decisions in the early 1970s were made within the framework of the new centralized bodies within the National Security Council: the Verification Panel and the Defense Review Committee. The theory was that arms control debates would be reconciled within the Verification Panel while political policy and military requirements would be brought together in the Defense Program Review Committee (DPRC)—both groups would be chaired by the President's Assistant for National Security. The result, however, was that the Verification Panel worked overtime while the DPRC atrophied. In retrospect, it is clear that the DPRC was bound to atrophy; for if the Secretary of Defense valued his institutional prerogatives, and especially if he was a skilled political operator (like Melvin Laird), he would protect this policy preserve.

In any case, two quite different processes are also involved. To a great extent, U.S. military planning has degenerated to budget management. Each armed service is wise enough to know that its share of the budget will not alter radically in any given year, and that the best it can hope for is a gradual long-term shift in resources to its programs. Thus, it would be almost inconceivable for the Air Force or Navy, for example, to argue simultaneously for two major new programs, because they would risk losing both (i.e., the B-1 and the air-launched cruise missile, or the *Trident* and sea-launched cruise missiles). The existence of the Office of Management and Budget—with a professional staff that concentrates on the defense budget, plus the usual domestic pressures for economies as well as mindless Congressional budget paring (mindless because it reflects no strategic design) all conspire to turn strategic planning into a bookkeeping operation. Take almost any budget proposal in the past decade: one will find numerous research/development items—for which little strategic rationale is evident, but for which small, almost innocuous amounts of money are requested—so as to be unprovocative and, ideally, unnoticed.

Since the principal vehicle for strategic planning is also one of the few management tools and means of discipline for the Secretary of Defense, naturally he would guard the process zealously. Attempts to inject political goals or even "Presidential" considerations face a massive wall of resistance from the outset. Moreover, the defense planning process is ponderous to the point that any impact is almost imperceptible. Advancing a new program means almost nothing unless the program is continually funded at adequate levels; but determination of what is adequate requires some long-term concept—some sense of doctrine for deployment and use. Rarely are such justifications to be discovered at the outset of development; generally, new programs are rationalized as providing a hedge against some threat or in the name of "flexibility." It is easier, of course, to eliminate a program. But that has inherent problems. The elimination of a new weapons program requires some sense that it is either (1) unnecessary; (2) unworkable; or (3) too expensive, even if necessary and reliable. But none of these criteria can be satisfied early in the planning process. Thus, major programs are generally challenged and cancelled later in their life. The B-1, for example, was cancelled only when it was ready for deployment; the *Trident* was nearly killed in 1973 when it was ready for laying of keels; the cruise missile nearly expired in 1973 when it began to show promise.

Given the inherent difficulties of shaping defense policy through budgetary manipulation, there remain two possibilities: (1) through doctrinal changes that imply new or different weapons, and (2) through arms control. Arms control lends itself well to infringements on defense policy. First of all, it is rather dynamic; the give and take process of negotiations requires innumerable tactical choices and occasional strategic decisions. The mechanisms for taking these decisions thus assume a life of their own and an inherent bureaucratic attractiveness. Gradually, there is an increasingly wide field for speculative endeavors. The premium is on reasonably rapid responses to negotiating situations; there is a pressure toward consensus and compromise, i.e., "negotiability" becomes an important consideration. At one point Kissinger's interagency Verification Panel banished "negotiability" from the litany of pros and cons for various options. It tended to give skilled political polemicists a tactical advantage. Often, however, the experts guessed wrong—especially in predicting whether the Soviets preferred an ABM ban or a MIRV ban.

Because of the very process of developing negotiating options, some imagination is needed to manipulate various combinations of limits and restraints on weapons systems. Without some clear guidance such as a general strategic plan (which scarcely exists in the Defense Department), there is a strong tendency to proliferate proposals affecting a broad range of weapons, and each proposal is, by definition, different from planned programs, i.e., "options."

The arms control process, moreover, has become continuous. There is virtually no period in which the bureaucracy is not preparing a position for negotiation or defending an existing agreement. This created an environment for bureaucratic guerrilla warfare against military programs, especially when coupled with the legal requirement for arms control impact statements. An excellent example of this is the Carter administration's evaluation of exotic systems—such as directed energy and lasers. The arms control impact statements for FY 1980 contain the following judgment:

> As the technology of directed energy weapons matures, it may raise some *significant challenges* to our arms control interests and policies. Thus . . . this technology deserves continuing attention from that point of view.[4] (emphasis added)

The foregoing raises the question of how an embryonic program, unrelated as yet to any strategy, could conceivably "challenge" arms control policy. The conclusion seems inescapable that arms control policy is fixed and immutable, while military programs are subject to challenge.

Two rough organizational models of arms control-defense integration have emerged in practice. The first model appeared during the Kennedy-Johnson era and featured lower-level coordinating committees and informal but high-level decision-making groups. The second model, from the Kissinger period under both Nixon and Ford imposed a more structured process, with permanent institutions, that gradually gained more influence and power.

The first model sought to bridge the expected military-civilian splits by forging agreed papers or consensus to apply pressure on progressively higher levels in the bureaucracy. This meant inevitably that the premium was on the lowest common denominator. The next level of consideration was thus confronted with yes or no decisions.

The Kissinger model in part reacted against the defects in this approach. The idea was to widen the scope for analysis and discussion of alternatives. Kissinger described this rationale in his recent memoirs:

A President should not leave the presentation of his options to one of the Cabinet departments or agencies. Since the views of the departments are often in conflict, to place one in charge of presenting the options will be perceived by the others as giving it an unfair advantage. Moreover, the strong inclination of all departments is to narrow the scope for Presidential decision, not to expand it. They are organized to develop a preferred policy, not a range of choices. If forced to present options, the typical department will present two absurd alternatives as straw men bracketing its preferred option—which usually appears in the middle position. A totally ignorant decision-maker could easily satisfy his departments by blindly choosing Option 2 of any three choices which they submit to him.[5]

Opening up the option process, however, risks deepening the military-civilian split, and, in effect, spreading the consequences over a broader range of issues than originally intended. Thus, when a position is under consideration by the president, the inter-agency split intensifies and the battle is conducted on strategic and tactical levels of implementation. When negotiations are active, individual members of the negotiating team have a wide field to stimulate Soviet comments that are then relayed back as "evidence" for or against options under consideration. This happened throughout SALT I.

Military participants in the arms control process have an additional recourse: They can integrate into their planning cycles certain weapons programs or testing schedules that then dictate negotiating positions. One of the most significant cases was the MIRV testing program in 1969, which became a test of political strength, rather than an occasion for cool examination of the various consequences of a MIRVed world. A testing moratorium was regarded as a sign of political weakness, and in the inter-agency debates, the Joint Chiefs and civilian defense officials adamantly argued for continuing the test program without change. (It must also be noted, however, that the Soviets showed no serious interest in stopping MIRVs, at least not until they had achieved their own capability.)

Probably, the most significant breakdown of the integrating mechanism occurred between 1973 and 1974, when a "new look" in defense planning emerged with Secretary James Schlesinger's presentation of "flexible strategic options"—at a time when post-SALT I negotiations were entering a crucial phase. On the one hand, the new strategy (actually a change in nuclear targeting initiated three years earlier) seemed to provide a strong lever for extracting Soviet concessions for a new agreement. But in June 1974, the Defense Department took a standard position: that the Soviets had to either abandon their new MIRV program or limit it to extremely low levels. Although it had a legitimate arms control objective, this position never specified what price the United States would pay; yet the Pentagon confidently argued that the Soviets could be persuaded to accept severe MIRV restrictions. Nixon explained his disquiet over the position adopted by the Defense Department.

> The U.S. military opposition to a new SALT agreement came to a head at the meeting of the National Security Council on the afternoon of June 20 when Secretary of Defense Schlesinger presented the Pentagon's proposal. It amounted to an unyielding hard line against any SALT agreement that did not ensure an overwhelming American advantage. It was a proposal that the Soviets were sure to reject out of hand.
>
> After the arguments on both sides had been stated, I intervened: "I think we should try to use this time to frame a more practical approach to this problem. We have to accept the fact that Secretary Schlesinger's proposal simply has no chance whatever of being accepted by the Soviets, so we should try to work out something consistent with our interests that will."
>
> There was a moment of silence, and then Schlesinger, who was sitting next to me, said, "But, Mr. President, everyone knows how impressed Khrushchev was with your forensic ability in the kitchen debate. I'm sure that if you applied your skills to it you could get them to accept this proposal."
>
> In my diary that night I recorded: "The NSC meeting was a real shocker insofar as the performance of the Chiefs, and particularly of Schlesinger, was concerned. His statement that he knew that Khrushchev had been very impressed by my 'forensic ability' and that, with my forensic ability, I could sell the idea that he presented, was really an insult to everybody's intelligence and particularly to mine."[6]

In sum, the organizational features are incidental to the larger problem. Neither the Johnson administration's model, the Kissinger model, nor the hybrid model that characterized the Carter administration guarantee that the antagonism between defense and arms control can be reconciled or at least moderated. The requirements, however, seem fairly simple: (1) a clear sense of strategic direction from the White House; (2) a specific military program to carry out these general objectives; and (3) an arms control plan that optimizes the chances of obtaining the military objectives through mutual efforts with the Soviet Union and other countries. The principal defects are that military planning is driven largely by marginal decisions about budgets, that arms control has become an end and not the means and is driven by negotiating tactics, and that the two processes are almost never in phase.

Arms and Negotiations

The ABM

The process by which strategic planning was distorted by arms control considerations began with the ABM decisions in the 1960s and early 1970s. The original decision bore little resemblance to long-range military requirements or strategy. In brief, a reluctant Secretary of Defense Robert McNamara adopted a tentative decision to proceed with an ABM system—mainly because of pressure from the president, who was concerned, not about strategic stability, but with the 1968 elections. It was almost inevitable that in this situation these conflicting bureaucratic-political tensions would be relieved through negotiations with Moscow. But once the option of negotiation was presented, it fed back upon military considerations. Thus, McNamara argued that an anti-Soviet ABM system would be destabilizing and provocative. He maintained that it could be used against Chinese nuclear attacks. It was a short step to argue that actually deploying ABM hardware would also undermine chances for the negotiations with Moscow. But for the military to support the ABM system, it had to be presented as one that could easily and rapidly be expanded.[7]

This "bastard system"—anti-Chinese in rationale, anti-Soviet in design—had all the ingredients for a confusing and ambiguous debate. It is scarcely surprising that ABM was almost constantly under some kind of review within the Executive Branch and on Capitol Hill and thus quickly became the focal point for negotiations that followed in 1969 and 1970. The fact that it passed the Senate by only one vote in 1969 made it seem inevitable that a coherent system would be rejected and that any reasonable Soviet offer would become the basis for an arms control agreement. This does not mean the final agreement was necessarily disadvantageous; it simply points up the inherent advantages of arms control in a situation where a firm military-strategic foundation has not been, or cannot be, created.

Mobile ICBMs

The increasing domination of arms control and its unavoidable backlash perhaps are nowhere better illustrated than in the evolution of the policy toward mobile ICBMs. A mobile missile, along with hardrock silos and point defense of ICBMs, were viewed in the early 1970s as potential answers to the threat of accurate Soviet MIRVs targeted against the *Minuteman* force in its fixed silos. When the chances for ABM deployment waned in the early 1970s, one might have expected mobility for American ICBMs to have enjoyed strong support. On the contrary, SALT cast a shadow over mobile missiles from the start, mainly because they were believed to be "unverifiable" and thus a threat to any agreement. From this, it was a short leap to call for a full ban on any mobile missiles. Only the short-sighted intransigence of the Soviets prevented a mobile missile ban at SALT I.[8]

Thus, in early 1971, the United States decided to shift more of its strategic efforts to sea, by developing *Trident*. Secretary of Defense Melvin Laird announced:

> The continuing Soviet strategic offensive force buildup, with its long term implications, convinced us that we need to undertake a major new strategic initiative. . . . It would be diplomatically and politically unacceptable for the U.S. to allow the Soviets to achieve a large numerical superiority in both land based and sea based strategic missiles. Moreover, there would be an increasing military risk that future technological advances in conjunction with much larger numbers of Soviet strategic missiles might offset the qualitative improvements we are planning for our land based strategic forces.[9]

This same statement briefly mentioned improved Soviet missile accuracies, but not mobile missiles. The Pentagon's Chief of Research and Engineering, John Foster, testified during the same period that ABMs and silo hardening were "counters" to *Minuteman* vulnerability and that other responses also included "relocation of the *Minuteman* missiles in some mobile mode." He added that *"At present there are no plans to deploy these counters*, but they are being studied."[10]

Indeed, Defense Department officials freely acknowledged that a new ICBM was not requested in this period, partly because of SALT. An Air Force officer, explaining the Air Force attitude toward a new mobile ICBM, said in 1974: "In the the last 10 years, there has been no formal Air Force proposal to the Secretary of Defense to work toward a jumping off point for a totally new ICBM system. While there have been a number of internal Air Force studies, this is the first formal ICBM systems technology program which . . . has been submitted to the Secretary of Defense." The proposal for a new ICBM had been held up because: "we would like to see what the SALT agreements were and the reaction that the Soviets were going to have to the SALT agreements."[11]

The attraction of both mobility, as a strategic option, and development of a new ICBM, however, had a strange impact on the SALT process. The first step, in the mid-1970s, was for the Joint Chiefs to reverse themselves and oppose any further effort to ban mobile missiles in SALT. However, at this point, the Air Force began to consider an alternative to the land mobile—which had never enjoyed much support in the Air Force and even less in the Office of the Secretary of Defense. This was an air-mobile ICBM system, possibly an adaptation of the *Minuteman*, to be carried on an aircraft. This was again to distort the negotiations, for by the time the post-Watergate negotiations resumed at Vladivostok in November 1974, the United States had to spend considerable negotiating capital to protect its option to deploy the air-mobile ICBM; thus the Vladivostok accord specifically provides that air-mobile ICBMs will be permitted and counted as one strategic vehicle.

The irony is that this hard-fought negotiating position quickly collapsed. First, the Defense Department lost interest in an air-launched ballistic missile—if only because it loomed as a budgetary competitor to the B-1 bomber. Second, the Soviet position changed; they came to favor a ban on mobile missiles at SALT, probably because their own mobile, land-based system (the SS-16) was proving to be inadequate. The Carter administration's SALT proposal of March 1977 would have banned all mobile ICBMs. It followed closely after the administration cut back funding for the MX and deferred its initial deployment from December 1983 to 1986. Thus, in the SALT II Treaty, air-mobile ballistic missiles (ASBMs) are banned from deployment or flight testing in the protocol period (through 1981), and so are mobile ICBMs. Both ASBMs and mobile ICBMs, however, are permitted under the treaty proper and would be counted as one launcher under the ceiling of 2,400. It has now become commonplace to assert that SALT did not create *Minuteman* vulnerability and thus could not solve it. But the record of interaction (or lack of it) between SALT and the issue of ICBM survivability suggests at least ambivalence, if not confusion about the relationship between means and ends.

Cruise Missiles

At the beginning of the SALT process, the cruise missile seemed destined for extinction. It had little or no support in the Defense Department. All the original U.S. proposals at SALT II would have banned long-range cruise missiles. Indeed, this was an early point of agreement with the Soviets, who were still developing and deploying a crude, cumbersome air-to-surface cruise missile. Washington's interest in cruise missiles as strategic weapons, as opposed to its interest in their use in tactical roles, was quite limited. In the early 1970s, cruise missiles were primarily seen as a means to improve the B-52 force's ability to penetrate Soviet air defense. The forerunner of the modern cruise missile—the subsonic cruise armed decoy (SCAD)—was a strategic decoy that incorporated the engine design of the current system. Given the Air Force's preoccupation with B-1, the Defense Department decided to cancel the SCAD program in 1973, apparently to eliminate competition against the proposed new bomber. Only a directive from the White House stopped the cancellation. The White House, however, viewed the SCAD as mainly a "bargaining chip" in SALT, since it seemed to have no strategic justification in its own right.

Once this decision was taken, however, Pentagon interest in cruise-missile technology revived. Its FY 1975 budget included 125 million for air-launched (ALCMs) and sea-launched (SLCMs) cruise missiles, with the deployment of ALCMs envisioned for the "late 1970s" and SLCM deployment designed to be available as a "strategic" version with a range of 1,500 miles fired from submarines. But these requests were not reflected in the U.S. negotiating position at SALT. It is not surprising that these programs came under Soviet negotiating pressures, and eventually became a major point of dispute. Thus, during the period between 1973—when the cruise missile was a candidate for extinction—and February 1978—when the B-1 was cancelled and the B-52 equipped with ALCM was elevated to a significant strategic system—a continuing ambivalence in U.S. policy was reflected at SALT: U.S. proposals swung from complete bans to various positions designed to preserve some or all of the cruise missiles options:

—The Ford administration proposed several variants mainly linked to the Soviet *Backfire* bomber, including, in January 1976, a ban on cruise missiles with a range over 600 km on heavy bombers, but with each bomber to be counted as the equivalent of a MIRV.

—The Carter administration proposed that all cruise missiles with a range falling between 600 and 2,500 km be permitted, but would have banned all such systems with greater ranges (March 1977). It then shifted to banning ground-launched and sea-launched systems for a three-year period, and finally arrived at a temporary ban (through 1981) on deployment, but not on testing.

The message in this case is fairly clear. Not until the Defense Department received a clear political signal for a cruise missile was it willing to consider a new strategic option. The most promising program, the ACLM, was protected in SALT, both at Vladivostok and in subsequent proposals leading to the SALT II Treaty. The SLCM and GLCM, however, had less bureaucratic support. The Navy, for example, was worried that its shorter-range anti-shipping version of the SLCM would be cut back in favor of a strategic version. Thus both GLCMs and SLCMs were vulnerable to arms-control attacks. Once again, the result was bureaucratic confusion reflected in the SALT II Protocol to the treaty.

Notes

1. See articles by Leslie Gelb and Richard Burt in *Foreign Policy*, no. 36, Fall 1978.

2. See the proposals of Sidney Drell, called *SUM*, in *Arms Control Today*, vol. 9, no. 8, Sept. 1979.

3. See Hedley Bull, "Arms Control: Stocktaking and Prospects," pp. 12–13, in *Problems of Modern Strategy*, Part Two, Adelphi Paper No. 55, ISS, March 1969.

4. FY 1980 Arms Control Impact Statements. Statements Submitted to the Congress by the President Pursuant to Section 36 of the Arms Control and Disarmament Act. Washington D.C.: U.S. Government Printing Office, March 1979.

5. Henry Kissinger, *White House Years*. Boston: Little, Brown and Co., 1979, p. 43.

6. Richard M. Nixon, *RN: The Memoirs of Richard Nixon*. New York: Warner Books, 1978, vol. 2, pp. 606–607.

7. See Morton Halperin, *Bureaucratic Politics and Foreign Policy*. Washington, D.C.: The Brookings Institution, 1974, p. 297 ff.

8. See John Newhouse, *Cold Dawn: The Story of Salt*. New York: Holt, Rinehart and Winston, 1973, pp. 25–26.

9. Melvin Laird, *Annual Defense Department Report FY 1973*. Washington, D.C.: U.S. Government Printing Office.

10. "Arms Control Implication of Current Defense Budget," *Hearings: Senate Foreign Relations Sub-committee on Arms Control*, First Session, June/July 1971, p. 49.

11. FY 1975 Authorization for Military Procurement, Part 6. *Hearings: U.S. Senate Committee on Armed Services*, March/April, 1974, p. 3322; testimony of General Cross, Deputy Chief of Staff, Research and Development.

7
Arms Trade Control

Richard K. Betts

> Because of the threat to world peace embodied in this spiralling arms traf-
> fic, and because of the special responsibilities we bear as the largest arms
> seller, I believe that the United States must take steps to restrain its arms
> transfers. . . . These controls will be binding unless extraordinary cir-
> cumstances necessitate a Presidential exception.
>   —Jimmy Carter, May 19, 1977

How quaint, how comical these words sound only a few years later.
Born-again cold warriors could be found peddling weapons all along the
"arc of crisis" in an attempt to bolster a new line of containment and
secure visitation rights for a resurgent projection of U.S. forces. Arms
sales are again normal rather than exceptional. This about-face was not
due simply to the shock of the invasion of Afghanistan, because the
policy was not just an artifact of détente. The program of arms trade
restraint had been crumbling from the moment of inception.
Philosophically flawed, practically infeasible, and never seriously implemented, the policy needed only the *coup de grace* administered by the
Soviets in December 1979.

What can be gained from a conceptual post-mortem of a policy relic?
First, his arms trade policy was a microcosm of the aggressive Wilsonian
idealism that permeated Carter's view of the world. It reflects the intensity of contradictions—more extreme than the normal contradictions
that every administration has to manage—in the president's ambitious
aims.

Second, these old impulses may be dormant rather than dead. U.S.
foreign policy tends to oscillate between complacent optimism and near-
hysterical alarm. In the first three years of the Carter administration the
pendulum swung in the latter direction. But once the dust settles,
adrenaline runs down, and the fluidity of alignments in the Middle East

bites U.S. leaders a few times, there may be a renewal of skepticism about arms transfers, if not a rebirth of hope in the evolution of world politics toward harmony. After all, it was barely two years after John Foster Dulles articulated the "roll-back" policy and the Soviets crushed the East German insurrection that we had "the spirit of Geneva." Even less time elapsed between the 1968 invasion of Czechoslovakia and the bloom of Richard Nixon's détente. Arms controllers argue that tension makes agreements on restraint more rather than less important, so the lobby for arms transfer controls will not die even if U.S.-Soviet confrontation remains intense.

Third, even if American leaders remain soberly disillusioned with the naiveté of Carter's original arms transfer policy, the question of restraint will not go away. Revival of containment does not justify all sales, because some customers are not proxies of either superpower, and want arms for purposes unrelated to U.S.-Soviet competition. The United States cannot give or sell all the weapons potential customers would like. Simple constraints of production capacity make it necessary to establish discriminatory priorities, and in many cases transfers will not serve U.S. interests. Just because Carter's conventional arms controllers had stars in their eyes does not mean that limitations are never advisable. A philosophical and operational basis still has to be found for integrating the benefits of arms trade for U.S. defense policy and the standard of restraint that may serve diplomatic objectives. Classifying weaknesses in the dominant arguments for arms trade control over recent years helps to put the problem into perspective.

Arms Control and Defense Interests

The relationship between U.S. security interests and the control of conventional arms trade is foggy. Where arms transfers and defense policy are directly linked—as in provision of weapons to close allies—there has never been any controversy. The only prominent question concerns the trade balance (how to make NATO arms purchases a "two-way street"), not whether there should be an absolute reduction of transfers. Where there is controversy—in regard to sales of weapons to "loose" allies or neutral Third World countries—the purposes of both transfers and the limitation of transfers are obscured by misty assumptions about security and responsibility in a fluid international system. Proponents of arms sales often make dubious arguments about how they benefit more than our pocketbooks, and opponents offer misleading nostrums about how limitations would secure more peace in the world. The role of arms sales[1] in supporting U.S. security has to be highly *contingent*, because interests outside Europe are diverse, conditional, and inconsistent, yet proponents and critics of sales tend to trap themselves in *categorical* assertions about the arms trade as a phenomenon in itself. Zealots on both sides have too narrow a conception of security. Crusaders against arms sales often do not take the recipients' military requirements seriously, and see proliferation of weaponry as a counterproductive indulgence that may propel the United States into self-destructive involvements in conflict. To avid arms salesmen, restraint means simply shooting ourselves in the foot, subordinating strategic self-interest to naive idealism or to foolish notions about our ability to twist despots' arms for the sake of their subjects' human rights. The former confuse destructive capability with destructive results; the latter suffer from vulgar realism, ignoring the long-term damage to strategic interests that the United States can incur from unnecessarily intense identification with some governments. Both suffer from moral absolutism and inadequate differentiation of interests, clients, and options. Proponents of both puritanical and promiscuous standards for arms sales offer a way to avoid difficult choices, but neither has ever offered a very sensible policy.

Extreme positions, of course, have never dominated policy. Arms transfers have always been limited, and the limits have never been drastic. Most participants in debate also agree that their opponents' arguments are valid in some cases. The problem is the intuitive *weight* attached to contending propositions. Arguments usually sit atop huge *ceteris paribus* clauses, and counter-arguments are usually depreciated as relevant only in minor and atypical instances. While détente was eroding but not yet dead, the high impact of intuition was due to the low clarity of notions about what U.S. security interests in the Third World are, how those interests affect each other, and how they relate to U.S.-Soviet competition. There is still probably only one principle of arms transfer limitation on which everyone could agree: do not give weapons to an enemy. Beyond that, there are a number of reasons that, even in the 1970s, the burden of clarification and proof should have fallen disproportionately on those who favor some systematic form of restraint in arms sales:

• The precedents for restraint are all discouraging. Nuclear arms control (simplified a bit by the small number of actors involved) is a new phenomenon and the verdict is still out. But there have been numerous attempts at international limitation of conventional arms trade since the Brussels Act of 1890. The best of these attempts were innocuous failures, the worst were fiascoes.

• There is negligible evidence that other arms suppliers are genuinely interested in restraint. In cases where a customer wants to buy, the sale does not threaten U.S. security, and alternate suppliers are available, there is a *prima facie* case that denial serves no U.S. interests.

• There is no evidence that reduction of worldwide totals of arms sales serves any of the axiomatic goals of arms control: to save money, reduce the probability of war, or reduce destruction in the event of war. The first goal is never served (except in terms of paternal supplier interest in keeping stupid *customers* from wasting *their* money). The second depends politically on the stakes of conflict and militarily on mutual deterrence, which is a problem of relative rather than absolute levels of arms. The third depends on how countries might otherwise spend their military budgets. It is likely that two states denied the purchase of a few expensive high-performance aircraft would kill *more* of each other, if they went to war, if they spent the same amount of funds on additional amounts of ammunition, small arms, artillery, and trucks.[2]

• Most arguments for limitation are made less in terms of benefits for U.S. security than in terms of altruism: benefits for the customers. Especially in cases where there is any trade-off between those two concerns, it is necessary to be sure that restraint does in fact benefit the clients. Arguments for this position are usually more energetic than empirical.

Integrating arms trade control with security planning requires that a number of very general questions be clarified and answers refined into less stark alternatives than we usually find in current debate. First, should arms transfers be considered a suitable subject for arms control? To a large extent the logic of nuclear arms control has been based on the goal of neutralizing the role of nuclear weapons and deflecting competition into other areas of military power. This assumption is certainly not shared universally, but the international consensus that nuclear forces should or can be taken out of the calculus of strategic interaction is immeasurably greater than the consensus favoring systematic limits on conventional arms trade. Second, in a world of more fluid alignments, growing Soviet capabilities for projection of power, and the combined expansion in several Third World areas of economic resources, nationalism, and frustration, what are the criteria by which to assess the utility, irrelevance, or counterproductivity of arms trade for U.S. security? Third, is it practical to try to formulate, negotiate, and implement any systematic arms control policy for an issue that is so thoroughly confounded with diverse and uncertain interrelationships of political, military, and economic costs and benefits?

Was There Really A Problem?

Except in regard to firm allies, for whom denial of purchases is not an issue, the impingements of arms transfers on U.S. defense policy are indirect. The biggest conceptual issue is whether arms trade limitation should be approached deductively, as a generic problem, rather than inductively, as a problem that has very different significance in specific geographic areas, and only then as a dependent variable. Proponents of limitation correctly believe that profligacy in sales has harmed client or supplier interests in certain cases, but they have yet to demonstrate that the "global" dimension of arms transfers has any relevance in itself.

If the United States or other suppliers have been selling too many arms, then customers must have been buying too many. If this is so, then which customers, and according to what yardstick? An obvious example is Iran, which many arms controllers pointed to well before the collapse of the Shah. It is notable, however, that even Carter's ambitious policy of restraint exempted Iran to a great extent, denying a few of the Shah's requests but maintaining a generous allotment under the aggregate ceiling. Moreover, in one shabby maneuver, the administration limited a U.S. sale, but allowed the Shah to get the hardware he wanted by agreeing to build the weaponry for a set of frigates but not the hulls (which were to be built in Europe).

Critics have also noted instances where the United States sold to both sides in a local conflict, and argue that it is somehow *ipso facto* absurd to play both ends against the middle. This finger-pointing begs the question of whether Pakistanis were any better off being killed by Indians with Russian arms rather than Indians with U.S. arms. And the argument addresses only the brand names of the weapons, not whether either side had bought too many. Whether India needed fewer weapons to deter China, or Pakistan needs fewer to deter India, is another issue. In both cases U.S. sales and grants were a direct function of security policy; for India, to contain China; for Pakistan, as a member of the Southeast Asia Treaty Organization (SEATO). The relevant criticism is that U.S. leaders misconceived how those countries could serve our interests, not that those countries bought more than they needed for *their* security.

The Carter administration's own data disprove the premise that arms sales were in an upward spiral at the time the new policy of restraint was imposed.[3] Moreover, the axiom that arms sales *in general* were ballooning unnaturally is usually made without reference to any criterion for a natural level. On the supply side, U.S. arms sales were commensurate with the U.S. industrial and technological position in the global economy, and were consistent with distribution of other exports.

Growth in arms trade has paralleled trends in world trade as a whole. On the demand side, Third World countries as a group have not bought arms in a pattern markedly inconsistent with their importation of other products. Countries have usually allocated increasing proportions of their Gross National Product (GNP) to defense as they have developed economically. In short, by aggregate measures, the arms trade has been an integrated and typical part of economic development and commerce.[4]

The postulate that developing countries have been buying more arms than they need is no more demonstrable than the argument that the suppliers themselves spend too much for their own defense. Since the suppliers have not notably reduced *their* military expenditures or deployments by arms control agreements, it seems rather presumptuous to ask insecure *clients* to put their worries away. The little success SALT has had to date has been through its attention to *equilibrium* rather than reductions, and MBFR has been hung up on defining an equilibrium as a prerequisite for reduction. Indeed, apart from the minor reduction of Soviet launchers required by the latest treaty, plans for the post–SALT II environment are marked by significant *expansions* of destructive power on both sides. If equilibrium is realistically the best that can be hoped for from arms control, then reductions of aggregate arms transfers are much less relevant than stabilizing disaggregated security equations among the customers.

Are Arms Sales Destabilizing?

"The virtually unrestrained spread of conventional weaponry threatens stability in every region of the world," said President Carter in announcing his policy of restraint in 1977.[5] The same assertion prefaces almost every brief for global limitations on arms trade, and the assertion is wrong. It mistakes a necessary or at most proximate cause for a sufficient or significant cause. It also implies a condescending and naive view of the Third World, as if backward countries would not be at each other's throats without the malign impetus of extra available weapons. States without the industrial capability to make their own weapons presumably cannot have the need for them that the supplier states have themselves.[6]

Propositions such as "It is widely accepted . . . that the lower the arms level, the lower the likelihood of war"[7] are rarely backed up by data. The assertion does not explain why most wars in recent years have been between states with *low* levels of arms (except for the American wars in Korea and Vietnam, which were not in the remotest way caused by arms transfers); in fact it suggests there is more danger of war between NATO and the Warsaw Pact than between Ethiopia and Somalia. High arms levels are not destabilizing, especially if they are in balance. *Revisionist policies* are what makes arms destabilizing; such policies, and risk-taking with even low levels of arms, are what prompts buildups—they are not created by them.[8]

Stability is by definition conservative, so a stabilizing supplier policy will just as often be one that disproportionately *increases* the arms available to the status quo power in a dispute. European stability in the summer of 1939 would have been enhanced rather than eroded by massive transfusions of U.S. hardware to France and Britain. As Quincy Wright, the late scholar of international law, noted, "Neutral arms embargoes if equally applied to all belligerents actually favor the aggressor, who is usually better prepared than his victim."[9] Some suppliers—Japan, Germany, Sweden, and Canada—purposely avoid sales in areas of tension. Such a Pilate-like policy avoids entanglement, but it does nothing automatically for stability.

Secular trends in arms transfers follow rather than precede the trends in conflict. The bulk of transfers went to Europe (*after* the Cold War began, not before) until the mid-1960s, then to Southeast Asia (*after* the war there escalated), and now to the Middle East and Persian Gulf. Perhaps Africa is next.[10] None of these areas were made more volatile by the transfers; the transfers were prompted by the volatility. Multilateral restraint on transfers will be most feasible where it can be popular with the customers—areas where there are no intense grievances, where states are motivated only to deter rather than compel, and where they would welcome an equilibrium that facilitates reduction of their defense burdens. Those areas, however, are not the source of the problem, because they are not where most arms are being sold. If stability in the sense of mutual deterrence is the goal of conventional arms control, the challenging areas will require discriminatory supplier policies, to re-equilibrate and maintain balances that discourage the resort to force. And if any of the suppliers support the aggrieved or revisionist party in the local dispute—as is likely in the cases most related to U.S. security interests—equilibrium will require competitive *increases* in transfers by other suppliers to the status quo party.

The salient fact behind such abstractions is that most of the important areas *are* ones where the two major suppliers have competitive interests, and the clients function as proxy vanguards in peripheral security. The problem in assessing how arms sales relate to U.S. security is the problem of identifying interests in the area, and the possible differences between the relevance of arms trade in regard to interests that involve military competition with the Soviet Union and those that do not. In what senses does the "global" arms transfer problem really overlap with national security, and where it does not, what might be gained or lost by attenuating the arms trade?

Standards for Framing the Problem

There is no consensus on these linkages or differentiations. Staunch opponents see arms sales in the Third World as serving few interests beyond greed. Staunch proponents see sales as automatic buttresses to containment or valuable sources of political leverage. The problem here, as in the preceding question of instability, is a fundamental difference in assumptions about international relations, which cannot easily be bridged by empiricism. Opponents of arms transfers usually identify with the idealist tradition or theory which runs from Kant's *Perpetual Peace* to the current academic schools of thought emphasizing "world order," "transnational" relations, and the "declining utility of force" engendered by economic interdependence. Proponents of the idealist tradition see war as unnatural and unnecessary, more often provoked by artificial catalysts than intractable conflicts of genuine interests.[11] Those on the other side identify with the *Realpolitik* tradition, advanced from Thucydides to Morgenthau, that views conflict as unfortunate but inevitable and national self-assertion as the enduring engine of world politics; order emerges from the balance of power, it cannot replace it. These basic differences in orientation account for most of the confusion about whether Third World military development can or should be avoided, and how it relates to superpower defense concerns. And such confusion must be resolved before stipulating criteria for judging the feasibility or danger of arms trade control.

Aggregate statistics about worldwide arms transfers are meaningless, as is the concept of a "general" arms race as opposed to specific disagreements between states about what their relative capabilities should be.[12] Absolute standards, even in regard to specific cases—about the amount or cost of arms—do not themselves indicate how transfers will affect regional security. The relevant criterion for sufficiency or excess is the net assessment of relative threat and the ratio between the client's power and interests. Small transfers may be devastating or large ones inadequate, depending on the power of the opponent. In 1975 the Soviet Union sent few arms to the Popular Movement for the Liberation of Angola (MPLA) in Angola, but they had a major impact on the outcome of the civil war.[13] Cheap, precision-guided munitions can also be effective against high-value tanks and aircraft, so a declining amount of funds spent on arms imports could coincide with absolute *and* relative increases in a country's military power.[14] The irrelevance of the global standard is no greater than the irrelevance of an undiscriminatory regional standard.

Blanket permissiveness or blanket restraint in sales to a region is sometimes justified as a "fair" or "equitable" policy. That is so only if suppliers are politically disinterested in the outcomes of regional conflict. And those are cases in which the suppliers' own defense planning concerns are no problem. Equitable provision or denial of supplies can produce inequitable outcomes because it only makes the other unequal variables determinative. Equitable purchases only reify the preexisting balance of military power, economic resources, and intensity of concern. Any simple categorical guidelines for arms transfers in general must include a stipulation "all else being equal," and all else is rarely equal.

An example of this problem in trying to refine global standards regionally was Carter's policy banning introduction of weapons with higher combat capability into an area. The official charged with supervising the policy cited the rejection of requests by both India and Pakistan for long-range strike aircraft as exemplary of this standard's logic.[15] That would be true at best only if military balances were judged by crude static measures—"bean counts" that abstract comparable elements from the integrated offensive and defensive capabilities on both sides. The impact of the denial on Pakistan, which has no hope of matching Indian manpower and can only clutch at the straw of a little firepower superiority to reduce its overall inferiority, was much greater. The only rational reasons for the ban (before the Soviet thrust into Afghanistan changed the basis of U.S. concerns) were that (1) the administration favored India politically and cared little about Pakistan's military insecurity, and (2) the administration perceived no vital U.S. security interests on the South Asian mainland that were compromised by Indian predominance. Arms sales restraint is easy to indulge where disinterest eliminates the desire to replace imbalance with equilibrium. Conversely, the United States gave generous amounts of arms to Pakistan in the 1950s, when anti-Communist mobilization of allies took precedence over regional balance. One proponent admits that an "open access" policy for arms sales would favor the dominant regional power, but sees this as usually consistent with U.S. interests.[16] Obversely, however, a blanket embargo would have the same effect.

There are many reasons why Carter's ban on introduction of more sophisticated weapons set an inconsistent standard. For instance, the computational methodology for statistics used in formulating the 1977 restraint policy exaggerated the relative level of U.S. transfers and especially obscured the *quantitative* significance of Soviet transfers.[17] In focusing on a qualitative restriction, therefore, the Carter policy hobbled an advantage U.S. transfers could offer to a client for offsetting an opponent's imports from the Soviet Union. Interpreted literally, the Carter standard would have prevented South Korea from getting F-16s until North Korea (with a larger air force to start) had gotten aircraft just as good: "The South Koreans would always be the last to get more capable equipment and could be in a constant game of technological catch-up."[18] Israel is a prime example of a U.S. client that has relied on a qualitative edge in arms to counter opponents' quantitative superiority. Most Israeli casualties have been inflicted by unsophisticated Arab arms (mortars, artillery) and the Israelis have used their own advanced weapons (aircraft) for counter-battery missions. If high-performance weapons were limited in the Middle East, then the arms control regime could disadvantage Israel disproportionately, at least in the short term.[19]

Tanks, artillery, and aircraft can be more destructive and useful for aggression than sophisticated precision-guided missiles (PGMs) or cruise missiles. Arms control standards for trade might more productively focus "on regulating 'old' rather than new technologies."[20] Importation of impressive numbers of PGMs might also discourage an opponent from buying more costly, high-performance penetrating systems—if he sees them as increasingly vulnerable.[21] This would be likely, if at all, only for states with defensive rather than aggressive motives. But it does suggest how restriction of some transfers might be facilitated by *promotion* of others.

Recognizing complexity and the need for much more conditionality in standards for arms trade limitation, however, does not mean that a finely-tuned, balance-regulating policy is practical. Agreeing both within and among governments on what constitutes a proper balance has proved awesomely difficult even in bipolar negotiations like SALT and MBFR. Third World environments pose a bigger challenge because (1) the smallness of most of the military establishments involved means that *any* increment of imported arms can alter proportional power significantly, and (2) multipolarity means that simple binary balances rarely exist.

Indian capabilities that may be at best adequate to deter China are far more than enough to imperil Pakistan. Multiple interactions make it difficult to calibrate or even anticipate outcomes. Senator Church was partly correct when he cited U.S. policy in Latin America to argue the impossibility of regulating stability by interventionary selling: In 1966 the United States sold A-4Bs to Argentina, then Chile bought *Hawker-Hunters* from Britain, after which Peru began negotiations to buy advanced weapons, and Argentina wound up seeking more sophisticated aircraft.[22] This does not prove that the original U.S. sale was inadvisable, or that the region would have been more stable in that sale's absence. It simply suggests that supplier control of local security situations may be too ambitious a goal to be served reliably by either generosity or timidity in sales policy. Global standards for arms trade levels are always irrelevant, but regional stability standards are often indecipherable.

Facing the Diffusion of Power

In the 1950s and '60s the relationship of arms transfers to U.S. defense policy was obvious: the former were an extension of the latter, as arms went mostly to allies. Not surprisingly, there was little interest then in restraining transfers, apart from the budgetary concern of limiting grant aid. By the mid-1970s sales had superseded grants, and three-quarters of transfers were going to Third World countries—most of whom offered at best tacit, tentative, or indirect support to U.S. security. As additional power diffused toward the East and South, arms traffic flourished. Critics of transfers can argue that the growth in arms trade is bad more plausibly than that it is unnatural, and proponents are more convincing when they say that growth doesn't affect U.S. security rather than suggesting that it clearly helps. Neither side has offered very subtle explanations for how the diffusion of power to neutral or equivocally aligned peripheral states affects the superpowers' military security.

Some radical analysts have seen the integration of arms trade with general economic trends as evidence of continued "feudal dominance" of the international system by the great powers.[23] The rise of the Organization of Petroleum Exporting Countries (OPEC) casts doubt on the usefulness of this characterization. Moreover, anti-colonialist resentment and *"dependencia"* rhetoric are now being directed at arms suppliers' *denials* rather than demands, against paternalism rather than exploitation.[24] Whatever cosmetic political benefits might be obtained from an arms trade limitation policy couched in terms of pacific moralism could be neutralized by the rejected customers' anti-hegemonist moralism. An amoral policy of promiscuous sales, on the other hand, would not wash the problem away. Nations will always resent sales to their enemies. Anger depends less on principle than on whose "ox is being gored."

One motive for refusing sales in the Third World is to prevent diversion of scarce resources from economic development. This is not convincing for three reasons: (1) Less-developed countries' (LDCs') military expenditures have not stifled development as demonstrably as critics contend;[25] (2) Most Third World countries do not spend much on arms, and where demand is high it is really the result of the diffusion of power since decolonization and the rise of OPEC. Unlike Europe, LDCs before 1960 "were not yet saturated with weapons and would require a good two decades to reach a comparable level of militarization;"[26] and (3) The OPEC nouveau riches are the most problematic customers for sales limitation policy, and scarcity of funds for development investment is no problem for them.

The only good reasons to deny sales to the nouveau riches have to be political. There is nothing illogical about Saudi Arabia's desire to have a level of military power more commensurate with the economic power it has to protect. To deny arms to such countries is to keep the diffusion of power truncated, to disjoin technical capability from economic, to deny the fungibility of their assets, and to legitimize the oil cartel's exploitation of our own vulnerability.[27] Geoffrey Kemp and Steven Miller note a different, sociological argument for arms trade reduction: rapid implantation of modern technology in LDCs can have revolutionary consequences and erode the basis for stability of the regime the transfers were designed to protect.[28] But this begs the larger question of whether the United States should encourage modernization in general. Arms imports are only a minor component in this process, other aspects of which can aggravate political instability much more. The case of Iran supports the argument, but it is doubtful the Shah would have averted internal challenge by curbing his appetite for weapons.

Finally, there is the concern that arms industries may become dependent on exports and increase supplier competition in the market. This may be undesirable for the suppliers (although the most ardent arms controllers are also usually those who are least alarmed by the overall increase in economic interdependence) but it does not necessarily hurt the recipients. Competition helps them to get more for their money. The market is far from a free one anyway. Between its oligopolistic nature and the frequent intervention of political considerations, customer choice is well circumscribed. A country may prefer to get second-choice weapons from a first-choice patron to entering a relationship with a suspect supplier.[29]

Stringent supplier limitations also encourage buyers to develop military production indigenously—an inefficient solution in terms of comparative advantage and a wasteful one in a global sense because it increases the total amount of production devoted to arms.[30] The pursuit of technological sovereignty via indigenous arms industries in many Third World countries is already visible, often being rationalized by spinoff benefits for civil economic development.[31] Indigenous production may enhance those states' independence, but it confounds the purpose of supplier restraint. Although Third World arms industries have a long way to go, their technological dependence will continue to pyramid, and the major suppliers can exercise collective control if they want to.[32]

I have emphasized the inconsistencies in rationales for rejecting requests to buy arms, and thus the dangers in claiming that any consistent, overarching standards for restraint exist. There, are however, good reasons for applying restraint, even inconsistently. For one, the long-term consequences of diffusion of military power are unpredictable, and by no means are they all likely to benefit U.S. security. In the past decade suppliers contracted for over $140 billion of arms transfer to LDCs. As Leslie Gelb testified, "Most of this equipment has not yet been delivered, much less absorbed. When these arms are delivered and when the recipients learn to use them, they will change the face of world politics. . . . in the process, our own technological advantage will recede."[33] A policy of meticulous discrimination by country-specific standards (rather than indiscriminate global or regional norms like "no first introduction of higher technology") would help to *manage* the diffusion of power. But as the previous section suggested, this kind of calibrated control of complex local balances is rarely feasible. Moreover, it is constrained by interests other than those of the customers.

Costs and Benefits

Regulating a regional equation requires cooperation of other suppliers. This means convincing suppliers that their interests, domestic as well as external, are served by limits on sales. Supplier interests, then, are more likely to determine policy, because they are more compelling and because they are easier to clarify than abstract calculations of local stability. U.S. schemes for stopping sales will have to incorporate the full range of costs and benefits to us, the British, French, and Russians, who together constitute the principal sellers in the market. The balance of interests is not the same for the United States and our allied suppliers, and certainly not for the Soviet Union.

Military

The least ambiguous intersection of arms trade with defense policy is where U.S. military capabilities are concerned. Transfers can function to extend U.S. force to allies or proxies who supplant our own deployments. In this respect sales can also increase cost-effectiveness by using cheaper indigenous manpower. By one estimate, South Korea can maintain twenty troops for the cost of one American soldier; for Turkey the ratio is twelve to one.[34] Transfers are also useful where the United States wishes to dissociate itself from a client without abandoning it completely (for instance, continued sales to Taiwan despite derecognition), or to compensate for reduction of U.S. presence (such as the force improvement plan for South Korea to underwrite Carter's original intention to withdraw the U.S. Second Division). Transfers have frequently been used to secure overseas base rights. The Western base structure has shrunk while the Soviet Union's has expanded. To the extent this trend was undesirable, use of sales to keep or obtain bases was sensible, irrespective of the Afghanistan shock.

The direct defense functions of arms transfers almost always take a back seat to diplomatic and political dimensions of strategy. Resupply of Israel in October 1973 reduced U.S. military power, denuding the European Command of much of its armor. The real but narrow military interest in solidifying base rights in Simonstown, to control the Cape Sea Route, is not enough to get NATO countries to breach the arms embargo against South Africa. Although Turkey is important to NATO and a valuable site for U.S. intelligence collection bases, Congress, nevertheless, cut off supplies when Ankara broke end-use agreements by invading Cyprus. (Partially as a result, when Congress subsequently dragged its feet in rescinding the embargo, Prime Minister Ecevit made noises about rapprochement with the Soviet Union—arguing that U.S. nonchalance about degradation of Turkish capabilities showed a refusal to take the Soviet threat seriously.)[35]

Uncertain survivability of clients whose arms imports are justified by their function as U.S. proxies can also give transfers a boomerang effect. The capture or retransfer of U.S. weapons may normally pose no major threat, if they fall into untrained hands and waste away for lack of maintenance and spares.[36] The U.S. arsenal acquired in 1975, though, did enhance Vietnam's military power, and certainly did nothing to inhibit the effectiveness of operations against Cambodia or China in 1979. The probable compromise of the F-14's *Phoenix* missile technology after the Shah's ouster obviously benefited the Soviet Union. And anticipated political profits from feeding the Shah's military appetite came home to roost as debits, giving Israel a generous argument for more aid than Washington wished to provide: Ezer Weizman complained that the U.S. arms left in the country could underwrite Iranian participation in pan-Islamic pressure against Israel.[37] *This* problem, more than the regional stability considerations cited by Carter, is what makes caution in sales of state-of-the-art technology advisable. In this context the rationale for restraint is independent of arms control considerations.

Economic

Many opponents of arms sales are also opponents of high defense spending. This position is consistent only as long as the level of threat to

U.S. interests is declining. Otherwise, there is a reciprocal relationship between sales to friends and cuts in American forces. This was the rationale behind the Nixon Doctrine's retraction of U.S. military power in the early 1970s. Since the blush came off détente in the mid-1970s, the perception of threat from the Soviet Union increased well before the Afghanistan event. Strategic rationales for trimming arms trade are harder to develop for supplier strategic interests than for customers' economic development interests.

The direct economic effects of limiting arms sales—for the suppliers—are negative.[38] Proponents of limitation cite the overriding import of other considerations, and the wastefulness of encouraging dependence on "inflationary" defense industries, but also denigrate the financial costs. Cahn and Kruzel cite Congressional Budget Office studies to show that savings on U.S. procurement costs due to arms sales (unit price reduction, R&D recoupment, etc.) amount to only about 7 percent, or less than half of 1 percent of total defense outlays.[39] At current levels, however, such percentages would approach hundreds of millions of dollars, hardly a negligible amount. For defense planners it is also notable that the Budget Office concluded that arms sales contribute substantially to the maintenance of the U.S. industrial mobilization base.[40] And for any country, a healthy indigenous military industry is a direct prop to strategic autonomy.

Western European suppliers initially put off Carter's negotiators by conditioning their willingness to limit sales on Soviet willingness and also with frank admissions of their own financial and industrial stakes in the arms trade. Their skepticism is understandable, considering the protectionism that has wrapped the U.S. market for military equipment. The "Buy American Act" placed extreme constraints on purchases of foreign wares. Relaxation came from unique cases that would benefit U.S. military capabilities.[41] Even without considering competing security reasons for sales, persuasion of other suppliers to practice restraint would require better integration of domestic policies.

Even then, European inhibitions would be too severe for arms controllers to explain away with the depreciations applied to U.S. economic losses. Although military exports contribute proportionally less to total exports and GNP for France and Britain than they do for the United States and Soviet Union, arms sales to LDCs are proportionally much more important to the Europeans. Three-quarters of British arms sales from 1966-75 went to non-NATO countries and, more than the United States, the Europeans tailor their production plans according to export potential and do not make only hyper-sophisticated weapons that are excessive for LDC needs.[42] Thus European recalcitrance about limiting sales outside the Alliance is comparable to U.S. foot dragging in making

NATO standardization a two-way street. Moreover, the goal of standardization conflicts with restraint in sales to the Third World. European countries will be reluctant to purchase U.S. weapons if they cannot support their own military infrastructures with sales elsewhere, and coproduction of U.S. weapons may be uneconomical if the arrangement prohibits other sales that would lengthen production runs and thus take manufacturing past the break-even point.[43] In this way the positive economic and international political sense of balancing Western military retrenchment with buildups of peripheral friendly forces is compounded by the negative economic and domestic political consequences of refusing arms sales.

It is hard to discern any way in which arms control in the area of sales would not exact a price from the United States and its allies. To make a cartel for limitations reasonable, the United States would not only have to negotiate market shares with other suppliers, but would ultimately have to reduce its own production capacity absolutely[44]—a formidable sacrifice. Yet if we admit the need to cultivate external markets in order to maintain the viability of industries in the Western democracies, then we actually validate Lenin's theory of imperialism. In this sense, hardnosed, self-interested dismissal of arms trade control would be a scarcely comforting basis for supporting Western defense. An alternative interpretation to Lenin's, more appropriate for a post-colonial world, is that a hegemonial policy conflicts with one motivated by industrial profit. The former requires tailoring weapons production to the supplier's own needs, and willingness to manipulate and cut off sales or make grants. The latter requires catering to customer needs, maximizing sales, and making no free gifts. The United States still fits the first pattern, while the British have moved from the first to the second.[45] All this still takes us no further than the previous discussion of customer interests: the need for contingent rather than consistent standards for sales.

Some observers react indignantly to the "if we don't sell others will" argument, in a manner similar to John Foster Dulles' fury when Nasser attempted to manipulate him by mentioning the Soviet offer to back the Aswan Dam project, or nineteenth century progressive reformers' revulsion at George Washington Plunkitt's distinction between honest and dishonest graft. In those cases, the rationales were viscerally repugnant to moral sensibilities, but pragmatically quite defensible, and evidence is scant that refusal to accept them left the refusers any better off. Financial benefit to suppliers should be a sufficient reason in itself for approving sales in the few cases where there are alternate suppliers available *and* no reasons against associating with the recipient. But there are few cases where both conditions are unambiguously present. The military and economic criteria for integrating arms trade controls with national strategy are much clearer and more tangible than the relevant diplomatic considerations.

Political

Arms trade outside alliance blocs affects security in terms of what the Soviets call the overall "correlation of forces," rather than the superpower military balance itself. This implies that arms transfers can improve or solidify influence with countries outside the blocs that confront each other in Central Europe. Those who favor an activist sales policy, however, claim too much when they say transfers can buy influence. Grants may buy influence because "beggars can't be choosers," but with cash sales the debt is usually paid with the invoice. Sales yield reliable leverage only when the customers have no alternative sources. These are usually desperate states like Taiwan, whose devotion offers more headaches than palpable strategic benefits to the United States. More often, the significant supplier influence *precedes* rather than follows the sale. Clients prefer to buy and rely on ideologically congenial patrons.

Indigenously financed buildups demonstrate a customer's commitment to independence. Were they willing to become vassals of the superpower they prefer, or Finlandized by the one they fear, they would need less military power. Once a cash sale is finalized the supplier's leverage declines, and the policies of China, Egypt, Somalia, Israel, and Turkey show their willingness to prevent arms dependence from determining their policies.[46] Recipients well recognize that arms are only a means to a political end and may even sacrifice decreases in dependence to intraregional interests. Saudi Arabia scuttled the nascent Arab Military Industries Organization (and Egypt risked and accepted the result) because of the primacy of the controversial separate peace between Israel and Egypt.

Critics of sales see many clients less as diplomatic targets of opportunity than as whirlpools threatening to suck the United States into problematic entanglements. The arms supplied may outlast the friendliness of the regime that bought them (or the regime itself), and the "umbilical relationship" requiring life-cycle support for logistics, maintenance, and training may leave U.S. citizens as hostages in the country.[47] The United States may also be reluctant to pull the plug by cutting off spares out of fear of damaging its reputation for reliability, or from a desire to woo a hostile government back (consider the resumption of parts supply to the Khomeini regime in late 1979—shortly before U.S. personnel were imprisoned in the embassy). The turning of leverage on its head, with clients manipulating patrons, is an old story for the Soviets as well as the

United States. Sino-Soviet rivalry, for instance, allowed Indonesia to exploit both Communist powers beginning in the mid-1950s. Even after the 1965 coup against Sukarno, the Soviet Union supplied parts and ammunition to the Indonesian army despite the fact that the supplies were used to butcher local Communists.[48]

The unpredictable reliability of customers has led many analysts to argue against letting the United States become the overwhelmingly dominant supplier in volatile areas because "dependence begets responsibility"[49] and diffusing responsibility "makes it easier for an administration to cut the supply line."[50] Attenuation of influence is worth avoidance of entanglement. The feasibility of keeping such a low profile, however—like the prospects for reducing transfers—may vary inversely with the strategic significance, U.S.-Soviet competitiveness, and appetite for arms in the region. The U.S. share of the arms market in Latin America dropped from 70 to 20 percent in the 1970s and the Carter administration could proudly cite an initiative for recipient restraint by eight countries there, but the acceptibility of the first development and the possibility of the second were largely due to the mildness of international tensions in the area.[51]

The Middle East cockpit, on the other hand, is more challenging. It is where the bulk of non-NATO sales have gone, and where limitations would have to be imposed to make a meaningful dent in the arms trade. (The revolution in Iran yielded a drop in total deliveries to the region, but this was no thanks to Carter's transfer policy.) The prospect for major reduction of arms sales *before* comprehensive peace in the area, however, is almost unimaginable, and even then if arms control were consistent with conflict limitation, that could be in the form of massive net increases (as a payoff to Israel, for example).[52]

Where U.S. restraint might really be used effectively for leverage—against Israel—it has been precluded politically. After the 1967 war, some officials wanted to delay transferring F-4s to get Israeli concessions (withdrawal from conquered territory or signature of the NPT), but Congressional pressure forced President Johnson to make the sale without any *quid pro quo*.[53] After the 1973 war the United States became the peacemaker because it *was* Israel's sole supplier and thus the only power with influence in Tel Aviv. But the influence depended on the political bond between the two and inducements were emphasized rather than coercion. President Ford's 1975 "reassessment" threat was hobbled by prior generosity. By that time, Israel was no longer dependent, for short-term operations, on U.S. parts and ammunition deliveries and could resist Washington's demands.[54] The United States could not even theoretically apply a "defensive weapons only" transfer policy (an implausible distinction anyway) because Israel has—for obvious reasons of geography and population—a defensive strategy based on offensive tactics. Washington was not even willing to wrestle with Israel over its use of F-15s for strikes into Lebanon. The only reasonable way to twist Israeli arms for concessions necessary for complete settlement would be to offer an ironclad guarantee to defend the 1967 borders with U.S. forces—an expansion of defense commitments as an arms transfer control solution, but a solution that appeals to few in the forefront of the movement for arms trade reduction.

U.S.-Soviet Relations

Retraction of U.S. military power and diffusion of power in the Third World would be complementary only if more of the diffusion were to U.S. friends than to Soviet clients. But Carter seemed to frame his arms trade restraint policy without fully recognizing this reciprocal relationship. Anglo-Saxon allies were officially exempted from the norms, but South Korea was not (although sales do continue there)—even as the president simultaneously announced eventual withdrawal of U.S. ground forces. Meanwhile, the American share of world military exports declined in the 1970s while the Soviet share expanded.

In earlier years the Soviets tried to use arms transfers to maximize their influence in a select number of countries while the United States spread its assistance more broadly,[55] but this pattern was probably a *reflection* of the global distribution of influence rather than a preferred Soviet strategy. The Soviet Union has discounted prices substantially for favored clients, and even provided arms to countries that suppressed Communist parties but maintained distance from the West. In the 1970s Soviet generosity tightened up, as C.O.D. terms replaced flexible credit and repayment, and arms sales became a vital source of hard currency.[56]

For most of the postwar period the United States was the only truly global military power, but in the past decade U.S. interest in power projection in the Third World fell faster than the capabilities for it, while the Soviet Union's capabilities began to rise to meet its interests. Thus it is not surprising that, until Carter's trauma at the end of 1979, Soviet interest in using arms sales to gain influence exceeded U.S. enthusiasm[57]—despite some embarrassing setbacks—and that they apparently took marketing advantage of Carter's unilateral restraint.[58]

Who was the sucker? Are arms sales an illusory advantage in the correlation of forces? Both superpowers had been bitten by ambitious transfer policies in the past—the United States in South Vietnam and Iran; the Soviets in Indonesia, Egypt, and Somalia. Such cases might have tempered the Carter policy's idealistic abnegation with a strong dose of realism. But given the prior circumstances in some of the unfortunate cases, it is not evident—even with hindsight—that grants or sales could or should have been avoided. And as the Sovietologist Herbert Dinerstein has suggested, whereas U.S. leaders usually respond to policy failure by looking for another policy, Soviet leaders often respond by looking for another opportunity. Wide and systematic limitation of transfers makes competitive sense only if the boomerang cases are typical rather than aberrational. It is remarkable, therefore, that Carter announced his sales restraint policy around the same time in 1977 that he announced other policies with contradictory implications: engagement of the Soviets in broad competition for influence in the Third World,[59] and vigorous inhibition of nuclear proliferation.[60]

Carter's policy was initially unilateral in the hope that it would prompt Soviet as well as European cooperation in comprehensive limitations. The reasoning must have been that restraint by both superpowers would prevent substantially unequal losses to their standing in the correlation of forces, and that such cooperation would moderate competition and thus improve the quality of peace between the global adversaries. Feasibility aside, there are three related questions about this notion: (1) would the politico-military benefits of arms trade limitation for the superpowers be symmetrical? (2) could the arrangement be concluded on any other basis than some measure of parity in market shares? (3) is essential equivalence in arms transfers practical, when total trade is reduced, without some sort of global condominium?

If arms trade outside NATO and the Warsaw Pact were terminated completely, the net benefit would accrue to the United States. The Soviets' ascendancy in marketing would no longer be relevant diplomatically; they would suffer financially from loss of hard currency and greater relative decline in overall trade balance, and the shrinking, but still large, disparity in force projection capabilities would give the United States a military edge in the Third World. Complete restraint, however, is no more possible than disarmament. Like SALT, arms transfer control will succeed, at best, at the margins. The administration originally believed the Soviets might favor bilateral restraint because it would lessen friction with us, because they had been burned by experiences in several countries, and because we could corner the market in an unlimited sales race.[61] This reasoning seems to assume, however, that Soviet motives and responses to experience parallel our own. It is noteworthy that the Russians agreed to talks on limitations at the same time there were rumors of Western arms sales to China, and in the negotiating sessions they proposed standards whose effect would just happen to be asymmetrically favorable to them. In opposition to U.S. initiatives to deal in terms of types and levels of arms transfers, the Soviet delegation proposed a geographic criterion: no sales to countries bordering the other superpower.[62]

If the Soviets agreed to the U.S. focus on global totals, though, they probably would not accept a freeze or unequal limitations, since either would codify American primacy—which existed, but was eroding in the market at the end of the 1970s. The thrust of arms control negotiations between the superpowers has been in the direction of symmetry—not of hardware configurations, but of gross dimensions of military power. In the 1950s the military component of the correlation of forces in Europe was characterized by countervailing superiorities: a U.S. nuclear advantage countering a Soviet conventional edge. In the 1960s the relative gap in both areas declined, and the Russians then scrambled for nuclear parity at SALT.[63] The United States continued to hold out for elusive conventional parity in MBFR. For arms trade control to be successful, both blocs would probably have to be allowed essentially equivalent sales. (There is no reason that proportional reductions from the current baseline should be any more acceptable to the East in this arena than it was to the West in MBFR.)

This kind of equivalence would be another push toward global parity for the superpowers. However, the West would have to shift its resources into other areas of competition where the Soviet Union would be less able to match those resources—such as foreign economic aid—or the net effect would be to Soviet advantage. If no confrontation developed between the United States and the Soviet Union, the superpowers would both benefit, but this didn't seem a likely possibility in 1980. Even if the Russians had never struck Afghanistan, how could the two states stabilize the coincidence or convergence of these developments? They could adopt a bilateral policy of benign neglect and disengage from the Third World. (Indeed, the fact that most LDCs want weapons for purposes that have nothing to do with the great powers is why their demand did not fall off when détente bloomed earlier in the decade;[64] that is why it is also hard to integrate much of arms trade policy with U.S. defense planning.) Otherwise, such stabilization would be hard to achieve without establishing what amounts to condominium. The Russians might be agreeable to a condominium (at least as long as they could still revel in the achievement, did not take it for granted, and were not tempted to exceed it). That way, the superpowers could have some degree of genuine interest in arresting the diffusion of power. But even before the recent reinvigoration of the Cold War, the United States took great pains to assure allies that it neither sought nor would accept condominium; such a prospect, furthermore, would increase the indignation that the Third World has already expressed against neo-imperialism. If Washington continues to proscribe such superpower collusion (as is likely, since domestic political pressures in the last few years are biased toward containment), the need to jockey through the complexity and fluidity of the global correlation of forces will preclude any negotiated limits on arms trade that are simultaneously substantial, reliable, and enduring.

Great Expectations, Modest Possibilities

President Carter's arms transfer policy was promulgated in PD-13. A flippant cynic would cite the number of the directive as an augury of its chances for success. Since tensions along the "arc of instability" were aggravated during the second half of the administration, the policy appears to have been put on ice—in effect, if not in theory. Only the Shah's collapse salvaged the attempt to reduce the dollar volume of sales, and only the Afghanistan invasion silenced the conventional arms control lobby for a while.

The dim prospects for meaningful limitations were not all Carter's fault, even before the new Cold War crystallized. Both opponents of the policy, who claimed it abandoned big financial and strategic benefits for nothing, and arms control enthusiasts, who saw it as an important step toward saving the world, were wrong: even before they were promulgated, the actual limitations were whittled to small proportions by exemptions and loopholes. Not much really changed, except the level of expectations created by the administration's excessive rhetorical commitments.

Prospects for progress on either side of the debate depend, paradoxically, on the adoption of a more realistic, coherent view that defines most of the issue away. Generic solutions are irrelevant and infeasible. Major arms sales outside formal alliances also have only secondary and highly variable significance for *either* global arms control or U.S. defense planning. For instance, the biggest chunk of arms sales must be evaluated as a subordinate component in political and diplomatic strategy toward the Middle East. Observers should fear, or hope for little from, the two principal alternatives for reducing sales—multilateral supplier negotiations or unilateral U.S. reductions—even if U.S.-Soviet relations should become more amicable.

Multilateral consultation for arms trade limitation was not Carter's brainchild. The International Security Assistance and Arms Control Export Act of 1976 directed the president to seek such discussions. Multilateral regulation could theoretically flow from tacit methods of agreement, such as mutual example, or from informal negotiations aimed toward market-sharing or supplier specialization.[65] Except where motives are both similar and perceptible, and where stakes are low for all the potential suppliers, these initiatives are likely either to abort or produce small results. However, small—rather than major—results are more likely to occur when tacit approaches are taken at formalized multilateral negotiations. What, then, accounts for the impetus to "conventional arms trade (CAT) talks"? It can only be hope or the assumption that it is desirable to try, not a belief that such talks are feasible or an expectation of major results.

In both SALT and MBFR, the United States was originally driven to serious negotiation more by tangible threats to security than by moral imperatives. For SALT the threats were, in general, the approach of nuclear parity and, in particular, Soviet development of a new generation of heavy missiles. At MBFR, the conventional Soviet threat was compounded by a new internal threat—the Mansfield Amendment. No such direct dangers of comparable interests apply in the realm of arms trade, where moral considerations are the driving force. Disembodied morality always yields to complexity and caution once the nuts and bolts are brought onto the negotiating table, and moral *obiter dicta* usually recede into confusion once they are placed in a concrete context of crosscutting allied, adversary, and customer interests.

Where recent arms control negotiations have produced fully accepted agreements between the superpowers, the basis has either been equal advantage (NPT), equal disadvantage (Partial Test Ban), or the apparent neutralization of the active utility of the weapons (SALT I[66]). The effect has also injected more competition into the unregulated dimensions of military power where negotiations—such as MBFR—have not succeeded. The successful negotiations were also quite tortuous, considering the results. The NPT has not ended the proliferation problem, and SALT is an elephant that labored for years to produce a mouse: the major achievement—the ABM Treaty—occurred in SALT I; SALT II offers more predictability but little to keep destructive capability from increasing.

Compared with these successful negotiations, the ambiguities of crosscutting military, diplomatic, and economic interests, and the multiplication of decision centers involved in conventional arms trade discussions present overwhelming difficulties. (It is not surprising that talks with the Soviet Union never got beyond the pre-bargaining phase of attempting to *create* negotiation.[67]) The barriers that these problems pose to suppliernegotiated sales limits could only be reduced if the consequences were less crucial to suppliers than they were in SALT or MBFR, and if they could more easily afford to take chances on an imperfect agreement. Other parties (the buyers) would suffer the most from any mistake that provided one customer in a region with military advantage. By the same token, suppliers are less pressed to find a solution to restraint. If reducing arms sales could clearly, rather than vaguely, enhance supplier security, suppliers might be more compelled to set aside other benefits that accrue from continuing sales. Western European suppliers weren't taking many chances with their economic stakes in arms sales by conditioning their interest in limitations on Soviet cooperation. The Carter administration reasoned that taking the first initiative might overcome other sellers' skepticism and bring them around to recognizing the wisdom of stemming the diffusion of destructive capability. However, the only mechanism that Carter's planners could find to implement their first initiative was a ceiling on sales—a reasonably pragmatic choice once the premise of aggregate reductions was stipulated. The principal official in charge of the policy argued that "a ceiling is no more arbitrary than a budget."[68] This notion is absurd, unless grant aid or delaying equipment for U.S. forces are at issue. A budget's purpose is to accommodate policy to scarcity by limiting outlays, not to limit intake. The budget analogy would really be more relevant to justifying *denials*, rather than approvals for profitable sales, or to the earlier phase of the arms trade—when transactions were more often gifts to allies who would fight the Soviets or Chinese on the same containment line.

The ceiling put planners through contortions precisely because it reversed the proper sequence of deducing means from ends. The ends of policy goals within regions had to be deduced from global limits on military means. The problem was recognized, in part, when the original policy announcement included so many exemptions and loopholes. Even then, however, the ceiling proved difficult to live with. Juggling the accounting to stay under the ceiling created an impression of insincerity. Construction costs—which doubled from FY 1977 to FY 1978—were excluded, although they subsumed runways and naval bases. Ceiling charges were also reduced by eliminating packing and shipping charges. Within the Executive's Arms Export Control Board, bargaining over purchase requests sometimes hinged on which permissions to delay until the following year rather than which to disapprove on their merits.[69]

When it was established, the ceiling had nothing to recommend it other than that no substantively objective criteria would work to assure aggregate reductions. That must mean either that bureaucrats assessing requests simply could not be trusted to follow orders and accord greater weight to arms limitation norms than to economic, strategic, or political sales incentives, or that when legitimate sales were considered inductively, the additive results invalidated the premise that previous aggregate sales levels were excessive. If reductions cannot be justified inductively by officials instructed in policy guidelines, the *a priori* policy of reductions itself cannot be justified.

Subordinating Arms Limitation to Arms Control

There is no necessary tension between good security and good arms control, but there can be tension between different goals of arms control. Saving money may conflict with preventing war if the former priority prompts one party to accept an unfavorable imbalance. Reducing destructiveness should deterrence fail, and maintaining technical stability may be conflicting goals if reducing prospective suffering increases propensity to risk. Weapon suppliers save money by selling rather than refusing, and Third World customers will suffer much more than their patrons if local deterrence fails. Enhancing stability, therefore, in the sense of discouraging resorts to force, should be the dominant one of the three classic arms control purposes in the policies of suppliers. The primacy of stability would also be consistent, in most cases, with U.S. defense policy.

Arms transfer control for stabilization may or may not require reductions. Stability depends on the varying weight and interaction of military, economic, political, and moral interests in diverse cases. In cases where the implications in all four dimensions point in the same direction, decisions are easy. As previous discussion has shown, though, there is no clear calculus to apply in cases where the implications are ambiguous or contradictory. Determining the basis for discrimination will inevitably be either arbitrary—as the ceiling constraint is—or uncomfortably subjective, general, and tentative, with one obvious consideration taking precedence over other ambiguous ones. Examples of such conditional guidelines are:

1. *Military* implications for American defense should usually be the first consideration in assessing purchase requests. This is a motherhood statement, however, which settles little in regard to controversial cases.

2. *Economic* profit is a constant interest, and should justify sales when there are no other reasons not to sell. There are no controversial cases, however, where there are no reasons not to sell. The weight of arguments against selling, and the availability of alternate suppliers to fill the request, should vary inversely.

3. *Political* considerations should dominate decisions where the United States has an interest in local developments—in a positive direction for reliable, vulnerable, and domestically stable quasi-allies, or in a

negative direction for customers with opposite qualities. This does not solve the problem of competing requests from local adversaries who are both important to the United States. There, the only solution is either to cut the Gordian knot with the offer of credible defense guarantees to replace indigenous defense capabilities, or to play it by ear and accept a messy outcome, as in the F-15 sale to Saudi Arabia against Israel's protest.

4. *Moral* norms should be primary in inhibiting sales where they overlap completely with *Realpolitik* (South Africa), secondary where the odiousness of the regime and the extent of the threat to it are both moderate (much of black Africa and Latin America), and tertiary where the objectionableness of the government pales beside the threatening alternative (South Korea).

Vaguely contingent rules of thumb are better than arbitrary ones, but they dim the possibilities of either devising an arms limitation policy *per se*, or decisively integrating weapons purchasers into a U.S. defense plan. This is just as well, since the only thing worse than confusion about how arms trade affects the correlation of forces would be a deceptively comforting false clarity. The answer is not to categorically abandon limits on arms sales, but to treat separate cases as dependent variables in regional diplomacy rather than elements of a global arms trade policy. This holds out the prospect of only modest progress, if any, in reducing the trade, even in the event—far from probable—that tension and competition between the superpowers decline. But that is the more realistic prospect, and in dampening expectations it will prevent the disillusionment and embarrassment that inevitably follows the oversell of undersell.

Notes

1. Except where otherwise noted, this discussion will deal with sales rather than grants. Grants are no longer a major part of arms transfers, and they are logically easier to evaluate in terms of the costs and benefits of restraint.

2. Sophisticated weapons "do not necessarily correlate with high casualties." Geoffrey Kemp, "Arms Traffic and Third World Conflicts," *International Conciliation*, no. 577 (March 1970), pp. 41–42.

3. Sales declined after 1974, and CIA projected that the long-term trend was downward. See Congressional Research Service, *Implications of President Carter's Conventional Arms Transfer Policy: Report to the Committee on Foreign Relations United States Senate*, 95th Cong., 1st sess., 1977, pp. 2–5. For customers in the Third World—the focus of most criticism—dollar volumes are also a deceptive indicator. Logistical and support functions (rather than actual hardware with direct destructive power) account for much of the volume because those countries lack military infrastructures. Lewis Sorley, *Conventional Arms*

Transfers and the Nixon Administration: A Policy Analysis, Ph.D. dissertation, Johns Hopkins University, 1979, pp. 126–127.

4. Philip J. Farley, Stephen S. Kaplan, and William H. Lewis, *Arms Across the Sea* (Washington, D.C.: Brookings, 1978), p. 99; Samuel P. Huntington, "Arms Transfer Policies," statement to the House Committee on Foreign Affairs, July 10, 1974 (mimeo), pp. 5–6; Jan Oberg, "Arms Trade with the Third World as an Aspect of Imperialism," *Journal of Peace Research* XII, no. 3 (1975) p. 222.

5. President's statement, May 19, 1977.

6. A panel peopled by several Carter appointees-to-be reported at the time of his election, "The rapid proliferation of highly sophisticated weapons to the Third World may foster militaristic tendencies and encourage national leaders to think of military, rather than political, means for resolving their international disputes. The influx of advanced weapons can create arms imbalances which may make military adventures appear more tempting. . . . Controlling the international arms trade is a prerequisite to lessening the likelihood of international armed conflict." National Policy Panel on Conventional Arms Control, *Controlling the Conventional Arms Race* (New York: United Nations Association, November 1976), p. 6. Such arguments reverse cause and effect.

7. Anne Hessing Cahn and Joseph J. Kruzel, "Arms Trade in the 1980s," in Cahn, Kruzel, Peter Dawkins, and Jacques Huntzinger, *Controlling Future Arms Trade* (New York: McGraw-Hill, for the Council on Foreign Relations, 1977), p. 39.

8. The Czech-Soviet arms deal with Egypt in 1955 is often cited as a destabilizing transfer, giving Israel an incentive to wage preventive war (the 1956 Sinai campaign) before Egypt could assimilate its new capabilities. The same argument is used to explain Pakistan's interest in striking India in 1965, as Indian capabilities were expanding as a result of the buildup after the 1962 border war with China. This argument does have some merit; the arms buildups were a proximate or marginal cause. But they were still mostly epiphenomenal. In both cases the political conflicts were so intense that it is almost impossible to conceive how attempts to achieve military advantage could have been avoided. To preserve military stability by abstaining from supply of the contenders, the superpowers would have had to disclaim the political imperatives of supporting their clients. At the height of the Cold War this alternative was, for better or worse, out of the question.

9. Quoted in Robert Harkavy, *The Arms Trade and International Systems* (Cambridge: Ballinger, 1975), p. 226.

10. Geoffrey Kemp with Steven Miller, "The Arms Transfer Phenomenon," in Andrew J. Pierre, ed., *Arms Transfers and American Foreign Policy* (New York: New York University Press, 1979), pp. 35–36.

11. A half-century old statement exemplifies the reasoning of many members of this school just as well today: "it is necessary to nail to the counter the fallacy of *si vis pacem para bellum* ("Who would desire peace should be prepared for war"). . . . Now there was a time when circumstances may have given some practical justification to this theoretically untenable position. Nations small and sparsely distributed over unorganized territories, small armies, simple weapons,

little or no international faith, unstable compacts, personal influence on international policies, may have made the method of preparedness the cheapest, safest, and most practicable, nay, the only one available. Today, the situation is the very reverse. The world has grown small for our power and resources. Only one opinion and one market cover the face of the earth. Wars absorb the whole population of the countries which engage in them, exact all their resources. . . . In this condition, preparing for war means securing . . . absolute control over the sources of supply and communications. . . . Preparedness leads therefore to the scramble for raw materials and territories, and thence to increasing causes of friction and possibilities of war." Salvador de Madariaga, *Disarmament* (New York: Coward-McCann, 1929), pp. 13–14. Written before Hitler's accession to power, this formulation looks peculiarly naive in its inattention to the causal impact of revisionist aims. Today, however, similar arguments are equally oblivious to the compelling force of territorial and ethnic disputes throughout the Third World. Why should we expect the process of national development and regional integration there to proceed with markedly less conflict than it did in European history? In recent years the primary utility of arms for the great powers has shifted. More than instruments usable for changing the status quo, they are now most useful for preserving it (through deterrence). See Klaus Knorr, "Is International Coercion Waning or Rising?" *International Security* I, no. 4 (Spring 1977), p. 94. This change, however, is largely a function of nuclear weapons, which arms controllers hope to keep out of the Third World. As the 1970s opened Geoffrey Kemp ("Arms Traffic and Third World Conflicts," p. 5) noted that a quarter of the states in the world were engaged in conflicts involving armed forces, and that if those who had used force in the previous decade and those preparing for it in the future were added, the proportion was over half. As the 1980s open, neither the record nor prospects appear any more promising.

12. See Samuel P. Huntington, "Arms Races: Prerequisites and Results," *Public Policy*, 1958, p. 42.

13. Kemp with Miller, "The Arms Transfer Phenomenon," p. 36.

14. Sorley, *Conventional Arms Transfers*, pp. 4–5.

15. Lucy Wilson Benson, "Turning the Supertanker: Arms Transfer Restraint," *International Security* III, no. 4 (Spring 1979), pp. 8–9.

16. Huntington, "Arms Transfer Policies," p. 15.

17. U.S. data subsumed services and construction while estimates on Soviet transfers rarely did. The statistics used also did not often reflect the significance of higher unit costs of American items. U.S., Central Intelligence Agency, *Arms Flows to LDCs: U.S.-Soviet Comparison, 1974–77* (November 1978); U.S. Congress, House, Committee on Armed Services, *Report, Indian Ocean Forces Limitation and Conventional Arms Transfer Limitation*, 95th Cong., 2nd sess., 1979, pp. 5, 11–12.

18. *Ibid.*, p. 12.

19. Charles M. Perry, "The Threat of Less-Advanced Arms: The Arab-Israeli Case," in Uri Ra'anan, Robert L. Pfaltzgraff, Jr., and Geoffrey Kemp, eds., *Arms Transfers to the Third World* (Boulder: Westview Press, 1978), p. 303 and *passim*. A supplier agreement to ban "escalatory" new-generation aircraft (see

Robert J. Pranger, "Towards Arms Control in the Middle East," *Middle East Problem Paper* No. 9 [Washington, D.C.: Middle East Institute, 1974], pp. 8–10), on the other hand might *eventually* benefit Israel. As Arab air forces obsolesced, Israel's *indigenous* aircraft industry could rebuild the qualitative advantage.

20. Richard Burt, *Nuclear Proliferation and Conventional Arms Transfers: The Missing Link,* Discussion Paper No. 76 (Santa Monica: California Seminar on Arms Control and Foreign Policy, September 1977), pp. 28–29.

21. S. J. Dudzinsky, Jr., and James Digby, "New Technology and Control of Conventional Arms: Some Common Ground," *International Security* I, no. 4 (Spring 1977), p. 151.

22. See David Louscher, "The Role of Military Sales as a U.S. Foreign Assistance Instrument," *Orbis* XX, no. 4 (Winter 1977), p. 960.

23. Oberg, ("Arms Trade with the Third World," pp. 215, 218) based this analysis on an application of Johan Galtung's model of structural imperialism to quantitative data on transaction flows.

24. As a Peruvian General complained, "The most tyrannical kind of dependence is military technological dependence." Quoted in David Ronfeldt with Caesar Sereseres, "U.S. Arms Transfers, Diplomacy and Security in Latin America," in Pierre, ed., *Arms Transfers and American Foreign Policy*, p. 135. It was easy to deny *grants* of arms without insult, since they were a cost to the supplier. With paying customers, though, it is ironic that liberal doves now make arguments for refusals to trade that must implicitly be based on the assumption that customers are either too stupid to realize they don't need the weapons, too corrupt to be trusted with them, or too illegitimate to decide how their countries' resources should be allocated, while conservative hawks favoring sales disingenuously criticize this attitude as inegalitarian, imperial, or racist.

25. See Emile Benoit, *Defense and Economic Growth in the Developing Countries* (Lexington: D.C. Heath, 1974), pp. 162, 168, and Stephanie G. Neuman, "Arms Transfers and Economic Development: Some Research and Policy Issues," in Neuman and Robert Harkavy, eds., *Arms Transfers in the Modern World* (New York: Praeger, 1979).

26. Jacques Huntzinger, "Regional Recipient Restraints," in Cahn *et al., Controlling Future Arms Trade*, p. 165.

27. Lucy Benson's "supertanker" metaphor is an unfortunate double entendre suggesting how rejected customers could view an arms supply embargo as no more moral than an oil embargo. Oil Minister Yamani related U.S. arms sales to continued Saudi support of the dollar and high oil production levels. Peter Osnos and David B. Ottaway, "Yamani Links F-15s to Oil, Dollar Help," *Washington Post*, May 2, 1978.

28. Kemp with Miller, "Arms Transfer Phenomenon," p. 71.

29. See Andrew J. Pierre, "Multilateral Restraint on Arms Transfer," in Pierre, ed., *Arms Transfers and American Foreign Policy*, p. 291.

30. See Quincy Wright's arguments quoted in Harkavy, *Arms Trade and International Systems*, p. 226.

31. See Donald J. Goldstein, "Third World Arms Industries: Their Own Slings and Swords," unpublished paper, Central Intelligence Agency, 1979, pp. 4–5.

32. Harkavy, *Arms Trade and International Systems*, chapter 6. Michael Moodie, *Sovereignty, Security, and Arms*, Washington Paper No. 67 (Beverly Hills: Sage, for the Georgetown Center for Strategic and International Studies, 1979), p. 83: "The trend in defense production in the Third World is broad but not deep."

33. U.S. Congress, House, Committee on Armed Services, *Hearings, Indian Ocean Arms Limitations and Multilateral Cooperation on Restraining Conventional Arms Transfers*, 95th Cong., 2nd sess., 1978, p. 16. In some areas, for instance, the United States is selling weaponry that could preclude military intervention by our own forces. American projection forces are "light," that is, lacking in heavy armor and organic firepower support. Their success (without high casualties) in landings may depend on the lightness of the local opposition.

34. Louscher, "Role of Military Sales," pp. 957–958.

35. Bernard Gwertzman, "Turkish Chief Sees No Russian Threat," *New York Times*, May 30, 1978.

36. See Kemp with Miller, "Arms Transfer Phenomenon," pp. 77–79.

37. Bernard D. Nossiter, "Weizman Says Israel Seeks Doubling of Arms Aid," *New York Times*, September 13, 1979.

38. For contrary views see Ann Hessing Cahn, "The Economics of Arms Transfers," in Neuman and Harkavy (eds.), *Arms Transfers in the Modern World*, pp. 173–183.

39. Cahn and Kruzel, "Arms Trade in the 1980's," pp. 66–67.

40. See Congressional Research Service, *Implications of President Carter's Arms Transfer Policy*, pp. 39–40.

41. See Lawrence Freedman, "Britain and the Arms Trade," *International Affairs* LIV, no. 1 (July 1978), p. 382. The policy was moderated in 1975, but for the most part exceptions have been unique weapons like the British *Harrier*. The Commandant of the Marine Corps specifically suggested that marketing *Harriers* to more foreign countries would ease the burden for the Marines, who cannot support the purchases very well alone. George C. Wilson, "New Marine Chief Favors 2-Sex Draft," *Washington Post*, July 6, 1979.

42. Freedman, "Britain and the Arms Trade," p. 381; Luigi Einaudi, Hans Heymann, Jr., David Ronfeldt, and Cesar Sereseres, *Arms Transfers to Latin America: Toward A Policy of Mutual Respect*, R-1173-DOS (Santa Monica: Rand Corporation, June 1973), Chapter IV; Lawrence G. Franko, "Restraining Arms Exports to the Third World: Will Europe Agree?" *Survival* XXI, no. 1 (January/February 1979), p. 16. LDC sales are vital to particular firms (e.g., Dassault-Breguet) and because most of the producers are totally or partially publicly owned, the British and French governments cannot escape political responsibility for layoffs due to sales contractions. "Cumulatively, the Europeans lag in civil aircraft, the small size of the European industry, the large scale economies in design and development, and the relative inability to shed workers in times of slump, imply that, under current domestic procurement and international trade conditions, countries such as Britain and France need to seek out export markets for military aircraft in order to maintain any indigenous technological capability in aerospace at all." *Ibid.*, p. 19. Some of the U.S. Arms

Control and Disarmament Agency's analyses of European exports are marred by problems with data. Edward A. Kolodziej, "Measuring Arms Transfers: A Problem of Sources and Some Sources of Problems with ACDA Data," *Journal of Conflict Resolution* XXIII, no. 1 (June 1979), pp. 222–223. For a French perspective on dependence on exports see Jean-Francois Dubos, *Ventes d'Armes: Une Politique* (Paris: Gallimard, 1974), pp. 182–186.

43. See Farley, Kaplan, and Lewis, *Arms Across the Sea,* p. 71; Paul Hammond, David J. Louscher, and Michael D. Salomon, "Controlling U.S. Arms Transfers: The Emerging System," *Orbis* XXIII, no. 2 (Summer 1979), p. 348; Eliot Cohen, "NATO Standardization: The Perils of Common Sense," *Foreign Policy* no. 31 (Summer 1978), p. 89; Colin S. Gray, "Traffic Control for the Arms Trade?" *Foreign Policy* no. 6 (Spring 1972), p. 161. Lengthening production runs gives producers great pricing flexibility for capturing sales because they can be based on marginal rather than average costs. John Stanley and Maurice Pearton, *The International Trade in Arms* (New York: Praeger, for the International Institute for Strategic Studies, 1972), p. 145.

44. Franko, "Restraining Arms Exports," p. 25.

45. Stockholm Institute for Peace Research International, *The Arms Trade with the Third World* (Stockholm: Almquist & Wiksell, 1971), pp. 32–34. Whereas the superpowers use arms transfers for diplomatic competition with each other, the intermediate suppliers—Britain and France—need independent production capacity, and thus sales, to hedge against changes in the relationship with their superpower ally. James Bellini, "National Defence Policy and Arms Sales," in *R.U.S.I. and Brassey's Defence Yearbook 1976/77* (Boulder: Westview Press, 1976), p. 17. Dependence is thus not only a problem of arms importers, but of intermediate exporters too, and it is the asymmetrical interests of the suppliers that place major barriers against coordinated limitations of sales.

46. Freedman, "Britain and the Arms Trade," pp. 387, 389–390. Gains in influence may be an illusory goal, but anticipation of *losses* of influence from denial of a client is more compelling, and accounts for the bulk of what remains of U.S. grant aid. Three-fourths of the Security Assistance appropriation requested in 1979 were a payoff for the two Camp David participants, Israel and Egypt. See Lucy Wilson Benson, "Security Assistance: FY 1980 Proposals," *Department of State Bulletin* LXXIX, April 1979, p. 43.

47. Robert Mantel and Geoffrey Kemp, *U.S. Military Sales to Iran*, Staff Report to the Senate Foreign Relations Committee, 94th Cong., 2d sess., 1976, pp. x, xiii, 52.

48. Uri Ra'anan, *The USSR Arms the Third World* (Cambridge: MIT Press, 1969), pp. 9–10.

49. Farley, Kaplan, and Lewis, *Arms Across the Sea*, pp. 113, 117.

50. Leslie H. Gelb, "Arms Sales," *Foreign Policy* no. 25 (Winter 1976–77), p. 22.

51. House Armed Services Committee, *Indian Ocean Force Limitations Report*, p. 5; Benson, "Turning the Supertanker," p. 13. There has been no major arms race in Latin America. See Einaudi *et al.*, *Arms Transfers to Latin America*, Chapter 3.

52. Kemp with Miller, "The Arms Transfer Phenomenon," pp 92–93.

53. William B. Quandt, *Decade of Decision: American Policy Toward the Arab-Israeli Conflict, 1967–1976* (Berkeley: University of California Press, 1977), pp. 66–67.

54. Thomas R. Wheelock, "Arms for Israel: The Limit of Leverage," *International Security* III, no. 2 (Fall 1978), pp. 127–130. Earlier Charles de Gaulle embargoed French arms to Israel, but most of the effects contradicted his aims. Paradoxically embargoes have tended to accelerate Middle East arms races. "Whenever one of the parties . . . felt that its future supplies of arms might be endangered, or when one source of arms closed while another opened without guarantee that it would remain open, there was a strong argument for buying immediately as much as possible." Yair Evron, "French Arms Policy in the Middle East," *The World Today* XXVI, no. 2 (February 1970), pp. 87–88.

55. Wynfred Joshua and Stephen P. Gibert, *Arms for the Third World: Soviet Military Aid Diplomacy* (Baltimore: Johns Hopkins University Press, 1969), p. 131.

56. *Department of Defense Annual Report Fiscal Year 1980*, January 1979, p. 269; Jo L. Husbands, "The Conventional Arms Transfer Talks: Negotiation As Proselytization," Paper for the American Political Science Association Convention, September 1979, pp. 15–17. The Soviets had taken a multi-billion dollar beating in Egypt and Indonesia, where their political influence evaporated, and without return payment for arms they would now suffer a substantial trade deficit with the Third World.

57. In Africa, for example, the Soviets supplied arms in 18 of 64 identified agreements, and the United States in only 3, while the USSR was even more prominent as a supplier in unreported transfers. James W. Abellera, "Appendix: The Arming of Sub-Saharan Africa," *AEI Defense Review* II, no. 6 (1978), p. 51. (The prominent role of Western European suppliers—in 48 of the identified agreements—substantially mitigates the significance of the disparity.) Washington has rebuffed purchase requests from African states that perform useful functions for the United States: Senegal (peacekeeping forces in Lebanon and Shaba) and Nigeria (support for policy in southern Africa). Chester A. Crocker and William H. Lewis, "Missing Opportunities in Africa," *Foreign Policy* no. 35 (Summer 1979), p. 154.

58. Leslie H. Gelb, Statement to the House Foreign Affairs Committee, *Department of State Bulletin* LXXIX, June 1979, p. 45.

59. Congressional Research Service, *Implications of President Carter's Conventional Arms Transfer Policy*, p. 16.

60. For conditional arguments that arms transfers reduce incentives for nuclear weapons see Burt, *Nuclear Proliferation and Conventional Arms Transfers*, and Richard K. Betts, "Paranoids, Pygmies, Pariahs, and Nonproliferation," *Foreign Policy* no. 26 (Spring 1979), pp. 176–178; for contrary arguments see Steven Baker, "Arms Transfers and Nuclear Proliferation," *Arms Control Today* VII, no. 4 (April 1977). See also Jean Klein, "Ventes d'Armes et d'Equipements Nucleaires," *Politique Etrangere* XL, no. 6 (1975). Cahn and Kruzel ("Arms Trade in the 1980s," p. 64) note that the only region showing a downward trend in arms

imports from 1965 to 1974 was South Asia. It is illustrative that since 1974 that region has become the most proliferation-prone in the world.

61. House Armed Services Committee, *Indian Ocean Forces Limitation Report*, p. 8.

62. Sorley, *Conventional Arms Transfers and the Nixon Administration*, pp. 167–168; Nicole Ball and Milton Leitenberg, "The Foreign Arms Sales of the Carter Administration," *Bulletin of the Atomic Scientists*, February 1979; "Arms Sales: Giving Notice," *Washington Post*, May 29, 1979. The Soviet position, while unacceptable, was really more rational since it was oriented to security outputs rather than technical inputs.

63. They exceeded it in SALT II but may lose it again by the late 1980s if the U.S. salves the wound by deploying MX, D-5, new penetrating bombers, and GLCMs in Europe.

64. Huntzinger, "Regional Recipient Restraints," p. 165.

65. Pierre, "Multilateral Restraints on Arms Transfers," pp. 308–310.

66. The challenge to SALT II from U.S. hawks is based on arguments that the limits are not equitable and do give exploitable utility to Soviet forces.

67. See Husbands, "Conventional Arms Transfer Talks," p. 3.

68. Benson, "Turning the Supertanker," p. 10.

69. U.S., Congress, House, Committee on International Relations, Hearing, *United States Arms Sale Policy and Recent Sales to Europe and the Middle East*, 95th Cong., 2d sess., 1978, pp. 45–47; Hammond, Louscher, and Salomon, "Controlling U.S. Arms Transfers," p. 334. One critic likened the spectacle to "watching President Carter try to cover up the continuing volume of U.S. arms transfers, as if he were the Amie Semple McPherson of evangelical disarmers." Bridget Gail (pseud.), "'The Fine Old Game of Killing': Comparing U.S. and Soviet Arms Sales," *Armed Forces Journal International*, September 1978.

8
Arms Control and the Indian Ocean

Richard Haass

In 1968, Great Britain announced its intention to withdraw from its remaining positions east of Suez. The reaction in the United States, then heavily burdened in Southeast Asia, was a mixed one: on one hand, there were those who feared the emergence of a post-British geopolitical vacuum that could be exploited by forces hostile to American interests; on the other, there were those who feared more the prospects of yet another U.S. commitment in Asia. The response that evolved reflected these opposing concerns and consisted of three principal elements: an attempt through détente to regulate competition with the Soviet Union for influence in peripheral areas; an effort, in part through military transfers, to expand the capacity of key, pro-Western local states to provide for their own defense; and the establishment of a modestly upgraded military (primarily naval) presence in the Indian Ocean.

After a decade of trying to protect American interests in the Indian Ocean area at a limited level of cost, U.S. policymakers can only reflect back on what is at best an uneven record. What is more important, however, is that the trends—revolution in Iran, the Soviet presence in Afghanistan, uncertainty in Saudi Arabia, widespread Soviet involvement throughout the ocean's northwest quadrant, new questions surrounding the price and supply of oil, the prospects of further nuclear proliferation—are worrying. The president's national security advisor felt it necessary (in December 1978) to characterize this part of the world as the "arc of crisis." This new perception "culminated" in the so-called Carter Doctrine, announced by President Carter in his 1980 State of the Union address: "Any attempt by any outside force to gain control of the Persian Gulf region will be regarded as an assault on the vital interests of the United States. It will be repelled by use of any means necessary, including military force." Perhaps more than any other single statement, this declaration signaled an end to the era of the Nixon Doctrine and its eschewal of the commitment of U.S. ground forces to Third World conflicts.

However significant, the above analyses and declarations fail to shed much light on specific policy options and directions. One question seems especially critical: In light of U.S. interests, and given the potential threat to these interests posed by the Soviet Union and a number of littoral states, what contribution can the "military instruments of policy" make toward the realization of U.S. objectives in the area? Put another way, what can be expected from arms, as well as from arms control, given the U.S. perspective in the Indian Ocean area?

Arms and Arms Control

The pairing of "arms" and "arms control" is deliberate. For some analysts, they provide but two means of reaching the desired ends of "stability" or "security." As such, they form part of the larger whole that is a sound national security strategy. For others, perhaps described better as advocates than as analysts, the two are viewed not so much as complements as competitors: more arms control tends to mean fewer arms; less arms control paves the way to more arms. Apparently, such an approach is inadequate; the relationship between arms and arms control is far more complex. In many instances, for example, the two are symbiotic: actual or expected increases in force levels can stimulate desires for arms control, while arms control negotiations (both ongoing or intended) can stimulate demands for force enhancement—whether to improve relative bargaining positions between negotiating parties or as a means of gaining domestic or bureaucratic political support for the negotiations.

There are other interactions as well. In some cases—for example, the decision by NATO to modernize long-range theater nuclear forces—political realities are such that no force improvement commitment was or is possible without an associated arms control initiative. Arms control can also alter the shape of actual forces by stipulating design or configuration requirements necessitated by verification procedures. In addition, the institutions of arms control can channel competition and innovation into weapons categories or deployment patterns not regulated by the regime.

Although the above is intended to be illustrative rather than exhaustive, two other points need to be made in addition to the basic one that the relationship between arms and arms control is anything but simple or straightforward. First, the two are hardly equals in terms of their impact on national security policy. With few exceptions the impact of arms control has been modest, tending at most to codify existing balances rather than to create new ones. This is particularly the case in the realm of general purpose (rather than strategic nuclear) forces, where unilateral planning decisions, however determined, have had a greater impact on U.S. security than have negotiated constraints. Second, it is important to point out that the relationship between arms and arms control is not necessarily the key to security policy or force planning. Phrased differently, one could argue that the sum of the contribution of arms and arms control does not equal either the totality of security policy or, more obviously, the totality of diplomacy. Only in the relatively unique realm of strategic forces can the argument be supported that there are direct trade-offs between the two with little else entering the equation. But the "purity" of the central strategic balance is not duplicated at "lower" levels of force where other instruments can more easily be substituted for, or used to balance, military ones. In the context of the Indian Ocean, the arms/arms control dichotomy is too narrow; quite possibly, neither arms control, nor local forces and facilities, nor both, may provide an adequate foundation on which to base U.S. policy toward the area.

Naval Controls: 1817 to the Present

Arms controllers have sought traditionally to establish limits on the inventories of selected forces of selected states. The approach can be indirect, as in the case with budgetary ceilings, or direct, applied either to inventories or to deployments with a designated area. Arms control can be directed toward the characteristics of forces or their use; whatever the object, approaches can be comprehensive or partial, bilateral or multilateral, quantitative or qualitative, explicit and formal or tacit and informal, and permit controlled growth of forces, zero growth, phased reduction, or elimination of the items (or activities) in question.

The potential scope of arms control is only partially illustrated by examining the precedents in the area of naval arms control. The first and probably most successful arrangement affecting naval forces was the 1817 Executive Agreement between the United States and Great Britain governing the militarization of the Great Lakes. Yet, the success of this first naval "zone of peace" and deployment regime (which by definition did not have a direct effect on the inventories of the parties) was less a tribute to the negotiations themselves than simply a reflection of the state of political relations that existed between the two states at the time. No naval arms race of any sort would have come about in the absence of any pact.

The next major naval arms control regime—the Washington and London naval treaties of 1922 and 1930, respectively—were at once more significant and less successful. Their importance resulted from the fact that the treaties included many of the key states of the day and that limits were stipulated on the prestige military forces of the day. Yet the arrangements lasted only so long as they placed no real constraint on the parties; that is, so long as they tended to reflect rather than restrict military strengths. In addition, the two treaties had the ancillary effect of redirecting or channeling competition and innovation into those classes of sea-based systems—cruisers, submarines, aircraft carriers—not covered by the regime. As such, the treaties became the first in a pattern of arms control arrangements unable to keep pace with either the political or technical dynamics of their era.

The Rush-Bagot deployment agreement, and the inventory approach of the two treaties during the inter-war years, represent but part of both the precedents and possibilities for naval arms control. The 1936 Montreux Convention instituted limits to the militarization of the Black Sea and the adjoining straits. Over time, however, loose interpretation and enforcement of neither the spirit nor the letter of the Convention has diluted its impact in peacetime; more importantly, the buildup of local forces has ensured that the battle for control of the Turkish Straits will be an intense one in war regardless of the Convention and its restrictions.

The most recent agreement regulating naval forces is the 1972 Soviet-American Agreement on the Prevention of Incidents On and Over the High Seas. The agreement is in effect a series of confidence-building measures (CBMs), although primarily of one type. In general, CBMs consist of steps intended to reduce the elements of uncertainty and threat inherent in the movements and activities of military forces in non-war conditions, thereby reassuring potential adversaries and reducing the chance for conflict. Within this general definition three types of naval CBMs can be envisioned: the establishment of procedures or "rules of the road" to lessen the chance of accidental conflict and reduce opportunities for intimidation and harassment of an adversary's vessels; the requirement that prior notification be provided for designated naval activities (inventory changes, transits, or deployments in a given area, port calls, exercises, etc.) such as the notices that are given before certain ground maneuvers under the CSCE (Helsinki) Final Act; and, if CBMs are defined in their broadest sense, the introduction of actual constraints on the use of naval or sea-based forces, in which case they become tantamount to activity controls.

The 1972 Agreement is largely a naval CBM of the first type. The pact establishes procedures for the two navies to avoid collisions, sets forth the principle of non-interference in the formations of the other party, and encourages both states to avoid conducting maneuvers in areas of heavy traffic. There are other regulations involving the use of signals, the prior notification of the involvement of submarines in exercises, and the distance to be maintained by surveillance ships from their objects of investigation. Simulated attacks by aircraft are banned. In practice, the agreement seems to have reduced the frequency of playing "chicken" at sea; yet such instances of interference are by no means obsolete, as was shown by Soviet behavior in the Indian Ocean in late 1978. More importantly, any claims that the agreement—even when honored—has had anything more than a marginal effect on the relations at sea between the superpowers lack substance.

Despite this uneven and generally unimpressive record, naval arms control continues to receive attention and support. Several factors account for this. Navies around the world continue to improve in quality (if not always to increase in quantity), and out-of-area deployments for the fleets of several states have become commonplace. The high cost of modern warships has similarly increased the visibility of navies. Resources moving on the sea as well as those found in and under it have also raised awareness of navies and their missions. Doubts about the survivability of surface ships in an age of widespread anti-ship missiles and submarines, the impact to the development of the Soviet Navy and the navies of other states, more general questions relating to the utility of force and thus both gunboat diplomacy and interventions from the sea—all have combined to challenge conventional wisdom surrounding the navy and have indirectly or directly increased interest in naval arms control. Indeed, it is only surprising that more attention has not come about.

The principal exception to this neglect, benign or otherwise, of seeking negotiated constraints on naval forces has involved those naval forces and facilities in the Indian Ocean. Support for some form of Indian Ocean arrangement has come from several sources. The advocates of longest standing are among the local or littoral states, many of whom have feared (and continue to fear) that the Indian Ocean would become a new and major venue of superpower competition and, at the same time, a new means for the superpowers to bring military force to bear directly on Third World states. For a long time, Indian Ocean arms control has been urged by various people in the United States, whether as a means of avoiding new and costly commitments in Asia or, more narrowly, a new and unnecessary form of competition with the U.S.S.R. Although the

Soviet stance has changed over time, and in any case is difficult to fathom, there have been signs of Soviet interest in Indian Ocean arms control—possibly in part for some of the same reasons just mentioned above; possibly as well to avoid alienating littoral advocates or even simply to seek some advantage over the United States.

Of earliest vintage is the effort to have the Indian Ocean declared and recognized as a "Zone of Peace." The theme evolved out of the formative stages of the non-aligned movement, and reached diplomatic, rather than actual, fruition when the United Nations General Assembly adopted a resolution in December 1971 declaring the Indian Ocean, along with the air space above and the ocean floor below, a zone of peace for all time. More specifically, the resolution consisted of two principal clauses, dealing with the "great powers" and all "user" states respectively. The first clause listed four stipulations, calling for no further increase in great power military presence in the Indian Ocean; elimination of all great power military installations in the ocean; banning nuclear weapons and other weapons of mass destruction from the zone; and, more generally, elimination of all military presence "conceived in the context of great power rivalry." Obligations for local and hinterland states, major maritime users of the ocean, and the great powers as well, were to preclude the use of the ocean by military vessels and aircraft for the purpose of threatening or using force against any local state.

That the resolution was passed at a time when the five most populous states in the world were involved in a war in South Asia is a coincidence both ironic and informative, as it has been factors both local and foreign that have combined to prevent the proposal from having anything more than a marginal impact. On one hand, the peace zone has been thwarted by the lack of common objectives among the local states themselves; beneath the *facade* of agreement there exist widely divergent notions about the peace zone and of what process should be used to *arrive* at an agreement. There has emerged a basic split between such relatively powerful local states as India, which has repeatedly emphasized the obligations of the great powers (and the United States in particular) to reduce their presence, and the smaller local states, who have expressed concern lest a relatively modest great power balance be replaced by the predominance of one or more local powers.

The Zone of Peace has also suffered from the resistance of the great powers. Among the five permanent members of the U.S. Security Council, only China has endorsed the proposal, and China is the only one of the five that has no naval presence in the ocean to withdraw. France has built an impressive military presence, both to indicate its concern for the flow of oil and to protect its more special interests and role in Africa.

Great Britain still manages an infrequent deployment into the ocean, and has voiced opposition to the peace zone in principle. Most important, however, has been the refusal of both the Soviet Union and the United States to endorse the measure. The Soviet Union, which uses its navy (among other things) to buttress its foreign policy initiatives in the area and claims it needs to deploy forces to protect this East-West highway, has opposed the measure while trying to place the onus of obstruction on the United States. The American position has traditionally been less equivocal, reflecting both legal concern and the more direct conclusion that any regime limiting only the naval presence of great powers would be a distinct disadvantage—given that the United States relies almost totally on sea-based forces to project a direct military influence in the area.

This is not to say that the Zone of Peace has had no impact. It has placed the advocates of increased naval presence on the defensive, and strengthened the arguments of those who have maintained that increasing naval presence might actually prove counterproductive to the realization of foreign policy objectives in the area. Over time, however, the proposal lost momentum, initially because its leading advocate—India—squandered its credibility through its own domestic and foreign policies and, more recently, through the Soviet policies, which, whatever else they might appear to be, are hardly consistent with the notion of reducing great power rivalry. (It should be noted, however, that the Soviet invasion of Afghanistan, the post-Afghanistan invasion/U.S. Teheran embassy buildup of superpower naval presence, and the American search for access to facilities in the area have ignited several local states to seek a new dialogue on the peace zone.) In general, though, the focus of arms control efforts in the Indian Ocean has moved over the past several years away from the Zone of Peace and toward the more modest but more pragmatic idea of bringing about some form of deployment constraint between the United States and the Soviet Union.

The NALT Alternative

Although the peace zone and any Naval Arms Limitation Treaty (NALT) are both forms of deployment agreements, the two differ in terms of process and degree. Whereas the Zone of Peace is in many ways an "imposed" regime and one which calls for the elimination of great power presence, any NALT arrangement would be voluntarily entered into and controlled by the superpowers themselves, and would simply limit rather than eliminate presence; indeed, the one series of bilateral NALT negotiations that came close to producing an agreement between the superpowers in late 1977 or early 1978 called only for a "freeze" on the levels of forces of the two parties.

The historical record of efforts to bring about some form of Indian Ocean NALT arrangement is a small one. Contacts between the states in the early 1970s yielded insufficient mutual interest to warrant holding serious negotiations. The most persistent advocates of an agreement were in the U.S. Senate, where proponents viewed an agreement not only as the best (if not only) means of heading off a superpower naval arms race in the ocean, but also as a means of preventing or at least postponing the proposed expansion of U.S. military facilities on the island of Diego Garcia. Congress actually voted in 1975 to delay the release of funds for the construction project, instructing the executive to use the "extra" time to assess Soviet willingness to enter into some form of a NALT pact. These instructions were resisted, initially on the grounds that arms control should only follow the establishment of an adequate military capability in the area, and later (after several months) on the premise that Soviet behavior in Angola made any such offer inopportune.

The period of executive branch resistance to Indian Ocean NALT abruptly ended with the inauguration of Jimmy Carter, who from the outset placed a surprising degree of emphasis on the need to pursue formal arms control in the Indian Ocean. More specifically, on numerous occasions President Carter referred to either the complete "demilitarization" of the ocean or, more modestly, some degree of mutual Soviet-American military restraint. The Soviet Union's response was typically mixed: although it seriously participated in the talks, it also continued to stress that elimination of all foreign bases, which from their perspective only included Diego Garcia, remained a prerequisite for any pact. Moreover, just when Soviet diplomacy appeared to become more flexible on this point—in early 1978 Soviet commentators publicly announced Soviet willingness to enter into a phased NALT arrangement permitting existing levels of ship presence and facilities—Soviet behavior became, in the words of the then Secretary of State Cyrus Vance, "inconsistent with a limitation of forces in the area." The increase in Soviet naval presence instituted in October 1977, and more crucially the more assertive (and aggressive) thrust of Soviet policy from the Horn of Africa to Afghanistan, clouded the entire notion of negotiating constraints on naval forces. As a result, after four sets of negotiations, the Indian Ocean talks were adjourned indefinitely.

This hiatus notwithstanding, Indian Ocean arms control remains on the agenda. Littoral state interest in the idea, although less than in previous years, continues to exist, and has increased parallel to the rise in the level of military presence in the ocean. Similarly, it is not improbable that calls for Indian Ocean NALT will once again be heard in the United States—be it to limit the role of an increasingly over-stretched and expensive U.S. Navy there, or to limit U.S.-Soviet rivalry in an increasingly unstable part of the world. As a result, the need to assess and reassess the entire question of Indian Ocean arms control remains an active one.

To attempt an assessment in the abstract is difficult and without much meaning; one must limit oneself to regimes that appear likely to be negotiated or at least proposed. Two basic regimes fit this description. On one hand, there is the basic deployment limitation that has already been the subject of bilateral consideration. The key question in this case will be the level of forces and facilities permitted. The second possibility is the introduction of a special series of naval CBMs to help regulate the nature and conduct of superpower naval presence in the Indian Ocean. In all cases, it is necessary to examine not only the negotiating difficulties that are likely to be encountered, but also the more fundamental considerations of the adequacy and the desirability of negotiated constraints. In this, the Indian Ocean NALT question is like any other arms control proposition; if such terms as "negotiability" and "desirability" seem by now to be well worn, it is because over time they have worn well.

Assessing NALT

The most difficult technical problem confronting any negotiation will be to arrive at criteria capable of reflecting and measuring capability. The capability of naval forces is determined by a number of factors—size, speed, range, staying power, armour, armament, and so on—and no yardstick, whether total ship numbers or tonnage, or some mixture of both, can suffice as an accurate standard. In general, broad numerical calculations are not representative of qualitative factors, especially in an era of growing disparity between the size of a platform and potential of the performance. As a result, there is little meaning in an equation of one 90,000-ton aircraft carrier with nine 10,000-ton cruisers, or even in assuming the relative equality of two vessels of equal weight. Similarly, in a deployment regime, the commonly used "ship-day" measure, which would equate one cruiser staying in the designated area for a week with either an aircraft carrier staying for the same time or seven cruisers staying one day each, is a grossly inaccurate and inadequate measure. The improved but more complicated ship-ton-day standard, incorporating the factors of numbers of ships, tonnage, and duration of stay, offers a more accurate measure, but one that still falls short of providing a direct reflection of capability.

Even the most perfect of regimes, however, would be incomplete if it only covered surface vessels. Somehow, the regime would have to also consider associated air power, amphibious forces, and on-board arms. There is the difficult matter of what to do about submarines—although they pose a major threat to surface ships, their relative invisibility (and need to remain so) creates major verification problems in a deployment limitation. There are also complications created by noncombatant vessels performing roles ranging from support to intelligence and communications. Most important, and as we will discuss below, are the implications of excluding forces that are neither naval nor based at sea but which possess a great capacity to affect matters both at sea and in the larger theater.

Equally difficult problems with definition and measurement surround the matter of facilities and bases. On one hand, there is the question of distinguishing between a facility and a base, as well as among ownership, control and simply access. Then there's the basic question of whether to place constraints on facilities, and, if so, to what extent. In the context of the Indian Ocean, it has been this consideration more than any other that has posed a "technical" obstacle to NALT; the Soviet Union has persisted in calling Diego Garcia a base (unlike, for example, its own one-time facility in Berbera) and, until recently, has made elimination of all "bases" a precondition for any agreement.

Two points should be made here. First, it is important to emphasize that many of the above negotiating difficulties are real rather than abstract. The U.S. and Soviet fleets differ at every level: individual vessels, total inventories, and deployment patterns in the Indian Ocean. Similarly, they differ in their dependence on floating support and in their access to support facilities in the Indian Ocean area. These asymmetries—which are the rule rather than the exception—will seriously complicate any formal negotiation.

Second, and as the last sentence suggests, there is an alternative to a formal and complex approach to Indian Ocean NALT. On one hand, negotiability can be improved by keeping any arrangement vague or even tacit and informal. Thus, one can envision some sort of negotiated commitment to keep force levels below a certain threshold, although specific stipulations would be rare or general in nature. The risk inherent in such an approach is that the arrangement lends itself to unilateral interpretation and invites violation. Similarly, negotiations can be simplified by limiting the object of agreement to surface combatants; the danger here is not so much that the agreement will then be violated, but rather that major changes in the military balance can come about *without* violating the agreement. If a vague arrangement invites violation, a partial or incomplete one tends to invite circumvention.

An alternative way to ease problems of negotiability that are likely to arise when seeking to develop a deployment-oriented regime would be to institute a series of CBMs for the two superpowers in the Indian Ocean. The two could agree to share information at regular intervals regarding the nature of their military presence in the ocean, as well as provide advance notification of deployments into the ocean. Similarly, advance notice of exercises, including information pertaining to their duration, location, and scope, could be made mandatory. To facilitate the exchange of data, some form of "Naval Consultative Committee," or NCC, might be established for the Indian Ocean; the technical problems involved in establishing and maintaining such a framework appear to be far more manageable than the problems involved in attempting to establish a more traditional arms control regime.

But questions of negotiability immediately lead to those of desirability; indeed, the two are, or at least should be, inseparable. One cannot consider desirability in the abstract, but only within the context of a specific regime. As a result, an assessment of desirability will come to reflect not only those forces and facilities affected by the negotiations, but also those that have not been constrained. Put another way, desirability must take into account not only the substance of the arms control arrangement, but also the net or resulting balance, of which the items affected by the regime will be only a part.

What would be gained from a limitation on ship deployments in the Indian Ocean is not readily apparent. The level of U.S. "floating presence" that existed for nearly a decade (until late 1979)—a small Middle East Force augmented several times a year by carrier or major surface combatant task forces—was barely sufficient in size and strength to manage flag-showing missions, make port calls, and cope with the most limited of contingencies. Reductions would not only have made these tasks much more difficult to fulfill, but would have tended to place the United States at a distinct disadvantage in relation to both littoral states and the Soviet Union—all of whom were, and are, less geographically dependent upon sea-based forces for constituting a military presence in the area. Since late 1979, the United States has increased its Middle East Force from 3 to 5 ships, and has maintained some 20 combatants (including as many as 3 carrier battle groups) in the Indian Ocean. The Soviet Union has similarly increased its naval presence. Yet, in light of the importance of U.S. interests and the growing Soviet capacity and disposition to intervene around the littoral, even a mutual "freeze" on floating presence would be of doubtful benefit to the United States. Such an arrangement would limit a form of presence that is more central to the U.S. military effort than that of others. In effect, it would do little to reduce the potential threat, while at the same time work to constrain a potential response and actual deterrent.

It is even harder to see the utility of activity restraints. To limit exercises or deployments along lines of frequency or scope in the name of building confidence begs a key consideration—confidence for whom? Although activity restraints might reduce the potential ability of adversaries to act against the United States, they would also weaken American ability to use naval forces for its own purposes. Again, so-called balanced constraints are not truly balanced in a context of unequal interests and unequal dependence upon sea-based forces.

The greatest questions about desirability concern the placing of constraints on the use of support facilities. At a minimum, limiting the scope or use of local facilities could be expensive, necessitating either the enhancement of "floating support" or the expansion of near but out-of-area facilities. The alternative is to reduce the level of deployments to that which a reduced level of support can maintain. More significant, however, is the change in the perception of interest and capability—and in actual capability—that would follow a reduction in local support. Important in peacetime and crisis alike, facilities (or bases) symbolize a latent capacity to introduce additional military forces into the area at relatively short notice. Should deterrence fail, or should some contingency arise that requires some form of increased military presence, facilities in and near the region would provide the best means of introducing and supporting augmented forces and operations. Indeed, this potential capacity to respond may be enhanced if arms control is used to compensate for any unexpected imbalances created by the arrangement. But with or without arms control, local facilities providing assured access and significant services possess an excellent mixture of attributes: a symbol of interest and capacity to act in peacetime, the ability to act in a crisis, and a reduced need to maintain large permanent forces and support (naval and otherwise) in the area.

The desirability and utility of CBMs are difficult to assess with any degree of certainty. Advance notification of exercises seems to be a reasonable measure to avoid unnecessary incidents, as does a more detailed application of the "rules of the road" principles found in the Incidents at Sea Agreement. But advance notice of deployments presents some problems. Counter responses might be brought about more quickly than they would have otherwise; one's own ability to respond might be compromised by notification requirements; and in all cases there is the fact that surprise and initiative might be forfeited, thereby reducing diplomatic gain or actually increasing the vulnerability of vessels. In general, although CBMs promise less arms control "rewards" than other regimes, they pose less in the way of risks; if some arms control in the Indian Ocean area is felt to be necessary for diplomatic or other reasons, a modest series of CBMs might offer the most prudent approach.

The problems with virtually any possible NALT agreement in the Indian Ocean—or elsewhere for that matter—is one of circumvention. The selection and isolation of surface combatants for special controls makes little sense given the role of submarines; similarly, the selection and isolation of all sea-based forces makes little sense given the ability of shore-based aircraft and missiles to reach targets at sea. Moreover, geographical factors continue to make the United States disproportionately dependent upon sea-based forces and local facilities in order to bring military power to bear on its interests in the Indian Ocean area; U.S. naval forces must be sufficient not only to counter, if need be, the sea-based forces and those land-based forces with maritime missions of potential adversaries, but must also project sufficient power to protect its interests on land. As such, local sea-based parity is inadequate considering the vital U.S. interests in the area, growing military strength of littoral states, Soviet naval aviation, Soviet land and air forces in its Southern military districts, and—perhaps most important—a growing Soviet willingness to move men and materiel into so-called peripheral disputes.

On balance, it is difficult if not impossible for the United States to justify a major commitment to naval arms control in the Indian Ocean. In part the problem is one of focus. So far, naval forces have not posed the greatest dangers to U.S. interests in the area. Since no naval arms race has materialized, containment is no problem either. At the same time, present naval forces—and especially facilities—give the United States an important capacity to introduce military power into the area should force become necessary and useful. Lastly, NALT holds little promise as a likely device to constrain those military capabilities that pose the greatest potential threat to U.S. interests from the Soviet Union and local states. In short, naval arms control would be more likely to constrain U.S. options at a time when such options are few, than to significantly alter the threat to the United States.

Given this perspective, it can be concluded that arms control holds out little or no promise to U.S. efforts toward furthering its interests in the Indian Ocean area. It is doubtful that constraints on sea-based forces, even if intelligently negotiated and reciprocally honored, would enhance the security of U.S. allies or provide the United States with a more favorable atmosphere in which to pursue its objectives; the post-arms control or subsequent balance of forces is unlikely to be an improved one. The greatest error of all would be to accept significant constraints on the scope and use of local facilities; more than anything else, those facilities provide an "insurance policy" should the use of force become necessary. All in all, it seems best to place Indian Ocean arms control, except perhaps for a limited set of CBMs, on the proverbial back burner for the foreseeable future. There is no justification for arms control efforts to become permanent in times of rapidly changing circumstances.

Assessing Arms

Does a significant increase in arms offer a more attractive policy option for the United States? At a minimum, this military posture should be approached with a good deal of caution. On one hand, the financial cost of expanding Indian Ocean deployments—at a time the U.S. Navy increasingly finds itself lacking sufficient units or sufficient funds to move and operate those it does have—must be considered; on the other, there is the matter of likely local and Soviet response. The most important question, however, is whether increasing local sea-based forces would serve a clear purpose.

To date, no one has challenged American "use of the sea" in the Indian Ocean. The low level of locally-based or deployed U.S. forces, however, makes it difficult to sustain the argument that these forces deterred any such attack owing to their inherent capability. Instead, to the extent that deterrence was a factor, it was achieved owing to ultimate, rather than immediate, U.S. ability to respond. The chief value of local forces in this regard may well have been in symbolizing some latent will and capacity to respond. Moreover, had a sudden and unexpected attack on the sea lanes taken place, there would have been little that on-the-scene forces could have done to prevent it from being initially successful. A range of systems in the inventories of almost all the littoral states could disrupt passage at sea, as of course could the far more capable Soviet fleet. There is no way to protect every vessel in peacetime against all potential threats; in normal conditions, on-the-scene forces provide more of a general deterrent than specific protection. While local forces have some ability to respond quickly and in the same locale, their peacetime contribution to maintaining free passage at sea appears to be limited. A far greater source of deterrence in normal circumstances stems not only from the latent (although still limited) U.S. ability to respond to many challenges in a military fashion, but also from its inherent ability to respond economically and politically at a time and place of its own choosing. Overall, given the range of instruments that a superpower can use to inflict damage on an adversary, local military forces contribute but one element of total deterrence.

Scenarios of war in Europe present other questions concerning utility of local sea-based forces. In a short war, the importance of the Indian Ocean and its oil supplies would be limited; conversely, as the duration of fighting grew, the value of such supplies would grow in kind. Yet to make this point is not to argue that the utility of those forces based in the Indian Ocean would also grow. Only if the threat to the supply of oil was primarily sea-based both in source and object—that is, if it were one posed by sea-based forces attacking tankers and their escorts—would local naval forces become the determining factor. However, it is far more likely that the Warsaw Pact would elect to disrupt the flow of oil through the far more efficient means of attacking sensitive oil installations, refineries and terminals, or by mining narrow passageways such as the Strait of Hormuz. In such cases, naval forces and sea-based air power would constitute but one component of a more capable and more varied force that would be required to meet the difficult challenge of protecting and defending these assets under attack.

It is also difficult to discern the optimal level of local naval forces needed to perform missions such as showing the flag and port calls. Arguably, a relatively modest force level is sufficient to carry out the important, but hard to measure function of naval diplomacy. Yet to the extent that political impact becomes a function of actual rather than potential combat capabilities, a far more capable presence is required to avoid projecting weakness or disinterest. More controversial is the subject of gunboat diplomacy, which as used here includes actions ranging from special shows of force (whether to intimidate or support) to actual uses of limited amounts of force. However, given such factors as an omnipresent Soviet Navy, impressive multi-force inventories of a number of littoral states, widespread anti-ship missiles, and strong nationalist sentiment resistant to superpower threats, it would seem that the opportunities for gunboat diplomacy to be used effectively will be fewer than in the past. Indeed, the record of U.S. gunboat diplomacy in the Indian Ocean over the past decade—the dispatch of a carrier task force during the 1971 South Asian War; the 1973 deployment during the Middle East War and Arab oil embargo; the spring 1973 show of force on behalf of Kenya; the early 1979 surge to demonstrate support for North Yemen and Saudi Arabia; the augmented deployments initiated late in 1979 when the U.S. Embassy was stormed in Teheran and when the Soviets invaded Afghanistan—indicates that at most such actions contributed but little to U.S. objectives at the time. In none of these instances (with the unique exception of the aborted attempt to rescue the American hostages in Iran) did the United States actually employ force to alter the local situation; instead, surge deployments were used to signal support for allies and communicate messages of warning to adversaries. If a conclusion can be reached from looking at these episodes, it would seem to be that shows—rather than uses—of force are to be expected and that shows, however impressive, are rarely decisive. Short of war, naval forces seem most important not for what they can achieve directly but for what they contribute to a climate or context in which other, more basic instruments of diplomacy can prosper; it would be overly optimistic, therefore, to expect major dividends from adding to the size and activity of forces located in the Indian Ocean.

Lastly, there is the need to consider the role of locally-based forces in a major or "half-war" contingency such as a Soviet invasion of Iran or an Iraqi attack in Kuwait. Unfortunately, even a cursory examination of recently initiated and planned U.S. initiatives—expansion of airlift and sealift capacity; prepositioning of support for combat units; increase in exercise schedules; negotiations of overflight, transit, and access arrangements with "enroute," near-regional, and regional states; the upgrading of Diego Garcia; the increase in local naval, marine, tactical air and reconnaissance presence and activity—would require a separate chapter or book.

What is more relevant for the purpose of this chapter, however, is that those forces deployed locally would contribute at most a small component of a force package required to cope with a major contingency. In conflicts of this scale, such forces could attempt to delay (through deep interdiction) an invasion force as well as protect key oil and military facilities. By so doing, these local forces would contribute in at least three ways: by gaining time for more capable forces to deploy to the region; assuring access to necessary military facilities; and protecting the key U.S. interest in the region—oil. In addition, simply introducing U.S. combat forces may be a deterrent. Most of the combat capability, however, must come from outside the region or area; more specifically, the key factors are likely to be the availability of properly "tailored" forces, adequate mobility, and an infrastructure capable of mounting and supporting combat operations. Thus, just as sea-based forces in the Indian Ocean constitute an insufficient foundation on which to build a meaningful arms control regime, so these forces are unable to provide the bulk of a meaningful military capability.

An Indian Ocean Policy?

While the presence of forces at moderate levels can serve as a useful adjunct of policy, significant increases in deployments would yield few benefits for the added investment, while the actual use of arms poses great questions involving utility, promise, and cost. If one may paraphrase—and no doubt distort—a thought of Richard Burt's: if it is wrong to ask too much of arms control, it is also wrong to ask too much of arms.

This is not to dismiss the potential contribution of either. The United States should consider some limited regime of CBMs for the Indian Ocean and use that format to press the Soviet Union for more general restraint in the area. The principle that sea-based forces should not be discriminated against, as they have been in negotiations to date, should be a guiding one. In addition, there is no reason to be defensive about the Zone of Peace so long as the littoral states are reminded of their own obligations under any general arms control regime for the area. This said, there is no role for arms control beyond such peripheral or even cosmetic steps. To negotiate a meaningful regime would require the inclusion and constraint of so many tools of diplomacy that it would be tantamount to proscribing competition in this area. Such an effort lacks credibility. Unfortunate or not, the balance of power in the Persian Gulf and Indian Ocean has become too critical a part of the global balance for competition to be negotiated away.

Equally, there is a role for locally-deployed forces to play. Peacetime naval diplomacy has made a discernible contribution to a major contingency. But given the size of the potential threat, acknowledged shortcomings in U.S. capability, and circumstances which preclude the establishment of a substantial American combat presence, reliance on only those arms which could be maintained in the region for the defense of U.S. interests appears highly unrealistic. Indeed, even assuming the optimum use of available warning indicators, the absence of significant crises elsewhere at the same time, and the availability of considerable forces with the means to move and support them, there are limits to what the United States can reasonably expect from arms in this part of the world.

Both arms control and arms, as was stated at the outset of this chapter, are elements of the military instrument of diplomacy, and in this part of the world the direct military instrument is, and will remain, unable to provide on its own a policy for the United States. (For what it is worth, the "indirect military instrument"—whether the threat of nuclear escalation, the threat of initiating conventional attacks elsewhere, or depending upon allies—is even less credible. In the first two instances, the balances all too often do not favor the United States; the latter is mostly precluded by a lack of capability and solidarity alike.) The flow of oil at affordable prices, the domestic stability of key allies, the impact of nuclear proliferation in South Asia, many forms of Soviet and Cuban intervention in the littoral—all will resist direct treatment by both arms and arms control. Instead, U.S. interests will depend more upon the adoption of a coherent energy policy, progress toward resolving the Middle East conflict, continued military transfers to local allies, greater involvement in the allies' programs for economic and political development, and the exercising of more effective leverage on the Soviet Union to moderate its probes and programs in the area. The most that can be expected from both arms and arms control is that they will help create an environment in which these other initiatives might have a better chance of prospering.

9
Limiting Strategic Forces

Charles A. Sorrels

Introduction

In June 1979, a SALT II agreement was signed by President Carter and President Brezhnev in Vienna. The agreement, the product of nearly seven years of protracted negotiations following the conclusion of SALT I in mid-1972 with an ABM Treaty and an Interim Agreement covering ICBM and SLBM launchers, included a treaty to last through 1985, a Protocol to expire at the end of 1981, and a Statement of Principles for SALT III.

Scrutiny of the SALT II agreements began in Senate hearings in July 1979. Substantial questions were raised about whether some key provisions of SALT II as submitted to the Senate were equitable, whether Soviet compliance with some provisions could be verified with confidence (especially in light of the loss of collection sites in Iran), and whether U.S. defense cooperation with its NATO Allies would be adversely affected, especially by the Protocol if it were later extended.

In early November, a majority (9-6) of the Senate Committee on Foreign Relations voted to report the SALT II agreements favorably to the Senate. In mid-December, a majority of the Senate Committee on Armed Services reached a negative judgment on military implications of the SALT II agreements for the United States.

It was then expected that the Senate would take up the SALT II agreement early in 1980. However, the Soviet invasion of Afghanistan in late December 1979 eclipsed the attention being given to SALT and worsened the prospects for SALT II receiving a two-thirds favorable vote of ratification in the Senate. President Carter asked in January 1980 that consideration of SALT II be removed from the Senate calendar.

The hiatus in the Senate debate on SALT II provides an opportunity to step back and broadly consider how the SALT process has worked in relationship to defense planning for U.S. strategic nuclear forces and how relevant SALT is to requirements for U.S. strategic forces in the

1980s. This chapter first reviews the expectations the United States—under the Nixon, Ford, and Carter administrations—has had for the strategic arms limitation process. It then explores several interrelated ways in which SALT arguably has or has not substantially facilitated defense planning, such as by reducing uncertainty in U.S. projections of Soviet strategic capabilities and facilitating U.S. measures to maintain stability in the strategic nuclear balance.

Assuming the United States and the Soviet Union will move into negotiations on SALT III (or a revision of SALT II), the chapter then considers some future negotiating outcomes. If extending into SALT III, the MIRV fractionation limits established in SALT II would be of high value to U.S. defense planning after 1985. Nevertheless, it would be realistic to have very modest expectations for what SALT III can accomplish. Largely because SALT II's constraints on Soviet and U.S. buildup of forces for the early to mid-1980s were disappointing, the agenda and expected results for SALT III are very demanding. First, the time frame for achieving a SALT III agreement will be even shorter than it was for SALT II—which achieved such disappointing results. NATO allies will be more directly involved in SALT III, complicating the diplomatic task and increasing the potential cost of divisiveness in NATO as a result of SALT. There is thus a clear possibility of overloading the SALT process in SALT III.

Expectations for SALT

The United States has had over a decade of experience with the SALT process, which began formally in Helsinki in November 1969. Since then, the government's expectations and assertions about the direct relevance of SALT to some central concerns in U.S. defense planning for strategic nuclear forces have gone through several phases.

In the SALT I negotiations from late 1969 through mid-1972, the Nixon administration had ambitious expectations about the potentially direct contribution of SALT to American security and defense planning. Early during the SALT I negotiations, the Nixon administration expressed the hope that a prospective agreement would prove to be an alternative to additional deployments by the United States "to offset" or respond to the growing Soviet capabilities the United States sought to curb in SALT I.[1] The Nixon administration entered the SALT negotiations concerned with two principal developments that the United States hoped arms control measures would address and alleviate: (1) a buildup of Soviet "modern heavy" ICBMs (at that time the SS-9) that could eventually pose a severe counterforce threat to the survivability of the American force of 1,000

Minuteman silo-based ICBMs, and (2) a prospective widespread deployment by both the United States and the Soviet Union of ABM systems that could reduce the effectiveness of second strike retaliatory forces. The United States was concerned that these developments would destabilize the strategic nuclear balance in a crisis by creating confidence in a first-strike advantage that could destroy a major portion of the other superpower's strategic forces, coupled with an ABM system that could degrade the effectiveness of second-strike retaliation by the opponent's surviving ballistic missiles. The United States was concerned not only with instability in the compressed time frame of a crisis but also over the longer term in the strategic arms "race" or competition. In particular, a widespread ABM deployment by both superpowers was expected to prompt a further buildup of strategic offensive forces to retain confidence in the ability of ballistic missiles to penetrate such ABM systems.

During the SALT I negotiations the Nixon administration expressed the hope that the Soviets might be evincing a "new commitment to stability." This hope was qualified with an explicit awareness as well that the Soviets might not share American interest in a "strategic equilibrium."[2] However, in asking Congress to ratify the SALT I agreements finally concluded at the Moscow summit talks in May 1972, the Nixon administration implicitly endorsed the conclusion or assumption that through SALT—especially in the ABM Treaty—U.S.-Soviet strategic doctrines had converged in stressing and acknowledging the importance of preserving mutual confidence in the survivability and efficacy of retaliatory deterrent forces.[3] Secretary of State William B. Rodgers, in his presentation to the Senate Committee on Foreign Relations, stated:

> Under this treaty, both sides make a commitment not to build a nation-wide ABM defense. This is a general undertaking of utmost significance. Without a nationwide ABM defense, there can be no shield against retaliation. *Both great nuclear powers have recognized and in effect agreed to maintain mutual deterrence.*[4] (emphasis added)

In 1973 and early 1974, the United States unsuccessfully proposed that SALT II place qualitative limitations on ICBM throwweight and offset Soviet advantages in numbers of ballistic missiles by retaining a U.S. advantage in number of MIRVed missiles. But by November 1974, at the Vladivostok summit between President Ford and Secretary Brezhnev, it was clear that the U.S. government no longer had high expectations for SALT's potential to deal directly with defense planning concerns—such as the growing vulnerability of the *Minuteman* force. Instead of attempting to use SALT to restructure fundamental aspects of the strategic balance, the Vladivostok accord reflected a more modest, but nevertheless important role for SALT: codification of some general aspects of parity or "political equivalence" in the strategic balance (for example, equal aggregate ceilings on strategic nuclear delivery vehicles). The terms of the Vladivostok accord were accordingly very general and left both sides with considerable freedom to pursue qualitative improvements in their force structure: the overall ceiling on strategic nuclear delivery vehicles in the Vladivostok accord was quite high (2,400), and the "subceiling" on MIRVed systems of 1,320 was so high as well, that it was not expected to curb the threat to, or thus obviate or postpone the need to replace the *Minuteman* force with a more survivable deployment. During the Ford administration, it proved impossible to translate the broad parameters of the Vladivostok accord into a completed SALT II agreement. Attempts through early 1976 failed to break a stalemate that existed fundamentally over whether and, if so, how to limit the Soviet *Backfire* bomber and the new U.S. cruise missile program.

The Carter administration soon made it clear that it had little regard for the unambitious Vladivostok accord and was anxious to boldly pursue "real arms control" with the Soviet Union—to achieve through arms control effective solutions to U.S. defense planning concerns, especially the expected vulnerability of the *Minuteman* force. For example, National Security Advisor Zbigniew Brzezinski noted early in 1977,

> It is our feeling that the framework defined by Vladivostok is so high in its numbers, so open-ended in its consequences, so susceptible to quantitative as well as qualitative improvements that in some respects it comes close to a misstatement to call any such arrangement arms limitations.[5]

By the end of 1977, Vladivostok was being described in less negative terms. In an interview, Carter said, "President Ford and Secretary Kissinger made great progress, I think, at Vladivostok and in their subsequent negotiations, to provide the first indication of equality."[6]

In March 1977, the Carter administration proposed to the Soviet leadership two basic options for concluding a SALT II agreement. One was a "deferral" option, concluding the agreed broad elements (ceiling and subceiling) of the Vladivostok accord but deferring attempted solution of the issues relating to the *Backfire*, cruise missiles, and mobile ICBMs. The option strongly preferred by the Carter administration, however, was the "comprehensive" one. Unlike the Vladivostok accord, the comprehensive proposal of March 1977 was intended to have major impact on the structure of each side's strategic nuclear forces. In addition to major reductions in the overall aggregate ceiling on strategic nuclear delivery vehicles (from 2,400 to 1,800–2,000), the comprehensive option included reductions in Soviet modern large ICBM launchers (from about 300 to 150), a subceiling of 550 MIRVed ICBMs, a sharp limit on flight testing (to only 6 per year) of ICBMs (to reduce confidence in accuracy improvements), and a ban on development, testing, and deployment of new types of ICBMs as well as mobile ICBMs. Such provisions, Secretary of Defense Harold Brown argued, would "deal with a key source of instability—ICBM improvements." The comprehensive option, he declared, could make ICBMs in fixed silos—such as *Minuteman* —"secure for another 10 years or more," making the need for a land-mobile ICBM, such as the MX, "less urgent." Through the comprehensive option, Secretary Brown concluded:

> Deterrence could then be achieved with higher confidence, fewer forces, more stability, and probably lower costs. . . . Arms control, thus, can make defense planning more effective and efficient in reaching national objectives.[7]

But the Russian leadership firmly rejected not only the comprehensive option but even the deferral—the "limited" option of March 1977. Although a general format of three tiers (a treaty through 1985, a Protocol of shorter duration, and a Statement of Principles for SALT III) for a SALT II agreement was agreeable to Secretary Vance and Foreign Minister Gromyko in May 1977, it took over two years to fashion the SALT II agreement that was finally concluded at the Vienna summit in June 1979 between Carter and Brezhnev. During the frustratingly long negotiations from 1977 through early 1979, the Executive Branch's hopes for a relationship between SALT and defense planning retreated toward the more modest expectations associated with Vladivostok—basically, codifying the current status and near-term trends (through 1985) in the strategic balance between the two military superpowers. The administration claimed that the agreement would not substantially affect the nature of the balance—especially if it extended the limitation of MIRV loadings (fractionation) on Soviet ICBMs until the treaty was to expire (December 1985). The administration also claimed that the agreement would not substantially affect American programs, but would facilitate U.S. unilateral moves to deal with the *Minuteman* force's vulnerability. This perspective was thus considerably more modest than the American view early in SALT I or in early 1977 that SALT should defer or substantially alleviate the anticipated problem of *Minuteman* vulnerability that was facing U.S. defense planners.

SALT and Defense Planning: The Potential and the Experience

Is this more modest perspective justified? In theory, several interrelated ways in which the SALT process and resulting agreements could serve or facilitate U.S. defense planning are by:

- facilitating intelligence on and reducing uncertainty in projections of Soviet strategic forces;
- limiting or reducing Soviet threats to the pre-launch and in-flight survivability of components of U.S. strategic forces;
- constraining the costs of the strategic arms competition, and
- enhancing or facilitating U.S. efforts to maintain stability in the strategic nuclear balance.

The remainder of this chapter will attempt to determine whether, in light of earlier negotiating experience, SALT can or cannot be expected to accomplish these objectives in the next decade.

Facilitating Intelligence and Reducing Uncertainty

U.S. intelligence provided a basis for U.S. concerns (for example, when its photographic satellites saw the initial Soviet ABM deployment around Moscow and the rate of Soviet ICBM silo construction) that led to negotiations in the first place. Moreover, acceptable SALT agreements were made *possible* because U.S. intelligence capabilities could verify Soviet compliance with some of the negotiated limitations or prohibitions. In addition, the limits to which intelligence could confidently estimate or assure were generally taken into account in shaping the provisions of SALT I and II. (For example, the Interim Agreement of SALT I limited the number of ICBM launchers, which in the case of silos can be easily monitored, rather than the number of missiles, which cannot be.)

Under the terms of SALT I and II, the Soviet Union is committed "not to use deliberate concealment measures which impede verification by national technical means of compliance with the terms" of the agreements. As SALT II includes some constraints on qualitative aspects—such as throwweight of ICBMs—that were not covered by SALT I, provisions relating to deliberate concealment become even more useful in assuring that the United States can collect intelligence data—such as unencrypted telemetry relating to parameters limited under the treaty.

The intelligence function of estimating the performance and deployment of Soviet strategic forces—which preceded, continues under, and would remain without SALT—is enhanced by SALT's provisions facilitating collection of intelligence. Although some changes in Soviet practice permitted under SALT II could degrade U.S. ability to collect intelligence, without SALT the Soviets would be free to implement widespread measures such as unrestrained concealment and deception—activities that are highly valued in Soviet military doctrine.

Unfortunately, the language in the SALT II agreement relating to telemetry encryption (Article XV, paragraph 3, Second Common Understanding) may not deter the Soviets from encrypting such important data: "Each Party is free to use various methods of transmitting telemetric information during testing, including its encryption, except that . . . neither Party shall engage in deliberate denial of telemetric information, such as through the use of telemetry encryption, whenever such denial impedes verification of compliance with provisions of the Treaty." The United States may have the burden of proof—thereby risking disclosure to the Soviets of the material's specific value to the United States—of arguing that an instance of encryption is contrary to the somewhat porous protection provided by SALT II.

Another potentially negative impact of the SALT process upon U.S. intelligence should also be noted. Even in the controlled context of the SALT II negotiations, the discussion of verification issues and of qualitative aspects that the United States wished to limit (and therefore presumably could monitor) may have facilitated Soviet awareness of the particular value of some types of data to the United States.

At the same time, it should be recognized that major surprises in qualitative improvements in Soviet strategic offensive forces occurred under SALT I and during the negotiation of SALT II. Within a year of the signing of the Interim Agreement of SALT I, which explicitly allowed modernization of ICBMs within constraints on increases in dimensions of silos, the United States was surprised by the scale and MIRV-carrying capabilities of the Soviets' fourth-generation ICBMs. By early 1973, the flight-test program revealed two successors (the SS-17 and the SS-19) to the widely deployed SS-11 as well as a successor to the SS-9 (the SS-18). The United States had expected two new MIRVed ICBMs, not three. Moreover, because the great increase in throwweight of the SS-17 and SS-19 came as a surprise, so did the number of MIRVs carried per missile. The United States had previously overestimated how soon the Soviets would develop a MIRVed ICBM, estimating an initial operational capability (IOC) in 1971, compared with the actual IOC in 1974.[8]

The SS-19 program, in particular, demonstrated almost three times the throwweight and substantially greater missile volume than the widely deployed "light" SS-11. The SS-19 program (along with the SS-17) thus undercut the attempt in the Interim Agreement to prevent conversion of the "light" SS-11 ICBM launchers into launchers of "heavy" ICBMs through limitations upon changes of silo dimensions allowed in the process of ICBM force modernization. Another surprise evidently occurred in late 1977 when the Soviets demonstrated qualitative improvements in the accuracy of the fourth-generation ICBMs sooner than expected, thereby increasing the threat to the survivability of the force of 1,000 silo-based *Minuteman* expected in the early 1980s.[9] With that development, a Soviet capability that the United States had hoped to delay or prevent when it entered the SALT I negotiations in late 1969 became a *fait accompli.* Moreover, this occurred four or five years before 1986, when the United States tentatively plans to begin deploying a new ICBM (MX) in a more survivable basing mode.

A further problem is the relatively short duration of the SALT II Treaty. In 1972 the hope was that a SALT II Treaty dealing with strategic offensive forces would become a comprehensive counterpart to the ABM Treaty in substance and duration. The time span of SALT II, which expires at the end of 1985, is so truncated compared with the long lead times required to develop and deploy strategic forces that the treaty would have little impact on U.S. and Soviet programs that are already under development. Thus, while U.S. defense planners must make assumptions about Soviet strategic capabilities *after* 1985 in order to plan the characteristics and scope of its own strategic programs for the same period, SALT II does not directly facilitate planning for this period. In planning for strategic programs post-1985, both superpowers, but especially the United States, will have to consider the possibility of "breakout" deployments by the other party to the soon-expiring agreement. This situation is not very different from the "arms race instability" SALT was supposed to curb or avoid.

Limiting or Reducing Soviet Threats

With the important exception of the ABM Treaty of 1972, SALT has not—for the time period covered by the agreements—substantially curbed Soviet threats to the pre-launch and in-flight survivability of U.S. strategic nuclear forces. The ABM Treaty of 1972 was an important accomplishment. It imposed major quantitative as well as qualitative constraints on ballistic missile defense, limiting ABM deployment to two sites (later reduced to one in a 1974 protocol) with 100 ABM launchers per site and limiting ABM radars both in number and in some qualities. The two permitted ABM deployment areas were so restricted and geographically separated that they could not provide the basis for a nationwide ABM defense. The treaty also prohibited some major qualitative improvements that could vitiate the effectiveness of the limitation on the number of launchers; it banned, for instance, the development, testing, or deployment of ABM launchers capable of rapid reload, ABM launchers capable of launching more than one interceptor missile at a time, and MIRVed interceptor missiles.

But neither SALT I nor SALT II attempted to affect the threat posed by air defenses, which are widely deployed in the Soviet Union, to the in-flight survivability of U.S. bombers and cruise missiles. The Soviet threat to the pre-launch survivability of bombers such as the B-52 through short-warning depressed trajectory SLBM attacks on bomber bases is also not constrained by either SALT I or the SALT II agreements. With Carter's cancellation of the B-1 bomber in mid-1977, the Soviet threat to the pre-launch survivability of the bomber/cruise missile force became a matter of greater concern—given the advantages of the B-1 over older B-52s in rapid base escape and hardening against some nuclear effects. Another important area not addressed by SALT is the threat posed by ASW (anti-submarine warfare) capabilities to the pre-launch survivability of SLBM-carrying submarines. (The United States has for many years had a substantial lead over the Soviets in ASW capabilities, but the long-term possibility of a Soviet breakthrough remains a matter of concern and a basis for expensive modernization in the case of the *Trident* I missile and submarine.)

More important, the growing threat posed by Soviet ICBMs against the silo-based U.S. *Minuteman* force was not significantly constrained by the SALT I Interim Agreement. The freeze on additional silo construction under the Interim Agreement did not, as Henry Kissinger and others claimed, curb the disturbing momentum in Soviet ICBM capabilities. Indeed, after 1972 the momentum accelerated. A major U.S. objective for SALT II, stated by the American delegation at the conclusion of SALT I in May 1972, was "to constrain and reduce on a long-term basis threats to the survivability of our respective strategic retaliatory forces." It was hoped that SALT II might limit throwweight and even reduce the level of launchers with large throwweight. By late 1974 at Vladivostok, the Ford administration (as noted earlier) had abandoned the effort to accomplish that objective. An attempt not only to constrain but also to reduce the Soviet ICBM counterforce capability was, as we have seen, attempted by the Carter administration in its comprehensive proposal to the Soviet leadership in March 1977. Even that option, however, was proposed at a time when the United States underestimated how far along the Soviets were in improving the accuracy of their fourth-generation ICBMs.

Constraining Costs

Constraining the costs of the strategic nuclear arms competition would seem to be a significant way for SALT to affect defense planning, by releasing resources either for non-defense needs or for other costly defense requirements—such as general purpose forces to enable sustained conventional defense of NATO/Europe. For perspective, however, it is important to realize that the direct costs of strategic nuclear forces have accounted for only about 6 to 7 percent of the defense budget in recent years.[10]

Given the general failure of SALT—with the exception of the ABM Treaty—to substantially curb U.S. defense planning concern for its strategic nuclear forces, it has been unreasonable to expect SALT to result directly in substantial budgetary savings or cost avoidance. Nevertheless, despite the general lack of a realistic basis for such an expectation, this argument has been extravagantly overstated in more than one administration—usually as part of an effort to sell a completed or prospective SALT agreement. Asserted budgetary savings from SALT understandably can have a strong appeal across the political spectrum as a tangible benefit compared with conceptual definition of objectives such as "stability."

In contrast to previous estimates, Secretary Brown's estimate in July 1979 of the "savings" or avoided expenditures to the U.S. as a result of SALT II was a modest estimate: "perhaps as much as $30 billion less expensive over the next decade," assuming the ABM Treaty of 1972 remained in effect. However, as in previous cases, detailed analytical support substantiating that estimate has proved difficult for the Executive Branch to provide. Perhaps the highest official estimates of the "cost avoidance" effect of SALT agreements were those of President Nixon in 1972 and the Congressional Budget Office (CBO) in early 1978. President Nixon claimed that if it were not for the recently concluded SALT I agreements, the United States would have to spend an additional $15 billion per year on strategic nuclear programs. In early 1978, the CBO told the Senate Budget Committee that the financial impact if SALT broke down would be a cost of $100 billion over a fifteen-year period. Secretary Kissinger in February 1976 warned and predicted that the alternative to a version of SALT II he then hoped might soon be concluded would be "an accelerated strategic buildup over the next five years" that "could cost as much as an additional $20 billion." To reach such a total required assuming, for example, that more *Trident* submarines would be built per year than shipyard capacity would in fact allow.[11]

The rhetoric of SALT has often given the impression that the process and its negotiated results are an alternative to a "renewal of the arms race." That impression has tended to obscure awareness that in fact an "arms race" or competition between the United States and the Soviet Union in strategic force developments has continued during the SALT process, and that the Soviet Union has done most of the racing—especially in terms of budgetary commitments and program momentum. It is of course true, as the Carter administration reiterated, that the United States "has not been idle" in the competition, with programs such as the *Trident* SLBM and cruise missiles. But over the last decade, Soviet procurement of strategic forces (offensive and defensive), in dollar costs, was about two and one-half times that of the United States. (In 1970 the Soviet procurement level was about twice that of the United States. In 1979 it had become nearly three times that of the United States. In the case of strategic offensive forces—ICBMs, SLBMs, and bombers—procurement by the Soviets in dollar terms exceeded those of the United States by about 90 percent over the 1970–1979 period; see Figures 9.1 and 9.2.)[12]

During the period 1969 through 1979 (and, indeed, through 1985 under the SALT II agreements submitted to the Senate) the only one major case of direct budgetary reductions associated with SALT is the phasing down of the U.S. ballistic missile defense program as a result of the ABM Treaty of 1972. Even in that clear case, however, estimating "savings" (or avoided costs) is an uncertain exercise, because the *Safeguard* ABM program was not a popular program and had been scaled down already in a response to Congressional opposition and doubts about not only its desirability but also its technical feasibility. In 1969 the *Safeguard* program—already reduced and reoriented by the Nixon administration from the *Sentinel* ABM program inherited from the Johnson administration—was sustained by only one vote in the Senate. Actually, hopes for SALT may have kept the *Safeguard* program alive. Perhaps a decisive argument for continuing with the expensive *Safeguard* program in the 1969 Senate debate was that it was necessary for U.S. bargaining leverage in the upcoming SALT I negotiations.[13] Thus, an estimate of the cost savings associated with the ABM Treaty is dependent on assuming that the *Safeguard* program is politically viable. Congress, as of 1972, had only approved four sites out of twelve in the overall plan developed by the Nixon administration. Assuming that the United States would have otherwise proceeded to a four-site ABM program, then the budgetary costs avoided as a result of the 1972 ABM

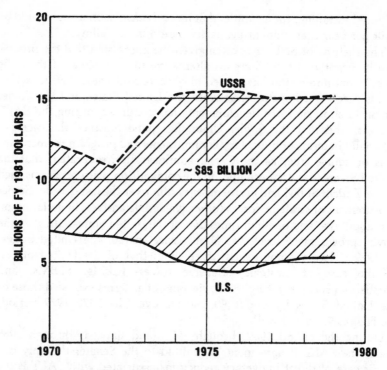

FIGURE 9.1   Strategic Offensive and Defensive Forces: A Comparison of U.S. Procurement Costs with Estimated Dollar Costs of Soviet Procurement, 1970-1979

Source: FY 1981 Department of Defense Program for Research, Development, and Acquisition, Statement of Dr. William J. Perry, Under Secretary of Defense, Research and Engineering, pp. II-12, 16.

Treaty (limiting deployment to two sites) and 1974 Protocol (reducing allowed sites to only one) would have been about $11 billion for the period FY 1972 through FY 1981.[14]

In terms of *indirect* effects of SALT upon the defense budget, the continuation of the SALT process and the euphoria associated with the SALT I agreements—as part of a détente atmosphere of moderated competition between the superpowers—probably lessened the *sense* of threat as an impetus to additional spending on strategic forces. Although the cancellation of the B-1 bomber in June 1977 was said to be independent of SALT, the negotiating context undoubtedly made it politically easier for President Carter to take the step. That decision, coupled with a deci-

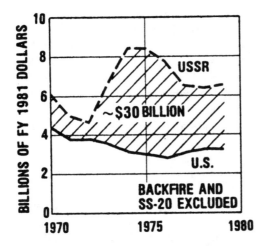

FIGURE 9.2 Strategic Offensive Forces: A Comparison of U.S. Procurement Costs with Estimated Dollar Costs of Soviet Procurement

Source: FY 1981 Department of Defense Program for Research, Development, and Acquisition, Statement of Dr. William J. Perry, Under Secretary of Defense, Research and Engineering, pp. II-12, 16.

sion to slow down by at least two years the schedule for the new ICBM inherited from the Ford administration (the MX), enabled the Carter administration to avoid significant increases in funding requirements for strategic forces in FY 1978 and later compared with the five-year defense budget envisioned by the Ford administration in January 1977.

Ironically, a broad and sobering review of trends in the strategic balance occasioned by Senate hearings on the SALT II agreements submitted by the Carter administration compelled the administration late in 1979 to propose an increase in projected defense spending for FY 1981 through FY 1985 in order to secure passage of SALT II.

Maintaining Stability

A major way for SALT to help the United States maintain stability in the strategic nuclear balance would have been for SALT to substantially curb threats to the pre-launch and in-flight survivability of U.S. strategic forces. As we have seen, that direct contribution has been lacking other than in the case of the ABM Treaty of SALT I in 1972. The ABM Treaty of 1972 and the 1974 ABM Protocol contributed to stability in the deterrent relationship by sharply curbing the threat that ABM systems could pose to the in-flight survivability of ICBMs and SLBMs, thus degrading confidence in the ability of their warheads to penetrate their targets. Although the ABM Treaty increased effectiveness of retaliatory forces, it did preclude one expensive option for dealing with the anticipated vulnerability of the silo-based *Minuteman* force—large-scale missile site defenses. Site defense of hardened targets such as reinforced concrete *Minuteman* silos or multiple protective shelters—although a technically very demanding task—may be feasible against a large-scale ballistic missile attack. Unlike the probably impossible task of attempting to protect or deny destruction of large, "soft" population centers, a site-defense system can be effective if it substantially dilutes the effectiveness of an attack. During the Senate consideration of the ABM Treaty in 1972, the Nixon administration requested some additional funding in the FY 1973 budget to accelerate the research and development for a site-defense option. Such an acceleration, it was hoped, would enable initial deployment shortly after the scheduled expiration of the Interim Agreement in late 1977— in the event that a comprehensive agreement on strategic offensive forces had not yet been completed as a counterpart to the ABM Treaty.[15]

But Congress could not sustain continued development of a site defense option as a hedge in the late 1970s at the level recommended by the Nixon administration in 1972. Insofar as budgetary support for continued research and development (R&D) of an ABM site-defense option was lessened because of the ABM Treaty (which allowed such R&D but precluded a large enough deployment to be effective), then the ABM Treaty indirectly reduced U.S. flexibility in the late 1970s to deal with the prospective vulnerability of the *Minuteman* force.

At the conclusion of the SALT I negotiations, on May 9, 1972, the U.S. delegation made a unilateral statement: "If an agreement providing for more complete strategic offensive arms limitations were not achieved within five years, U.S. supreme interests could be jeopardized. Should that occur, it would constitute a basis for withdrawal from the ABM Treaty. The United States does not wish to see such a situation occur, nor do we believe that the USSR does. It is because we wish to prevent such a situation that we emphasize the importance the U.S. government attaches to the achievement of more complete limitations on strategic offensive arms." If not in 1972, over time this "threat" by the United States to link continued support for the ABM Treaty to achievement of a comprehensive counterpart limitation on strategic offensive forces must have seemed rather empty rhetoric to the Soviets, given the sharply curtailed U.S. ABM R&D efforts after 1972.

It is noteworthy that, in contrast to the United States, the Soviet Union maintained a vigorous research and development program for ABM systems after 1972. Consequently, in the early 1980s the Soviets may be in a better position to "break out" of the ABM Treaty or take advantage of a negotiated revision of its terms than the United States.

Site defense is not, of course, the only option for coping with the threat to the survivability of the silo-based *Minuteman* force. Nevertheless, although SALT left other options open, the U.S. response to that long-anticipated threat was probably slower in large part because of the euphoria (described, in retrospect, as a "tranquilizer effect" by the Joint Chiefs of Staff in 1979 testimony on SALT II) produced by the ABM Treaty and Interim Agreement. The reassuring atmosphere produced by SALT was not the only factor accounting for the relatively slow response to *Minuteman* vulnerability. Another important factor was probably the Air Force's own efforts to assure that the B-1 program did not have to compete in the late 1970s with the new MX ICBM program for funds. However, that constrained budget situation was, in turn, made more likely by the détente atmosphere associated with the continuation of SALT negotiations. By early 1974 it became apparent that the *Minuteman* force was not only threatened by "modern heavy" Soviet ICBMs (SS-9/SS-18) but also by new "medium" ICBMs (the SS-17 and SS-19). Secretary Schlesinger, in his Annual Defense Department Report in March 1974, noted that with reasonably expected refinements in their guidance mechanisms, the SS-19s and SS-17s could "achieve a respectable hard target kill capability during the early part of the next decade." His FY 1975 budget request included $37 million for "advanced ICBM technology" (MX). Secretary Schlesinger stated in his FY 1975 report that "we intend to pursue this new development at a very deliberate pace, pending the outcome of the current SALT negotiations."[16]

Shortly after the Vladivostok accord of November 1974, MX missile development was adjusted to a slower pace, allowing about two more years of effort. The reduced pace was attributed to a reappraisal of the realistic initial operational problems of new Soviet ICBMs targeted against the *Minuteman* force (including "fratricide" effects of one warhead's detonation on another) and a more optimistic appraisal of the effectiveness of the silo hardening program to enhance and prolong the survivability of the existing *Minuteman* force.[17] Nevertheless, it is hard to believe that the atmosphere of the continuing SALT process was not also a significant factor in slowing the MX, particularly given Secretary of State Henry Kissinger's exaggerated claim in November 1974 that the

Vladivostok accord was a "breakthrough" which would place a "cap" on the "arms race" for a decade.

After nearly two more years of study, the Ford administration in its FY 1978 budget proposal in January 1977, called for an accelerated MX program. The missile design emphasized increased throwweight and high accuracy, enabling greater hard-target kill capability. A survivable basing mode was also emphasized, with the "primary basing concepts, at this time concealing mobile missiles in either underground trenches or hardened shelters." Secretary of Defense Donald Rumsfeld said: "The objective is to provide missile basing at a large number of aim points, each of which must be assumed to be equally likely to contain a missile." This "multiple aim point" basing mode was intended to be, unlike a smaller number of silos, "relatively less sensitive to the Soviet hard target threat."[18]

The Carter administration, amending the Ford FY 1978 budget in early 1977, sharply reduced the funding and deferred full-scale engineering development on the MX, which under the Ford FY 1978 budget might have been deployed in early 1984. Secretary of Defense Harold Brown said at the time that "the deferrals and revisions that we have made do give us additional options to see what happens in a Strategic Arms Limitation negotiation and I think it's almost certain that our subsequent program will depend upon what happens in that negotiation." He also noted a need to defer full-scale development "while we consider what basing system makes sense."[19]

In fact, a decision to proceed with full-scale development of the MX and a final approval of a basing mode did not come until the summer of 1979, after nearly two and a half years of further study and review of basing modes and missile options.[20] Finally, shortly before the conclusion of SALT II in June 1979, President Carter approved full-scale development of the MX missile. In early September, he decided upon a basing mode for the MX, using multiple protective shelters (MPS). These decisions would enable an initial operational capability for the MX in mid-1986 and full operational capability of the "baseline" program of 200 MX missiles amidst 4,600 shelters in late 1989. Under the MPS basing mode, each MX missile (with 10 MIRVs) is moved periodically on a transporter carrying an erector/launcher from one hardened shelter to another in a cluster of 23 shelters, and in a manner intended to deny the Soviets knowledge of which shelter within each cluster actually contains an MX missile. The shelters within a cluster would be spaced at spurs along a road at intervals far enough apart to preclude destruction of two shelters by one Soviet warhead aimed between them. By proliferating the aim points the Soviets would have to attack in order to destroy MX missiles, the MPS mode of deployment could reduce the Soviets' first-strike incentive, thereby contributing to stability in a crisis. Although the MX would have a more lethal counterforce capability against Soviet silos that the *Minuteman* III provides, the enhanced survivability of the MX would mean that—unlike the *Minuteman* force—the MX would not be a "use or lose" force and that the United States would not be pressured to rely upon a "launch under attack" tactic for its ICBM force.

A program as expensive and as critically important to the future U.S. strategic nuclear force posture as the MX program should clearly be undertaken only after a very thorough and necessarily time-consuming deliberative process, weighing a wide range of considerations (including environmental impacts). It would have been unreasonable not to expect a new administration to take a hard second look before proceeding with the nature and pace of the proposed MX program inherited from its predecessor. Not only the validity of the requirement for the MX but also the technical soundness of the proposed means of meeting such a requirement should have been thoroughly scrutinized. (For example, there was concern that the "buried trench" deployment mode for the MX, favored at the end of the Ford administration, could prove particularly vulnerable due to propagation of nuclear shock waves down its length.) A reasonable time for a responsible "second look," however, was not almost two and a half years, particularly when Soviet missile flight tests in late 1977 demonstrated a more rapid pace in accuracy improvements in the SS-18 and the SS-19 than had been previously expected.

The protracted length of the Carter administration's decision on the MX can be attributed in large part to SALT. For a start, risks involved in delaying a decision probably seemed politically more tolerable because of the atmosphere created by SALT II negotiations. The Carter administration itself expressed optimism in its March 1977 comprehensive proposal that SALT could finally be converted into "real" arms control that would substantially curb the destabilizing threat to the *Minuteman* force and thereby postpone significantly the need for an MX as a response to that threat. Concerns with compatability of MX basing modes with SALT verification were also a major basis for prompting reassessment of basing modes and considerations of even more expensive basing options, such as an air-mobile MX, in early 1979.

In sum, since the beginning of 1977 the scheduled availability of the MX in a survivable basing mode has been delayed at least two years, from early 1984 to mid-1986. Ironically, because of delays in which SALT played a major role, the MX program will proceed on somewhat of a "crash program" basis, contrary to the "arms race stability" that the SALT process and agreements were supposed to foster.

In addition, the initial "baseline" deployment of the MX in multiple shelters will be more expensive because of a basic design choice driven largely by SALT-related verification concerns. In SALT II negotiations in the summer of 1978, the Soviets had objected to the vertical protective shelter basing mode for the MX as being a violation of both the ban under SALT II on the construction of new fixed ICBM silo launchers and the prohibition of deliberate concealment measures.[21] As a design choice, President Carter approved horizontal rather than vertical shelters, even though studies had indicated that the vertical shelters were not only the least expensive option (compared with horizontal shelters and covered trench) but also the lowest risk in terms of confidence in estimated hardness.[22] At the time of Carter's decision in early September 1979, the cost the baseline horizontal shelter MPS deployment was estimated to be as much as $7 billion ($33 billion compared with $26 billion) more than for a vertical shelter mode with equal numbers of shelters.[23]

Although both the vertical and horizontal shelter MPS deployment would have overall design features to aid the Soviets in verifying U.S. compliance under a future SALT regime, the horizontal shelter is believed to be easier to verify. As envisioned, at periodic inspection intervals, some portion of the MX deployment would be "opened up" to enable the Soviets through national technical means (such as photographic satellites) to count the number of missiles actually deployed within clusters of shelters (only one MX missile among 23 shelters, under the baseline program). Opening a horizontal shelter along its length (using removable "viewing ports") provides a more confident viewing opportunity for Soviet photographic satellites than would opening up the smaller "lid" or door on top of a vertical shelter. The verification task facing the Soviet Union in attempting to determine how many MX missiles the United States has produced and actually deployed in an MPS basing area is, of course, much less difficult than the task facing the United States in trying to establish how many ICBMs the Soviets might produce and deploy in an MPS basing mode, given the closed character of Soviet society. It may well have been concern about the difficulties the United States would face if the Soviets adopted an MPS basing mode that finally led the Carter administration to choose horizontal shelters. If the Soviets were to adopt their own version of an MPS basing mode for a portion or most of their ICBM force, the United States would have only low to moderate confidence in estimating Soviet missile deployment and Washington thus would face a considerable "breakout" problem—the possibility that Moscow could fill its purportedly empty shelters with missiles in a short period of time.[24] But it seems highly unlikely that the Soviets would pursue an MPS basing mode instead of pursuing a variant of the type of road-mobile deployment Moscow has already deployed—the SS-20 IRBM, beginning in 1977.

Assuming that the Soviets would be inclined to pursue a mirror image of the U.S. MPS system, at considerably extra cost to the Soviets than a road-mobile system, may be an example of a somewhat ethnocentric presumption that somehow the United States not only tutors the Soviets on the meaning and importance of "stability" in the strategic balance but also sets a standard for new strategic systems that the Soviets will seek to emulate. Nevertheless, the possibility that the Soviets might be interested in an MPS basing mode, perhaps largely because of the "breakout" potential it facilitates, cannot be entirely dismissed.

It is argued that the horizontal shelter MPS option has an important inherent, "backup" feature that enhances survivability compared with the vertical shelter option: a "dash" capability, enabling relatively rapid reconfiguration or reshuffling of the location of the missiles among the shelters. If the United States had reason to conclude that the uncertainty of the location of the missiles had been lost through Soviet reconnaissance or other means, a "dash" capability would enable relatively rapid movement of missiles from one shelter to another. The loading and unloading of a vertical shelter is inherently more time-consuming than for a horizontal shelter. (It has been estimated that with the horizontal shelter system the entire force of MX missiles could be repostured in new locations within about 12 hours, whereas about 48 hours would be needed to reshuffle vertical shelters.) Such a "dash" capability is an attractive feature and appears, generally, to be operationally realistic. Perhaps it would include placing some portion of the MX force in "constant motion," and awaiting receipt of tactical warning before rapidly dashing into a nearby shelter during the flight time (about thirty minutes) of the Soviet ICBMs.

Some design changes in the horizontal shelter system to make it less expensive have reduced the degree of "dash" capability originally advertised for the system, and further review of operational considerations (including reliability) and Soviet tactics of attack may lead to further modifications of the "dash" as an operational mode for the MX.

Nonetheless, the record strongly suggests that the decision to adopt a considerably more expensive horizontal shelter MPS basing mode was chosen primarily because of verification concerns. Thus, arguing that the additional expense for the horizontal mode with its "dash" feature is an investment for survivability, rather than for compatability with SALT, may be stressing a military virtue that was a byproduct of political necessity (in other words, insistence on a basing mode regarded as more amenable to verification).

SALT III

Can we expect SALT to do better in the future? The discussion below addresses the desirability and feasibility of some of the major negotiated outcomes that have been suggested for SALT III.

Deep Reductions

The SALT II Treaty, as submitted to the Senate, sets an initial aggregate ceiling for ICBM launchers, SLBM launchers, heavy bombers and ASBMs (air-to-surface ballistic missiles capable of a range in excess of 600 km.) of 2,400 and then reduces that ceiling to 2,250 as of January 1, 1981, with reductions to that lowered ceiling to be completed by December 31, 1981. The Soviets will have to reduce by 104 launchers to comply with the initial ceiling of 2,400. The United States, given that its current operational deployment is considerably below 2,400, will only have to dismantle or destroy about 30 launchers (probably some of the 230 B-52s already mothballed and "cannibalized" in storage) to comply with the lower ceiling of 2,250.

The Joint Statement of Principles for SALT III includes an agreement to pursue "significant and substantial reductions in the numbers of strategic offensive arms." "Deep reductions" in SALT III would presumably involve at least 20 to 25 percent (or about 16 to 25 percent as called for in the March 1977 comprehensive proposal).

As generally appealing as "deep reductions" seem to be, there are reasons to question or qualify the desirability—as well as the significance of the budgetary impact—of such a step. Substantial reductions in some types of launchers would not necessarily produce commensurate budgetary savings. The 450 silo-based *Minuteman* II ICBMs account for almost half of the U.S. ICBM force and about 20 percent of total U.S. strategic nuclear delivery vehicles, and yet the elimination of the *Minuteman* II force would only have avoided about 2 percent of the FY 1977 budget request for strategic offensive forces, for example.[25] First, deep general reductions in launchers cannot prudently be considered in isolation from other, especially qualitative, characteristics of the strategic balance prior to and after the implementation of the deep reductions. For example, as the Carter administration noted in 1977 in discussing its comprehensive proposal, unless the Soviet heavy ICBMs are substantially reduced, the destabilizing counterforce potential of the large MIRV payload of the SS-18 becomes even more destabilizing, and a more potent threat to the survivability of a reduced target base in the United States. Moreover, at substantially reduced levels the strategic balance would be more sensitive to cheating and breakout. One of the major arguments for the adequacy of verification of SALT II is that at existing weapons levels, the strategic balance is unlikely to be upset by the scale of any cheating effort that could be achieved before it was detected. At substantially lower levels of allowed launchers, the risk that a Soviet program—either covertly, or in declared breakout—could upset the strategic balance before the United States could implement long-lead compensating reactions would be considerably more worrisome. An additional reason for caution or doubt about the desirability of deep reductions is that substantial reductions in the aggregate levels of strategic launchers could serve to magnify the significance of the theater nuclear balance, especially in long-range theater systems (such as the SS-20 and *Backfire* bomber) where the Soviets have an advantage that is already troubling.

Are "deep cuts" feasible? The Soviet willingness to go beyond the reduction of relatively obsolescent launchers that they were required to undertake to comply with SALT II ceilings (from 2,400 to 2,250) is open to question. However, given that the *Backfire* bomber is not counted under the SALT II Treaty, the Soviets might agree to some modest further "reductions." Their compensation would be the ability to continue building up their uncounted *Backfires* to a force level of about 350 in 1985, at a production rate of thirty per year consistent with the Brezhnev assurance to the United States at the 1979 Vienna summit. Yet, if the Soviets become more concerned about the growth in Chinese and Western European nuclear capabilities, Moscow's willingness to consider deep reductions may be even less in the 1980s, despite their large and improving theater/peripheral strike forces such as the SS-20 mobile, MIRVed IRBM.

The Joint Statement of Principles for SALT III states that both parties will continue "to seek measures to strengthen stability, by among other things, limitations on strategic offensive arms most destabilizing to the strategic balance." Presumably, for the United States such measures would include reductions of heavy ICBMs. It has been argued that the Soviets will become so concerned with the prospective counterforce potential of the MX missile system to destroy most of the Soviet silo-based ICBM force, that they will finally see a general need to reduce their reliance upon such systems and, in particular, will develop an incentive to reduce their heavy ICBMs (perhaps emphasizing mobile ICBM deployment for survivability) and agree to do so under SALT III.

Nevertheless, it seems unlikely the Soviets would undertake such a move without getting something quite substantial in return. The Soviets would probably demand major curtailment or cancellation of the MX program in exchange for reducing their SS-18 force by half (to 150 launchers, as proposed by the United States in March 1977) or eliminating it from their force structure. Without such a cutback or termination of the MX program, the United States would be building up to at least 200 new ICBMs with increased counterforce potential against hardened Soviet silos while Moscow magnanimously reduced its most threatening system, the SS-18. Finding a negotiated basis for avoiding the large costs of the controversial MX program could have a rather strong attraction to some. Unfortunately, if sharply reducing or terminating the MX program of 200 missiles were exchanged for reducing by half or eliminating the Soviet force of about 300 SS-18 launchers (on its face a bargain for the United States), the large force of SS-19s would still remain as a major threat to *Minuteman* survivability in the early and late 1980s—a problem the MX was supposed to address through enhanced survivability. Thus, although a reduction or elimination of Soviet heavy ICBMs remains a desirable negotiated outcome, it could well require a U.S. "payment" that would make the net negotiated result unsatisfactory.

Extending Limits on MIRV Fractionation

The provision (Article IV, paragraph 10) of the SALT II Treaty that limits the number of MIRVs that the Soviets may test (and thereby reliably deploy) on their SS-17, SS-19 and SS-18 ICBMs is perhaps the most useful provision in the treaty in terms of limiting Soviet counterforce threat potential in a way that directly facilitates the survivability of the MX in an MPS basing mode. The "freeze" on the number of MIRVs that have been flight tested as of May 1, 1979, legally limits the SS-17 to four reentry vehicles, the SS-19 to six reentry vehicles, and modern heavy SS-18 ICBM to ten reentry vehicles. The "cap" on the SS-18 during the period of the treaty is regarded as the most significant because of the potential of the SS-18 to carry as many as 20 or more warheads. Even within the MIRV fractionation limits, under the terms of SALT II the Soviets are allowed to deploy about 6,000 MIRVs on their ICBMs through 1985. (See Table 9.1.)

As we have seen, the warhead yield and accuracy available to the Soviets in their MIRVed fourth-generation ICBM program will enable them in the early 1980s to destroy nearly all of the 1,000 silo-based *Minuteman* ICBMs, using two warheads against each such silo and still having a residual force of about 4,000 ICBM reentry vehicles "for use against other targets."[26] The MIRV fractionation allowed the Soviets under the "limits" of SALT II is clearly so high that it does not relieve the threat to *Minuteman*. Instead, the value of the MIRV fractionation limit to American defense planning is primarily in the post-1985 time frame,

TABLE 9.1
Permissible Deployment of MIRVs

Fourth-Generation ICBMs		MIRV Limit/Missile Under Treaty	MIRVs: Maximum Allowed Deployment Through 1985
SS-18	308	10 RVs	3,080
SS-19	250/400*	6 RVs	1,500 -- 2,400
SS-17	262/112*	4 RVs	1,048 -- 488
Total deployment			5,628 -- 5,928

*Illustrative allocation between SS-17 and SS-19 to keep within subceiling of SALT II of 820 MIRVed ICBM launchers (including 308 SS-18s).

after the SALT II Treaty expires under its terms. It is in that later period (1986 to 1990) that the United States plans to deploy 200 MX ICBMs amidst 4,600 multiple protective shelters.

It can reasonably be argued that prior to the MX deployment period, the Soviets would not in any event have had much incentive to fractionate significantly beyond their present capabilities because, until the accuracy of the fourth-generation ICBMs is further improved, lighter weight/lower yield warheads placed on the missiles would actually reduce the hard target kill probability (per MIRV) against *Minuteman* silos. It can also be argued that, *even within* the fractionation limits of SALT II and the subceiling of 820 MIRVed ICBMs, the Soviets will be permitted to have such a large number of high-yield, highly accurate MIRVs in their fourth-generation ICBM force that they will be in a position at the expiration of SALT II to pose a severe threat to the baseline MX system, even with 4,600 shelters. The possibility that Moscow may be able to pose a nearly overwhelming threat to even large-scale MX deployment is suggested both by the high levels of MIRV-loadings on Soviet ICBMs permissible under SALT II and the accuracy improvements that could reduce the number of MIRVs they would have to expend against the *Minuteman* force—leaving a larger "residual" for use against the MPS/MX deployment. Accuracy improvements in the SS-18, demonstrated in flight tests in December 1977 and expected to be incorporated in the operational SS-18 force by 1982–1983, will enable the Soviets to confidently consider using only one SS-18 MIRV—rather than the two previously required—to destroy a *Minuteman* silo.[27] Thus, even before the MX begins deployment in mid-1986, the Soviets, requiring perhaps as few as 1,000 to 1,200 MIRVs (depending on the assumed operational reliability of the SS-18) to destroy all of the *Minuteman* silos, could have at least 1,800 SS-18 MIRVs left over for use against the initial MPS/MX deployment as well as another 2,800 MIRVs atop the SS-17/SS-19 force. This Soviet MIRV potential of 4,600 could grow *legally under SALT II limits* by another nearly 2,400 to 2,700 MIRVs if the Soviets replace 512 SS-17/SS-19s with an allowed "one new type" ICBM with ten MIRVs, still staying within the high subceiling of 820 MIRVed ICBMs under SALT II. In sum, the Soviets in a sense already "have in the bank" sufficient ICBM MIRV loadings needed to pose a severe threat to an initial MX deployment amidst 4,600 shelters. Compared with the *Minuteman* silo, a horizontal shelter will be a relatively soft target, against which only one MIRV from either an SS-18, SS-19 or SS-17 would have the required yield and accuracy for confident destruction.[28]

The prospect of a Soviet threat to MX under SALT II highlights how formidable a negotiating task faces the United States in SALT III. As negotiations of SALT III or a revision of SALT II proceed, the MX program seems unlikely to provide U.S. negotiators with much "bargaining chip" leverage of the sort that Washington possessed with the *Safeguard* ABM program during SALT I talks. The *Safeguard* program was near initial deployment early in the SALT I negotiations and involved an area of technology in which the Soviets were concerned the United States had established a substantial and useful qualitative superiority—which might widen rather than narrow in the near term—over their own, then current, ABM efforts. The MX program will not possess these attributes. Unlike the U.S. ABM program in the early 1970s, the MX program may be seen by the Soviets as essentially a "catch up" effort to match Moscow's prompt counterforce potential. Unlike the ABM, the mobile MX embodies concealment techniques that the Soviet Union, as a closed society, can probably more easily exploit than the United States. The potential to expand the MIRV loading of the MX missile from 10 to 12 seems unlikely to convince the Soviets that restraint through arms control would be to their advantage, especially in view of their own option to use the SS-18's throwweight potential to carry 20 or even more MIRVs instead of the 10 legally permitted under SALT II. Given that the Soviets during the course of the SALT II negotiations linked their acceptance of MIRV fractionation limits with a limit on the average force loading of ALCMs set at 28 on U.S. bombers, one important basis for American leverage in securing an extension of the MIRV fractionation limitations might be to pursue a cruise missile carrier aircraft program that has the potential to raise the average loading considerably above 28 ALCMs. But

U.S. momentum to provide some leverage to extend the MIRV fractionation limitations would probably have to include a more active program to research and develop an ABM site-defense option to complement MX deployment (thereby increasing and complicating the Soviet requirement for attempting to overwhelm an MPS system).

As we have seen, the Soviet Union may not desire a larger number of MIRVs than those permitted under SALT II, believing it can cope with an MX force of 200 missiles and 4,600 shelters. But if the Soviets come to believe that Washington will build several thousand additional shelters, then the Soviets will have an incentive to pursue further fractionation of their ICBM force beyond that permitted by SALT II. They may come to take seriously the possibility of a "race" between Moscow's deployment of additional reentry vehicles (RVs) and Washington's deployment of additional protective shelters for the MX. In considering such a "race," the Defense Department argued in mid-1979 that it would be "easier and cheaper for us to add hard aim points to the MX system than for the Soviets to add missiles or reentry vehicles to attack it."[29] By early 1980, the claim had become more modest. The Soviets might become hesitant to pursue such an RV/MPS "race" because of a lack of cost advantage to them (although a cost disadvantage has not dissuaded them from pursuing massive air-defense deployments that are more expensive than the U.S. strategic bomber program such defenses would counter). However, the Soviets simply may not regard as credible the political will of the United States to pursue such a race with an open-ended MPS deployment, given the controversy that surrounds the MX program—in particular, the considerable local opposition generated just by the prospect of initial baseline shelter deployment in Utah and Nevada. Moreover, realizing that the MX/MPS program has been characterized in the United States as "not making sense without SALT," withholding agreement on extending the MIRV fractionation limit may be seen by the Soviets as a way to encourage the demise of the MX/MPS.

All the same, the Soviet leadership may decide it is *not* in their interest to "race" against shelters by adding to their silo-based ICBMs RVs that will become increasingly vulnerable to counterforce attack by the MX. Instead, the Soviets may well be motivated by the threat from MX to pursue mobile deployment of some of their ICBM force to increase its survivability. Not only would it cost the Soviets more per RV to try mobile deployment (to have feasible mobility it would seem unlikely to involve a heavy ICBM of the throwweight class of the SS-18), but if they chose a road-mobile concept, accuracy for a counterforce attack role could be degraded somewhat compared with silo basing.[30] If the principal Soviet response to the MX/MPS deployment is to pursue mobile deployment for some Soviet ICBMs, this suggests an intriguing possibility. In some cases, perhaps the Soviets can be induced toward a posture more compatible with U.S. concepts of stability, more surely as a result of American unilateral force changes (which involve an element of threat to the Soviets) than through attempted diplomatic "tutorials" by U.S. negotiators in the SALT dialogue on the meaning of stability and Soviet self-interest in having some restraints.

The Soviets may not, of course, follow the path that logic, from the perspective of the U.S. Defense Department, suggests they should pursue. The United States, therefore, clearly must consider the implications for its MX/MPS program if SALT fails to extend MIRV fractionation limits. Such a scenario of a massive Soviet buildup in ICBM MIRVs beyond the 6,000 or more already allowed under SALT II was considered in the Carter administration's agonizing deliberations on whether to proceed with an MX/MPS program. The MPS basing concept technically would be "highly resilient" to substantial increases in the inventory of Soviet warheads that could be used to attack the MPS/MX system. By greatly expanding the shelters, the United States could continue to face the Soviets with an adverse exchange ratio: that is, the Soviets would have to expend considerably more warheads than they could expect to destroy (an extension of the situation in the baseline case where the Soviets would have to use 23 MIRVs in hopes of destroying 10 MIRVs on one MX amidst 23 shelters—a warhead exchange ratio of 2.3 to 1).[31] Assuming a buildup of the Soviet MIRVed ICBM counterforce threat beyond that which is allowed under SALT II, one "worst case" possibility considered by the Defense Department would require increasing the shelters from 4,600 to a total of 13,500 and increasing the MX missiles from 200 to a total of 400. This major expansion of the MX program was estimated to add $26 billion to the "baseline" program costing $33 billion in FY 1980 dollars. Under the "emergency conditions" associated with a U.S. response to a severely threatening Soviet buildup, it was estimated that the United States could build 2,000 shelters per year.[32] After perhaps doubling the number of shelters in the baseline—from 4,600 to 9,200—the Defense Department also estimates that it would at that point become "highly cost-effective" to deploy a site-defense ABM system amidst the MPS deployment for the MX. In particular, the low-altitude defense system (LoADS), currently in research and development stages, is designed to complement the MX with ABM interceptor missiles and radars that take advantage of the concealment afforded by shelters. That would continue to force the Soviets to attack every shelter, while the United States would only have to defend one shelter in a cluster; the

Soviets would have to assume that each shelter they attack might be defended, requiring additional RVs to overcome that defense.[33]

Thus, the basic rationale of the MX/MPS program would not become invalid if SALT limits were to expire, especially on MIRV fractionation. If the United States assumed that SALT would not resume after a hiatus of a year or so, then some design features of the MX/MPS system could be reconsidered. For example, the additional cost of the horizontal shelters might not seem worth a gain in mobility over vertical shelters that are compatible with verification under SALT. The throwweight of the MX missile could be increased if SALT constraints were lifted, but the additional encumbrance thereby to mobility would make that a questionable option. (Indeed, a lighter weight ICBM in the class of the *Minuteman* would have some attraction for facilitating mobility, but the lead time for such a new *Minuteman* might be little, if any, shorter than that for the MX missile.)

In any event, given the severity of the Soviet threat to the survivability of MX in the baseline MPS basing mode, even with 4,600 shelters, it would seem a good idea to give increased priority to research and development of a future ABM site-defense option that could assure sufficient survivability of MX missiles against even a severe Soviet MIRV threat. The United States should not allow itself to be in a position in the mid-1980s whereby a Soviet ABM "breakout" is realistic but an American option to add defensive protection to the MX is handicapped by lack of budgetary funds and technology. Depending upon Soviet developments and willingness to extend MIRV fractionation limits at a tolerable negotiating "cost" to the United States, Washington should consider whether to revise the ABM Treaty of 1972 to permit site defense in designated ICBM areas. Under its terms the ABM Treaty is subject to review at five-year intervals, the next being in 1982 and 1987. (Given Soviet concerns with future vulnerability of its silo-based ICBMs to U.S. attack and with prospective growth in French, British, and West German nuclear threats, Moscow may be interested in revising the ABM Treaty.

Limiting Theater Nuclear Systems

Western Europe has long lived with a major asymmetry in long-range theater nuclear forces favoring the Soviet Union. In the past this has not caused great concern because U.S. advantages in the strategic nuclear balance seemed to offset Soviet advantages in the theater. However, the emergence of parity in the strategic balance and erosion of some areas of U.S. advantage (such as in accuracy and numbers of warheads), combined with Soviet moves to improve and increase its advantage in the theater nuclear balance with such systems as the SS-20 and the *Backfire* bomber, have prompted considerable concern in Western Europe that the Soviets are seeking to gain an intimidating advantage in long-range theater nuclear delivery systems.

In early December 1979, NATO made a fundamental decision to approve the production and deployment of U.S. long-range theater nuclear missiles in Western Europe. Deployment is scheduled to begin in 1983, with a force goal of 464 GLCMs (ground-launched cruise missiles) and 108 extended-range *Pershing* II ballistic missiles. These new systems, on ground-mobile launchers and under U.S. control, will be capable of striking targets in the western U.S.S.R. The decision was prompted primarily by the continuing buildup of the SS-20, which began in 1977 and had reportedly reached a level of 120 directed at Western Europe during 1979, with one SS-20 being deployed per week.[34] Although the continuing Soviet buildup of SS-20s galvanized NATO to approve the GLCM/*Pershing* II deployment plans, a consensus to make such a controversial decision was only possible by coupling this step with an offer to the Soviet Union to negotiate limitations on U.S. and Soviet long-range theater nuclear systems in SALT III. In early December 1979, it was assumed in NATO that SALT II would soon be ratified and SALT III negotiations would begin shortly thereafter, perhaps resulting in a negotiated "solution" affecting trends in the theater nuclear balance in a way that could possibly obviate the need to actually deploy the GLCMs and *Pershing* IIs in 1983.

The landmark decision by NATO in December 1979 was not unanimous and the consensus may not prove durable, especially given the persistent propaganda campaign launched by the Soviets in hopes of unraveling or reversing the NATO decision—which Moscow characterizes and condemns as a provocative Western move that circumvents SALT II and jeopardizes the future of East-West détente in Europe. A combination of an alluring "peace offensive" and threatened Soviet responses if NATO does not reverse its decision may succeed in undermining consensus within NATO on approving GLCM/*Pershing* II deployment. To counter Soviet pressure, NATO has formally declared its intention to pursue a policy of "two parallel and complementary approaches:" on the one hand, attempting to achieve in SALT III some agreed constraints, while on the other hand pursuing military modernization programs to affect the theater nuclear balance in the mid-1980s through a unilateral buildup that would also provide some necessary negotiating leverage in the arms control negotiations.[35] It is hoped that the uncertain prospects for arms control negotiations will not be allowed to become a premature basis for postponement or unilateral curtailment of the "hardware" programs, controversial as they may be in some nations where they may be based.

What is desirable as well as feasible in SALT III as a negotiated outcome relating to the theater nuclear balance is uncertain. NATO has declared a difficult general goal: achieving "a more stable overall nuclear balance at lower levels of nuclear weapons on both sides," applying the principle of *"de jure* equality" in establishing ceilings and rights to deployment.[36] Given the major asymmetries favoring the U.S.S.R. in long-range nuclear delivery systems based in the theater, and the strong Soviet motivation to retain a potentially intimidating advantage *vis-a-vis* Western Europe (including "escalation dominance" in a NATO/Warsaw Pact conflict), seeking parity in the actual balance as a negotiated outcome seems unrealistic. In any event, concern by some Western Europeans with the "decoupling" of U.S. strategic nuclear forces may lead them to doubt whether parity in a compartmented theater nuclear balance is a desirable goal. And even if a negotiated outcome desirable for the West and acceptable to the Soviets can be identified for long-range theater nuclear delivery systems, problems of categorizing and comparing weapon systems with flexible mission and quite disparate capabilities will be formidable. For example, "dual capable" aircraft such as the U.S. F-111s based in Britain are not only theater nuclear delivery systems but also high value assets to NATO for delivering conventional munitions. Should all the F-111s be counted—including those, based in the United States, that might be used in quick response to a contingency in the Persian Gulf or to support South Korea? The allocation of *Backfire* bombers between Soviet Naval Aviation and Long Range Aviation is reportedly about equal. Should they all be counted? How would Soviet requirements for peripheral attack capability against China be considered in establishing limits upon SS-20s that could strike either Chinese or Western European targets in some locations or, in any event, be moved readily in a crisis? An SS-20 delivers three MIRVs. A GLCM and *Pershing* II each carries a single warhead. Are SS-20s and GLCMs and *Pershing* IIs to be counted in the same way? In the case of the SS-20 predecessors—the SS-4 and SS-5 systems—the United States estimated that in 1976 the Soviets had a refire capability with "over 1,000" missiles supporting about 600 launchers.[37] Should launchers or missiles be counted? If launchers are counted, and if the GLCM's transporter-erector-launcher carries four missiles and the SS-20 launcher does not, then how is that difference to be treated? What confidence could we have in verifying the number of missiles (especially for the reloadable SS-20 system), compared with launchers?

Questions of how to categorize and count some systems with flexible missions and systems with great differences in capability have been faced and solutions found in earlier phases of SALT; thus, SALT III would not be unique in that respect. Perhaps the questions offered above will not prove insurmountable. In its December 1979 communiqué NATO proposed that negotiations in SALT III initially concentrate on U.S. and Soviet long-range theater nuclear missiles. The Soviets, however, seem unlikely to agree to initially exclude some allied systems, such as the British and French SLBMs, that concern them. Therefore, some sensitive topics of sovereignty might be raised in NATO. But the principal basis for concern about the feasibility and the desirability of limiting theater nuclear forces at SALT III outcomes is political; the problems of definition and categorization of systems to be covered are not. It will be very difficult to maintain consensus and resolve within NATO over the several years that are needed to stabilize theater nuclear balance through continuing unilateral defense programs as well as arms control negotiations. The difficulty that U.S. administrations had in pursuing a policy of "two parallel courses" during the long SALT II negotiations suggests the even greater difficulty for a coalition of allied governments.

Given the differences of perspective within Western Europe and between the United States and Western Europe on the priority of theater and strategic nuclear issues on the agenda of SALT III, the negotiations may tend to highlight differences of national interest within NATO. U.S.-Soviet agreement on some issues relating to "central systems" may seem to some allies to be at the expense of satisfactory solutions to their "theater" concerns. This occurred, for example, in 1977 when the Protocol emerged rather suddenly in SALT II, placing limits—that NATO allies feared might be later extended—upon future U.S. "forward-based systems" for theater nuclear roles (GLCM and SLCM) without any counterpart limits on Soviet long-range theater systems such as the SS-20. Even if one assumes that consensus and political resolve to pursue parallel paths can be maintained in NATO, the disparity in status of programs—with deployment of the SS-20 and the *Backfire* already underway and likely to reach a level of several hundred by 1985, and the GLCM and extended range *Pershing* not operationally available until 1983 at the earliest—suggests that the bargaining leverage will not favor NATO in negotiations to limit such long-range theater systems. In attempting through SALT III to influence the balance in long-range theater nuclear systems toward a less unfavorable situation for NATO in the mid to late 1980s, the choice seems to be "damned if we do, damned if we don't," given the political imperative to place heavy emphasis upon a hoped-for arms control "solution" and the political strains within NATO that such negotiations may well produce.

American Defense Policy and the Future of SALT

The foregoing suggests that unless, in light of ten years of experience, expectations about what the SALT process can reasonably accomplish are scaled down, the future of the SALT process may become endangered by overloading it with too demanding an agenda. Scaling down expectations about what SALT can reasonably accomplish is not a disservice to the potential of arms control, but instead may well be necessary to preserve it from a collapse or openly acknowledge failure that not only dims the future of arms control, but also damages and possibly poisons broader relationships between the United States and the Soviet Union and within NATO.

As the United States proceeds into SALT III or a revision of SALT II, any administration should recognize that—despite the appearance of words such as "strategic stability" in the generally phrased "Joint Statement of Principles" for SALT III—the United States does not have a basis for wisely or indeed safely assuming, even after a decade of dialogue in SALT, that the Soviets share U.S. conception of and concern with "stability" in the strategic balance, which the United States has believed SALT should enhance. Therefore, the United States should not expect that the Soviets will be inclined to help deliberately fashion a SALT III agreement in a way that will facilitate American unilateral efforts to preserve the survivability of critical components of its strategic deterrent. SALT thus cannot be expected to be or to be responsibly described as "an alternative to an arms race," obviating the need for substantial, very expensive unilateral efforts by the United States to preserve its definition of stability in the strategic nuclear balance.

Maintaining stability and at least rough parity in the strategic balance will realistically be accomplished primarily through other such unilateral U.S. efforts than from SALT. Maintaining stability and "essential equivalence" in the strategic balance should obviously take priority over shaving funds from the small portion of the defense budget allocated to strategic forces. In cases where a new U.S. program—such as long-range ALCMs—strengthens deterrence and contributes to stability but also complicates completion of a phase of SALT negotiations, pursuing the program and assuring reasonable flexibility to introduce it to the U.S. arsenal should take priority.

In addition, the basic components of U.S. strategic forces—such as land-based ICBMs—should not be allowed to become so dependent on SALT provisions, such as limits on MIRV fractionation, that Soviet violations or abrogation would sharply alter the military balance. Responses to clearly emerging Soviet threats to pre-launch or in-flight survivability of U.S. strategic forces should also not be significantly delayed—as was the case with the response to *Minuteman* vulnerability—in hope of securing cooperative restraint by the Soviets through SALT. SALT should facilitate—not encumber—responses to some problems facing defense planners. Carefully managed competition by the United States, including an emphasis on diversifying the components of its strategic arsenal, rather than being antithetical to maintaining stability, is critical to the difficult task of preserving it. SALT will not even be relevant to some critical aspects of strategic equation in the 1980s, such as the need to improve the initial survivability and endurance of command, control, and communications (such as airborne command posts) supporting strategic forces.

Placing SALT in perspective, however, means not only scaling down expectations but also recognizing a core contribution to stability that SALT can make if it is structured with that principal contribution in mind: reducing some uncertainties in projections of the strategic balance that are a basis for defense planning. Providing some greater degree of predictability in the strategic nuclear balance is a modest but important contribution to defense planning that SALT agreements can make—*if* they are long enough in duration to facilitate planning for strategic forces that typically take at least a decade to proceed from development to deployment. As we have seen, one of the major shortcomings of the SALT II Treaty as negotiated and submitted to the Senate was the relatively short duration of the agreement—only through 1985. Perhaps the political impact of such a duration is even more troubling. If 1985 is considered a deadline for completing an acceptable SALT III agreement, it pre-sets a near-term political alarm clock for U.S.-Soviet relations. It also preschedules strains and anxieties within NATO, especially given the limitations upon theater systems that SALT III is expected to consider. Thus, as the military significance of successive SALT agreements becomes relatively minor, the political significance can nevertheless be magnified by deadlines that schedule potential crises or stress points in East-West negotiations.

Because the lead time from development to deployment of a strategic weapon for the United States has come to be about ten years, if SALT is to reduce significantly the uncertainty in projections of Soviet strategic capabilities used in defining the nature and scope of requirements for U.S. strategic forces, its time span for agreement should be at least a decade. (Even with such a duration, however, the United States would still have to hedge programmatically against the contingency of a Soviet abrogation or breakout from an agreement.)

In terms of facilitating U.S. defense planning by reducing uncertainty,

SALT agreements that attempt to limit fewer aspects of the threat, but for a longer time, would seem clearly more valuable than agreements that attempt to affect or control more threat parameters, but cover a shorter time frame and probably take longer to negotiate. In considering how SALT agreements of long duration can contribute to U.S. defense planning, it is important to recognize how new agreements have aided American intelligence, via the prohibition on interference with national technical means (such as photographic satellites) and the ban on deliberate concealment measures that impede verification by national technical means of compliance with SALT provisions.

At the same time, it is also important to recognize the risks associated with SALT provisions that pose perhaps too demanding verification requirements upon U.S. intelligence. The SALT II Treaty imposes more difficult verification tasks upon the intelligence community than did the Interim Agreement of SALT I which, unlike SALT II, did not attempt significant qualitative constraints on strategic offensive weapons but instead focused basically upon quantitative limitations upon deployment of ballistic missile launchers. The more demanding qualitative restrictions attempted in SALT II were subject to some serious doubts about verifiability, especially after the loss of collection sites in Iran. The Statement of Principles for SALT III endorses the pursuit of "further qualitative limitation" as well as the requirement that "further limitations and reductions of strategic arms must be subject to adequate verification by national technical means." There is a risk, if not a danger, that these two imperatives will be incompatible, even if there is some progress in establishing "cooperative measures" (such as more useful schemes for prior notification of ICBM test launches than there were under SALT II) "contributing to the effectiveness of verification by national technical means."

Ability to verify compliance with critical provisions of SALT agreements has been and should be an important consideration in shaping and evaluating such agreements. If agreements have provisions which impose too demanding requirements for verification upon the intelligence community, then not only the SALT process, but also efforts to moderate tensions in the superpower relationship, may be jeopardized by the poisonous atmosphere that can be generated by charge and countercharge of violations of some provisions that are so difficult to verify that ambiguity and suspicious doubt necessarily surround questions of compliance with them.

On the other hand, it should be kept in mind that although it is imperative that feasibility of verification not be neglected in shaping and evaluating SALT agreements, verification is not an end in itself. In some cases the contribution to stability in the strategic balance by some force developments that pose unavoidable uncertainties in verification—such as mobility and concealment to enhance the survivability of ICBMs—is a more important goal than high-confidence verification. Establishing ground rules for mobile ICBM deployment—such as designated deployment areas—that do not jeopardize concealment of individual launchers but facilitate somewhat greater confidence in estimating force level of launchers deployed, would be an important and difficult task for SALT III.

As noted earlier, one of the key arguments for adequacy of verification of SALT II was that the scale of cheating that might proceed before detection would not be enough to upset the strategic balance. "Substantial reductions" or "deep cuts" could make the balance more vulnerable to breakout and make much less convincing the claim that the balance could not be upset by cheating or covert preparations for breakout. The risks associated with uncertainties in verification would be more worrisome under a SALT III regime that involved "deep cuts."

Scaling Down Expectations: A Difficult Imperative

Scaling down expectations about what arms control can accomplish of use to defense planning will not be an easy task for political leadership. More than one administration has been powerfully tempted to claim that much will soon be or has recently been accomplished in SALT. What at times has been a penchant for predicting imminent "breakthroughs" in SALT has probably weakened U.S. bargaining leverage with the Soviet leadership. It will be harder to scale down expectations if the SALT III agenda must include a topic in which considerable hope has already been generated among Western European allies: limitations upon long-range theater nuclear systems. How that sensitive subject is handled will affect the political cohesion of NATO. There will be impatient hope within Western Europe that SALT III can rather quickly reach a "solution" to the problem of a growing imbalance of long-range theater nuclear delivery systems that favor the Soviet Union—such as the SS-20— thereby obviating the controversial deployment of new U.S. long-range, land-based theater missiles in Western Europe scheduled to begin in 1983. U.S. explanations of the substantive and diplomatic complexity of SALT III, including limitations upon central systems that may be linked by either or both superpowers with any agreement on limitations relating to theater nuclear systems, may prompt suspicion rather than support from U.S. allies. Some allies will question whether the United States is jeopardizing the prospects for maintaining (or restoring) East-West détente in Europe by "stubborn" positions on issues relating to central systems that are of much less direct importance to some NATO allies. Without very skillful diplomacy by the United States in the context of allied expectations about SALT III, divisiveness between the United States and its Atlantic allies—long an important objective of Soviet foreign policy—may become a costly byproduct of the SALT process.

Notes

1. Richard M. Nixon, *U.S. Foreign Policy for the 1970s*, Report to the Congress (February 18, 1970), p. 124; see also *Foreign Policy for the 1970s* (February 9, 1972), p. 160.
2. Nixon, *U.S. Foreign Policy for the 1970s*, Report to the Congress (February 25, 1971), pp. 159, 168, 188, 192.
3. In a broader context, Dr. Kissinger articulated the rationale for the SALT I agreements. He told Congressional leaders that an "adequate political foundation" (i.e., a broadly based détente between the superpowers) had been established to prevent the SALT agreements from becoming isolated and vulnerable to collapse as had the Washington Naval Treaty and the Kellogg-Briand Pact of the 1920s:

> For the first time, two great powers, deeply divided by their divergent values, philosophies, and social systems, have agreed to restrain the very armaments on which their national survival depends. *No decision of this magnitude could have been taken unless it had been part of a larger decision to place relations on a new foundation of restraint, cooperation, and steadily evolving confidence. . . .*
> The final verdict must wait on events, but there is at least reason to hope that these accords represent a major break in the pattern of suspicion, hostility, and confrontation which had dominated U.S.-Soviet relations for a generation. (emphasis added)

Quotation from Dr. Henry A. Kissinger, "Briefing to Congressional Leadership," The White House, reprinted in Hearings of the Senate Committee on Armed Services, *Military Implications of the Treaty of the Limitations of Anti-Ballistic Missile Systems and the Interim Agreement on Limitation of Strategic Offensive Arms* (1972), p. 122. (Hereinafter identified as SASC 1972)
4. Strategic Arms Limitation Agreements, Hearings, Senate Committee on Foreign Relations (June–July 1972), p. 5. See also Ambassador Gerard C. Smith, press conference in Moscow, May 26, 1972, referring to Article I of the ABM Treaty, "In effect it says that neither side is going to try to defend its nationwide territory. This is an admission of tremendous psychological significance, I believe, *recognition that the deterrent forces of both sides are not going to be challenged.*" Dr. Kissinger briefed the Congressional leadership in June 1972 at

the White House, and stated in a review of the SALT I negotiations that "both sides more or less agreed at the outset that a very heavy ABM system could be a destabilizing factor." Reprinted in SASC 1972, pp. 99 and 119.

5. April 1977 Press Briefing.

6. Television interview, December 28, 1977.

7. Harold Brown, Address on Arms Control and Strategic Nuclear Planning, University of Rochester, N.Y., April 13, 1977.

8. *Allocation of Resources in Soviet Union and China—1975*, Hearings, Joint Economic Committee, Subcommittee on Priorities and Economy in Government (94:1, Part 1), pp. 32–33, 97–98.

9. Richard Burt, "Search for an Invulnerable Missile," *The New York Times Magazine*, May 27, 1979, p. 34.

10. Harold Brown, *Annual Defense Report for FY 1980*, p. 114; Donald Rumsfeld, *Annual Report for FY 1977*, pp. 50–51.

11. Senate Committee on Foreign Relations, Hearings, *SALT II Treaty* (Part 1), p. 117; President Nixon, News Conference, June 29, 1972; *Public Papers of the President, Richard Nixon, 1972.* Washington, D.C.: U.S. Government Printing Office, 1973, p. 711. Department of State Bulletin, February 23, 1976, p. 209.

12. Statement by William J. Perry, "The FY 1981 Department of Defense Program for Research, Development, and Acquisition," pp. vi–11, 16–17 (excluding the *Backfire* bomber and the SS-20 IRBM systems). In the case of ICBM procurement, the Soviet outlays over 1970–1979 were about three times those of the United States. For SLBMs/SSBNs, Soviet procurement was about 130 percent larger. Only in the case of strategic bombers (assuming the *Backfire* excluded), did U.S. outlays exceed those of the Soviets for procurement for the period of 1970–1979.

13. SASC, 1972, p. 132.

14. *SALT and the U.S. Strategic Forces Budget*, Congressional Budget Office, Background Paper No. 8, June 1976, p. 5.

15. SASC 1972, pp. 5, 51, 65, 141, 221.

16. James B. Schlesinger, *Annual Defense Department Report for FY 1975*, pp. 46–47.

17. Senate Committee on Armed Services, Hearings, FY 1976 (part 10), p. 5231; FY 1977 (part 6), p. 6373.

18. Donald Rumsfeld, *Annual Report for FY 1978*, pp. 129–130.

19. Press Conference, February 21, 1977.

20. For some background of the history of studies, see Senate Armed Services Committee, Hearings, FY 1980 (part 6), pp. 3477–3518, 3536–3537.

21. Senate Foreign Relations Committee, Hearings, *SALT II Treaty* (part 4), pp. 406, 433–434, 447, 473; (part 1), pp. 484, 486. (Hereinafter SFRC.)

22. SASC, FY 1980 (part 6), p. 3478; SFRC, Hearings, *SALT II Treaty* (part 4), pp. 403, 406, 433–434, 447, 473; (part 1), pp. 484, 486.

23. SFRC, Hearings, *SALT II Treaty* (part 4), pp. 403, 427, 477 (FY 1980 dollars).

24. SASC, FY 1980 (part 6), p. 3538.

25. Substantial reductions in some types of launchers would not necessarily produce commensurate budgetary savings. The 450 silo-based *Minuteman* II ICBMs account for almost half of the U.S. ICBM force and about 20 percent of total U.S. strategic nuclear delivery vehicles, and yet the elimination of the *Minuteman* II force would only have avoided about 2 percent of the FY 1977 budget request for strategic offensive forces, for example. "SALT and the U.S. Strategic Forces Budget," Congressional Budget Office, June 1976.

26. Harold Brown, Statement on MX System, May 6, 1980, p. 1; and "FY 1981 Budget Estimates (Research, Development, Test, and Evaluation)," U.S. Air Force, April 1980, p. 11.

27. Testimony of Dr. Perry before the Subcommittee on Military Construction, Senate Appropriations Committee, May 6, 1980.

28. Estimate of 600 psi provided in Dr. Perry's Statement on the MX System, March 25, 1980.

29. SFRC, Hearings, *SALT II Treaty* (part 1), p. 117.

30. SFRC, Hearings, *SALT II Treaty* (part 4), p. 464. General Lew Allen, Chief of Staff of the Air Force, has noted that if the Soviets chose to fractionate the SS-18 from 10 to 20–30 warheads, that would provide a more favorable exchange ration for the MX, using one of its MIRVs to destroy 20–30 instead of 10 SS-18 MIRVs. See letter to Senator John Stennis, Chairman of the Senate Armed Services Committee, February 28, 1980, p. 5.

31. Unless the U.S. has an MX/MPS deployment considerably beyond the baseline of 4,600 shelters—in order to provide confidence that the system cannot still be overwhelmed by the Soviets, the prospect of an adverse exchange ratio may *not* deter the Soviets if they, in a sense, can afford to be profligate in targeting MIRVs against MX/MPS. This point is implied in General Allen's statement of the basic rationale for the MX/MPS, which added a sentence beyond that in Harold Brown's statement on the same point:

> Thus a rational enemy, *if* starting from a position of anywhere near parity, would be deterred from attacking because such an attack would cause the relative balance to shift against him. *But an unfavorable exchange ratio might be acceptable if the attacker began with an inventory so large he could overwhelm us.* (emphasis added)

Quotation from Department of Defense, Statement on the MX System, by Dr. Perry, May 6, 1980, p. 9.

32. SFRC, Hearings, *SALT II Treaty* (part 4), p. 477.

33. Department of Defense Statement on the MX System, May 6, 1980, pp. 10–11.

34. Burt, Richard, "The SS-20 and the Eurostrategic Balance," *The World Today* (Feb. 1977), pp. 43–51; Kaiser, Karl, "Western Security at Stake," *New York Times*, March 7, 1979.

35. NATO Communique, December 12, 1979.

36. NATO Communique, December 12, 1979.

37. General George Brown, JCS *Military Posture Statement for FY 1977*, p. 71.

10
Restraints in Outer Space?

Geoffrey Kemp

The purpose of this chapter is threefold: first, to examine the near-term military uses of outer space and some of the technical steps the United States can take to insure that these military activities are secure in time of crisis and war; second, to ask whether it is in American interests to negotiate with the Soviet Union greater regulation of arms competition in outer space; and third, given the technical and economic dynamics of space-related activities, whether it is in U.S. long-term interests to agree to restrictions on the military and commercial exploitation of space.

While, in the short run, there may be advantages for the United States in pursuing outer space arms control negotiations with the Soviet Union, provided that an active and comprehensive program for defensive and offensive satellite operations is continued, over the long run—say, the next thirty years—new weapons technology and the rapid commercial expansion of space activities raise fundamental questions about the desirability and feasibility of legal limitations on U.S. activity in outer space. Hence, the United States should proceed very cautiously before agreeing to further bilaterial or multilateral military and economic restraints on outer space activities.

I will first discuss the military uses of outer space and alternative ways, including arms control negotiations and new weapons deployments, of ensuring the survivability of U.S. military space-based systems. This will be followed by a wider-ranging discussion of futuristic issues in the military and economic dimension that may have a profound effect upon national security in the period ahead.

The Military Uses of Outer Space

In the past decade the growth of military activities in space has been phenomenal. Both the United States and the Soviet Union rely heavily on space-based systems for a myriad of military activities, including command, control, communications, and intelligence (C^3I); weather forecasting and navigation; surveillance and early warning; verification of arms control agreements; and electronic warfare. In the near future, new generations of space systems will revolutionize several of these activities, especially navigation and real-time reconnaissance. The next decade may also see the deployment of land-based and space-based anti-satellite systems (ASAT), some of which may make use of high-energy lasers (HEL) or, conceivably, charged-particle beams.

It is important to note the symmetries and asymmetries in the military uses of outer space by the two superpowers and the respective advantages each side is assumed to have in the various mission-related technologies. For only if an assessment of the importance of space systems is made on a mission-by-mission basis can the benefits and costs of regulating these military activities be accurately considered. It is not possible in this chapter to cover all the developments in military space, but the most important emerging military technologies include the following:

C³I Systems. Satellites have become an integral but not totally indispensable element in the C^3I systems that would be used in general nuclear war. From an investment perspective, the United States would appear to have more immediately at stake than the Soviet Union, since U.S. space-based C^3I systems are believed to be more sophisticated, and hence more valuable from a military standpoint, while the Soviet Union has built great redundancy into its own communications satellites. On the other hand, since the Soviet Union places such great emphasis on C^3I as part of its overall war-fighting doctrine, it, too, has a great deal at stake in outer space, even if its systems are cruder and more redundant.[1]

Weather Satellites. The next generation of defense meteorological satellites is currently being developed and will provide much better real-time data on weather patterns and cloud formations in central theaters of operations. The military implications of such capabilities could be very significant in regions such as Europe and Northeast Asia. Furthermore, the ability to beam direct weather information into carrier-based aircraft—which is currently planned by the U.S. Navy—would have a significant impact for power projection and the use of airpower at sea.[2]

Navigation. Improvements in satellite navigation may well revolutionize tactical air, sea, and land operations. In this context, the United States appears to have a lead over the Soviet Union. For instance, when the NAVSTAR global positioning system (GPS) comes into service in the mid-1980s, it will provide a three-dimensional navigation capability of extreme accuracy for military units, including tactical aircraft operating in inclement weather; ground forces operating at unit level; ships and submarines; transport aircraft, and, possibly, strategic cruise missiles and ballistic missile reentry vehicles. NAVSTAR will provide a continuous fix on positions, with accuracies between 10 and 100 meters. The consequences for tactical warfare have not been fully thought through, but this may well be one of the more remarkable military developments in the 1980s. It is expected that the final GPS system will consist of 24 satellites in 3 circular "o" bits, each providing around-the-clock coverage of the world. The satellites will be in geosynchronous orbit at heights of 11,000 nautical miles. According to official testimony, the current plans for the GPS "provide a significant margin of safety from current generation Soviet ASATS."[3] Total cost of the system is not yet fully known.[4]

Ocean Surveillance Systems. In the important area of ocean surveillance, the Soviet Union is believed to have developed a substantial lead. The crash of *Kosmos* 954 and its onboard nuclear reactor in Canada in January 1978 drew attention to the sophistication that the Soviets have achieved in their ocean satellites, which have probably been operational since 1974. It is feared that second-generation Soviet systems will be able to achieve real-time targeting data on NATO warships, a factor that could have a decisive influence upon the outcome of a war at sea. Given the great importance the West attaches to its ability to maintain open sea lines in times of war, a military requirement to neutralize these satellites in wartime is compelling. This is, therefore, one arena where the Joint Chiefs of Staff have assigned a priority for U.S. ASAT systems.[5] The United States is developing its own ocean surveillance system (code name *Clipper Bow*). However, this is not expected to be operational until 1983.[6]

Electronic Warfare. Both the United States and the Soviet Union are known to have developed satellites with the explicit purpose of spoofing and jamming each other's electronic warfare capabilities. Since most of this information is closely held, not many details have been made public except that this area of activities is bound to grow—especially since so many of the technologies associated with eavesdropping and ferreting are required for verification missions that are essential to the successful implementation of arms control agreements.

Verification and Reconnaissance Systems. As suggested, the importance of satellites for detecting military deployments and developments on either side becomes crucial for the "national means of verification," long replacing the manned aircraft, except for very specific missions in remote areas. The United States has plans to develop much larger, orbiting radars that would be able to spot extremely detailed activity on the ground and, in particular, would provide almost instant warning to troop deployments and, obviously, missile attacks. The ability to maintain systems like this is an essential part of the early-warning capability in a military context quite apart from the arms control verification requirements. However, it is important to distinguish between these two tasks and the respective utility of satellites for performing them. Most experts believe that U.S. space-based systems can perform the "early-warning" mission with a high degree of confidence. There is less confidence concerning verification, which in this context means the ability to detect activities in the Soviet Union that relate to Soviet military programs. Satellites can be "deceived" and sometimes the data they obtain is ambiguous. This uncertainty can best be controlled if other, independent, means are available to provide a check, such as ground-based listening posts.[7]

Anti-Satellite Systems The most important task for an ASAT system is to degrade the operational capabilities of the enemy satellite. Thus, techniques designed to confuse, spoof, manipulate, and blind enemy satellites may be as relevant as those designed to physically destroy the enemy satellite. Since the destruction of satellites would be relatively easy to detect, it could give the adversary a clear signal of intent and, thus, valuable warning time. In contrast, an ASAT system that merely downgraded the performance of enemy satellites would be harder to detect and thereby might provide less warning in time of hostile enemy actions.

There are several methods that can be used to interfere with or destroy satellites. These include ground-based systems (high-energy lasers on top of mountains offer promising results); air-based systems (the U.S. Air Force is presently preparing a bidders' list for developing and deploying an anti-satellite space defense launch missile—known as the prototype miniature air-launched segment [PMALS]—which will be carried on a modified F-15A);[8] and, thirdly, space-based systems. It is this last category that has caused the most concern in the United States in view of the intensive series of tests the Soviet Union has conducted over the years in its attempts to develop a satellite killer.[9] Once in space, an anti-satellite killer can use different methods to seek out and neutralize satellites, including conventional explosives; the use of grit to damage and destroy the satellite; and lasers to blind or destroy the electronic circuitry and power systems. It is also possible to "steal" an enemy satellite by sending up a manned vehicle such as the U.S. Space Shuttle.

With regard to the respective vulnerability of satellites, several points have emerged from public discussion. The Soviet Union is ahead in testing operational ASAT systems, but the United States has an active program and, in technical terms, may have more sophisticated concepts that could eventually reduce and perhaps overtake the Soviet lead.[10]

Neither the United States nor the Soviet Union presently has the capability to threaten satellites placed at high orbit (10,000 miles or more). However, according to testimony by Lt. General Thomas Stafford, the homing intercept technology being used to develop the Air Force's ASAT will have the capability to attack some Soviet satellites in synchronous orbits. This is an important capability because Soviet C^3 satellites operate in these orbits.[11] It is the lower-altitude satellites that are most vulnerable and, while the United States has fewer, more sophisticated, low-level satellites, for geographic reasons the Soviet Union is not easily able to place satellites in geostationary high orbit. Instead, the Soviet Union has to put its satellites into orbits that have very high apogees (some 40,000 miles) and low perigees.[12] When in the high orbit, Soviet satellites are visible from the United States, even though they will be invulnerable to the proposed U.S. ASAT weapon. On the other hand, their low perigee will make them very vulnerable to the U.S. system.

An Anti-Satellite Treaty?

In June 1978, the Soviet Union and the United States began talks in Helsinki to discuss ways of restricting the testing and deployment of ASAT weapons. An ASAT treaty would follow logically from the 1967 Treaty on the Uses of Outer Space, the 1972 ABM Treaty, and the proposed SALT II Treaty. Proponents have argued that it is in the interests of both superpowers to seek cooperative ways to preserve their existing military investments in outer space irrespective of previous agreements.[13] It is also argued that the loss of forward ground-based intelligence facilities in Iran for monitoring Soviet missile tests has added new importance to space-based systems.

As of mid-1980, details of the ASAT negotiations were sparse, but several points have emerged to indicate the inherent technical complexities of the subject and the different perspectives the two sides have on the question of definition and scope. Three basic issues need to be mentioned before considering the advantages and disadvantages of seeking arms control agreements on anti-satellite operations. First, what is the definition of an ASAT weapon? Second, can an ASAT treaty be verified? Third, what provision should or could be made for the use of ASAT systems against other countries, such as China?

The first and second issues are closely related. Given the numerous legitimate military and commercial space-related activities that the United States and Soviet Union and, eventually, other countries will continue to carry out, how can one decide what capabilities and techniques fall within the rubric of an ASAT agreement? At various times the Soviet

Union has raised the question about U.S. directed-energy programs, which are discussed in the next section, and has also insisted that the Space Shuttle be counted as a potential ASAT weapon. While it is true that the Shuttle could be used to place ASAT killers in space and could conceivably be used itself to "capture" Soviet satellites, the suggestion that the Shuttle be included in any agenda is out of the question and is probably a bargaining tool.

On the assumption that there could, in theory, be an agreement to restrict research and development, testing, deployment, and use of ASAT systems, it is felt that a treaty covering research and development would be very difficult to define—let alone implement. Any formal restriction on the use of ASATs, therefore, while easy to define, would be relatively worthless from an arms control perspective. This leaves the possibility of restrictions on testing and deployment. Provided that an agreed definition of "testing" could be found, it might be possible to restrict certain activities relating to air- or space-based ASAT systems using national means of verification. However, to successfully verify compliance concerning the testing of ground-based ASAT systems might require on-site inspection. Even if a deployment ban could be negotiated, there remains the danger of "breakout"—the possibility that the Soviet Union, while formally agreeing to ASAT restrictions, could proceed in secret to develop a new ASAT system that it could suddenly deploy in time of crisis. Given the past record of Soviet clandestine activity and the impossibility of restricting research and limiting testing, especially of ground-based systems, "breakout" must be regarded as one of the key problems in ASAT negotiations.

Another substantive issue relates to third countries. As China improves its space program and starts developing a manned space effort, the problem will intensify. By the 1980s, China could have its own C^3 spacecraft and have developed a synchronous orbit capability.[14] According to some reports, the Soviet Union wishes to retain the capability to attack Chinese and possibly NATO spacecraft and only wants to agree not to attack U.S. satellites. The United States wants spacecraft of "mutual interest to either country" to be protected under a treaty. The U.S. negotiation position has been that the Soviet Union should cease ASAT tests, dismantle its present ASAT capabilities, and agree to adequate verification procedures. The Soviets evidently have responded by including the Space Shuttle in their definition of ASAT capabilities, and by agreeing to a ban on activities to "damage, destroy or displace" satellites—*provided* that they could circumvent the ban under certain circumstances, through a "hostile act" clause.[15] (It has been reported that the Soviet Union wishes to retain the broadest possible definition of what a "hostile act" might be, which would permit it to include direct broadcast communication satellites that could beam radio signals to Soviet citizens!)

Quite aside from the inherent complications in the ASAT negotiations, what, at this stage, can be said about U.S. interests? There would be advantages to both sides if neither side developed ASAT capabilities, in that expensive procurement programs could be slowed down and possibly abandoned. On the other hand, there are scenarios in which it would be highly advantageous for the United States to be able to destroy certain Soviet satellites, particularly those engaged in ocean reconnaissance and C^3 missions. From the Soviet point of view, the ability to destroy the increasingly accurate American navigation systems as well as U.S. C^3 must rank highly on their agenda of military tasks in war. It can also be argued that as technologies for military uses of outer space improve—including the development of effective ways to use directed-energy systems for certain missions—it is inevitable that the military requirements for satellite protection and destruction will increase. Given the many activities these systems perform, the Soviet Union is bound to consider U.S. satellite capabilities in its war plans. Similarly, the United States cannot afford to forego the possibility of developing effective ASAT systems, given the potential advantages it has in space technology and geography. It has also been suggested by General Stafford that space may be "an alternative arena for a show of force." According to this viewpoint, "conflict in space does not violate national boundaries and does not kill people and can provide a very visible show of determination at relatively modest cost."[16]

This leads to the more specific question as to whether or not Washington should pursue ASAT negotiations, and what it should seek if it does. As with most arms control issues, there is a sharp division of opinion on the question. Whereas some believe that our technological commitment to space and high dependence on surveillance and navigational programs makes it necessary to initiate negotiations to control anti-satellite capabilities, others feel that by avoiding such negotiations the United States could more reliably counter Soviet potential in that area while developing its own offensive capabilities. The debate is really over what options provide the greatest security for the United States: attempts to block the development of a new and highly volatile arena for competition, or a decision to willingly enter a new realm where U.S. technological skills will give us an advantage in weapons innovations and foil.

Critics of ASAT Negotiations

Critics of the talks stress that important problems plague negotiations with the Soviets when unfavorable asymmetries characterize the programs to be controlled: first, how to get the Soviets interested in negotiating seriously; and second, how to control the negotiating process so as to avoid prolonging their advantage? According to some observers, the latter question is particularly worrisome when negotiations get under way too soon after programs are initiated and while the adversary has a significant testing lead.

The argument against arms control initiatives in this area has a significant time component. Critics believe the United States must acquire a better understanding of the vulnerabilities that our system will have over the next five years before acting to constrain them. Then, the argument goes, if we proceed with negotiated restraints, we should do so cautiously in recognition of the dynamic nature of space technology. It may be that the unitary systems that we seek to control today will have become obsolete in less than a decade.

Critics do not accept that the current relative dependence of the United States on satellite systems should dictate arms control solutions to Soviet ASAT capabilities. Instead, they feel that the United States can still investigate back-up programs to provide redundance—a need that was identified as far back as the 1950s.

Advocates of ASAT Negotiations

Supporters of ASAT negotiations argue that satellite owners tend to be the victims of satellite killers in ASAT war games. Since both sides value their space-based systems, each would be poorer for unrestricted ASAT competition. But given its growing dependence on such systems, the United States has a special interest in capping the Soviet Union's offensive program despite Washington's technological advantages. For there are basically two alternatives for the future: permitting both sides to rely on space-based assets, or backing out of space technologies for the performance of these missions. The Carter administration chose the former, which means letting the Soviets have neither a monopoly on ASAT nor hegemony in outer space. Therefore, funds for ASAT were budgeted at the same time that attempts were made to prevent competition in this technology through negotiations. Thus, advocates of negotiations argue that if we really want to develop our space program, ASAT negotiations are a first step. In this view, if SALT is any indication, such talks are less likely to tie our hands than to focus attention and even stimulate appropriations. If we postpone negotiations, the Soviet program is as likely to mature as our own. In short, there is no evidence that the anti-satellite gap would be more easily closed in the absence of negotiated limits than with them.

Advocates also stress that ASAT negotiations would not eliminate the need for developing anti-satellite counters because there is clearly no guarantee that such discussions would be successful. However, since the window for restraint exists now, it should be held open long enough to explore the extent to which a durable relationship can be achieved.

Critics respond to this line of reasoning by asking how one designs an arms control agreement that is based on "the mutual interests" of both parties when the doctrinal and programmatic base of each diverge? In addition, critics are skeptical of the desirability of an anti-satellite test ban when this would leave the United States substantially behind in operational capability. When the technology is so new and the impact of constraints is so uncertain, designing a desirable agreement may well be impossible.

To which point the advocates respond:

- It might be desirable to approach the negotiations as a two-phased endeavor—first seeking a test ban to cap Soviet programs, then focusing on equity for a second-stage accord.
- Recognizing that achieving an ideal agreement is a quixotic goal, one can still design an accord that will leave us on a particular step of the technological stairs. Accepting such an accord does not require prophetic judgment so long as a unilateral termination clause is included.
- From a military point of view, it is in our interests to raise the threshold for anti-satellite warfare since we face vulnerability with or without a treaty. Negotiated restraint could raise the stakes for first use, providing valuable time.
- Negotiations need not trap us into significant inferiority. Certainly, in the absence of early agreement to freeze both programs, we would continue our plans to test. Moreover, the Soviets would take negotiations seriously. They seem to be concerned about the Shuttle program, and probably regard ASAT as a deterrent as well as an offensive capability.

Some critics question whether the primary issue is survivability. For it is not conditions of peace with which we must be concerned, but rather with crises—such as another Korean, Middle East, or European conflict—when treaties are abrogated. With or without an ASAT treaty, in such instances one must anticipate dealing with an adversary that has

ASAT capabilities, since the potential for breakout will always exist. In this regard, it can be argued that we would be better off without an ASAT treaty, which, in turn, raises the question of whether we should emphasize ASAT programs or the development of defensive systems.

Longer-Term Perspectives

Directed Energy Weapons

In the spring of 1977, a furor was caused in U.S. defense circles. It was stimulated, in large part, by an article in *Aviation Week & Space Technology*. The thrust of the article, which made constant references to statements by former head of U.S. Air Force Intelligence, Major General George J. Keegan, Jr., was that the Soviet Union had achieved a major technical breakthrough in the development of charged-particle beam technology. It quoted a U.S. official as saying that "after ten years of work at the site and after developmental testing of the beam for over a year the only thing required was to scale the device for weapons application." It went on to say "that could be accomplished by as early as 1978 with a prototype beam weapon and it could be in an operational form by 1980 some officials believe."[17] This estimate was disregarded in official circles as wildly exaggerated. However, the press coverage given to the subject and details given about Soviet programs were sufficiently precise to inspire concern about very serious security violations and to suggest the possibility that the Department of Defense and the Intelligence community had underestimated the Soviet capabilities.

Whatever the truth of the initial disclosures, there can be no doubt that interest in the directed-energy technologies has increased. The Department of Defense has increased its activity in this arena, although, as mentioned earlier, such U.S. programs as high-energy lasers were already making dramatic progress despite low-key publicity, or, to put it another way, good security.

Two questions emerge. What is the status of directed-energy technology? And what are the implications for U.S. defense planning and the U.S.-Soviet military balance if effective directed-energy weapons should prove to be feasible for strategic warfare in the decades ahead? The first point is that there seems to be greater promise of an early breakthrough in the practical application of high-energy lasers for weapons than in charged-particle beams. It is estimated that the United States has spent about $2 billion on laser weapons to date and plans to spend at least $200 million in 1980.[18] The U.S. Army, Navy, and Air Force all have research programs on various applications of directed-energy weapons, coordinated by the Defense Advanced Research and Projects Agency (DARPA). The Air Force is working on the concept of an airborne testbed for high-energy laser weapons that it hopes to test in the near future. The operational implications of the Air Force program relate in the first instance to the possibility of developing an airborne anti-missile capability that could enhance the protection of strategic bombers operating over hostile air space. The Navy is testing possible applications at sea, as well as laser countermeasures, and the Army and DARPA are exploring space and space-related laser technologies for a variety of missions. Evidently there have been some major breakthroughs in tactical laser weapons in recent years. The first success was in 1973 when the Air Force shot down a wing drone using a high-energy gas dynamic laser. Three years later—in 1976—the Army used a high-energy electric laser to destroy winged and helicopter drones. In March 1978, the Navy, using chemical lasers, successfully engaged and destroyed a tow anti-tank missile in flight.[19] According to the Defense Science Board, the most promising military use for lasers may be in outer space. Such lasers could be used to protect U.S. satellites against Soviet ASAT systems. According to a 1979 Arms Control Impact Report to Congress, if laser satellites were deployed in sufficient numbers (less than ten), not only could they defend against Soviet attack, but it would also take only two of them to destroy all Soviet low-orbit satellites in less than 24 hours.[20]

Particle-beam weapon research in the United States is closely coordinated by DARPA and includes the Navy's *Chair Heritage* Program on naval uses of particle-beam weapons for the protection of aircraft carriers and cruisers against Soviet nuclear-armed cruise missiles. In addition, the army has a ballistic missile defense advance technology program for particle-beam weapons. This program has potentially important implications for outer space and could be covered by the ABM Treaty of 1972, which prohibits the deployment of anti-ballistic missile systems in outer space.

As suggested, Soviet developments in laser and particle-beam technology are the subject of great controversy within the scientific community. The Defense Intelligence Agency reportedly believes that a Soviet prototype short-range particle-beam weapon will appear in the 1980s, although there is a lot of skepticism on this point in some circles. However, there seems to be less skepticism over the Soviet Union's ability to deploy lasers in space for anti-satellite weapons. According to a C.I.A. study reported in the *New York Times* in May 1980, the Soviet Union has *already* developed a ground-based anti-satellite laser and could deploy a space-based laser by the mid-1980s.[21]

It does appear that the Soviets have expended a lot of money for research into laser and beam technologies. Two facilities are frequently mentioned in the press—one at Sarova near Gorky and the other at Semipalatinsk. The latter facility may be devoted to perfecting miniaturized explosive generators for pulse power, which is necessary for a long-range particle-beam weapon. This technology is related to the development of magnetic fusion in which the Soviet Union is known to have made a large effort. However, some American scientists argue that these are civilian technologies involving nuclear fusion capabilities rather than weapons research.

If there were technical breakthroughs in these technologies for weapons application over the next decade, two things are clear. First, the operational difficulties of using lasers or particle beams for ballistic missile defense, as distinct from anti-satellite operations, seem overwhelmingly high at present.[22] The number of battle stations that would be needed in space to effectively protect either the United States or the Soviet Union is related to the lethal range of the system. Thus, a laser or particle-beam weapon with 1,000 kilometer lethal radius would require up to 406 battle stations to cover the globe; with 5,000 kilometer lethal radius the number would be 21, whereas weapons with an effective range of 10,000 kilometers would permit the world to be covered from only 9 battle stations. Obviously, if the Soviet Union or the United States were to develop effective beam or laser capabilities, there would be a revolutionary effect on the strategic warfare capabilities of both sides—depending upon when the systems were introduced and how effective they were. Some experts who have speculated about such matters argue that in the event that such a breakthrough occurs within this decade there would still be numerous countermeasures the offense could take to neutralize or confuse laser-beam ABM weapons.[23] In fact, those speculations are analogous to those debated in the late 1960s on the potential effectiveness of ground-based ABM systems. Others, however, believe that the basic technology for a laser anti-missile system exist. It is suggested that chemically-powered lasers being developed by the TRW Corporation provide the best opportunities. An anti-missile space-based laser system would have three critical components: the laser itself, which would weigh several tons; a detecting and tracking system; and a system for directing laser beams to target (so-called "pointing technology"). It is believed that this last component poses the most technical problems for a laser anti-missile battle station.[24]

If some of these difficulties could be overcome, it is fair to ask whether a technology that moves us toward systems that can provide active defense against nuclear attack from outer space would necessarily be against U.S. interests. Such developments would reflect a shift in the cost-exchange ratio in favor of such defense so that reliance on offensive nuclear doctrines such as massive retaliation and assured destruction could be downgraded. A critical concern, assuming some breakthrough, would be the time-frame in which either side introduced its space-based ABM system. Some have argued that if there is a breakthrough in technology and both sides have access to it, the United States would have an advantage given the Space Shuttle program and the enormous lift capability it will have in the 1980s. On the other hand, if the Soviet Union is ahead in the basic technologies, there is no doubt that it could improve lift techniques to assemble battle stations in space if costs were not considered a major factor.

All in all, it would seem that speculation about the ABM potential of laser and beam weapons will continue and intensify into the 1980s, even though most informed experts in the scientific and engineering communities still think that the technical and economic problems involved with applying ABM to these systems (as distinct from tactical uses on the battlefield and possibly for anti-satellite warfare) work against their near-term utility.

The Commercial Exploitation of Outer Space

Unless there is a radical change in leadership and the criteria for setting national priorities, future generations of Americans may well remember the 1970s as the period when the United States lost its world primacy, not only because of diminished military power—although this is undoubtedly an important issue—but also because of a national failure to develop the unique advantages and opportunities offered by the exploration of outer space. Yet this is a propitious moment for the United States to reassert its determination to dominate outer space technology and the numerous economic opportunities that could flow from such a decision. The symbol and substance of this opportunity is the Space Shuttle, which is expected to complete its first, long delayed, flight in 1981. The Shuttle will reduce the costs of putting payload into space. The consequences of this technology are potentially as important as the development of the railroad was in the 19th century, when vital new land frontiers were opened up to economic development.

Support for commercial exploitation of outer space falls into two schools of thought: the conservative and the futurist.[25] The difference between the two schools has to do with the time-frame for the industrialization of space.[26] The conservatives argue that one does not need to exaggerate the potential bonanza of outer space in order to justify from an economic, social, political, and military standpoint the investment costs in the Shuttle (although some would argue that there are cheaper alternatives to the Shuttle program). Space has already become indispensable to a myriad of earth-based activities; what the Shuttle will do is make these activities more sophisticated and almost certainly cheaper. In this context, a boom in the development of communication satellites is expected, since the Shuttle will permit the deployment of more complicated and larger satellites or antennae "farms" in orbit; those could, if necessary, be repaired on station. This, in turn, will coincide with new technologies to permit the use of smaller and cheaper receiving stations on earth. For this reason, a range of new communications tasks will occur in the next decade—including electronic mail and much wider use of satellites for radio, television and telephone services. The legal, political, and economic implications of the communication revolution in outer space have generated a host of complicated problems, including antagonism between the developed and less developed countries; wavelengths assigned to less developed countries in new satellite systems; and the legal rights that equatorial countries have over satellites placed in geosynchronous orbit over their territories. These disputes are likely to increase in the future as part of a growing conflict over the legal rights of nations to exploit space.[27]

Other arenas in which the conservatives place great hope include information gathering for meteorology, weather forecasting, and earth resource management. These technologies can have great benefits. For example, satellites may be able to predict long-term weather changes and the climatic impacts of industrialization on various parts of the world. The value of such forecasting to farming, airlines, fisheries, the building industry, shipping industry, and even the tourist industry is considered to be in excess of the cost of developing the satellites and paying the lift costs to put them in orbit. Breakthroughs in remote sensing satellites, which are used for resource management, offer equally positive pay-offs. Satellites used for agricultural forecasting can distinguish wheat from corn and healthy from diseased crops; they can tell if the soil is too wet or dry, can identify pest infestations and, therefore, be of great use in guiding crop production and crop management. Other agricultural uses include the capacities to detect how many sheep and cows can graze off a particular plot of land and what the arable land conditions are likely to be in the months ahead. They can be used for discovering scarce minerals, guiding forestry planning, predicting river flooding, monitoring irrigation, guiding urban land use in planning, tracking icebergs, monitoring ship movements, locating schools of fish, and even looking below the ocean surface and the earth's crust. The pioneering achievements of NASA's land resources and mapping satellite (LANDSAT) are such that many nations are seeking to gain access to the data that these systems provide (a factor that also raises delicate political problems, since all users of the LANDSAT data have access to detailed pictures of neighboring countries).

In almost every case it can be argued that the economic benefits of these systems far outweigh the intitial investment costs involved. For the future there are also possibilities for manufacturing products in space that make use of the unique vacuum and gravity-free environment. These include vaccines, large crystals for electronic applications—such as computer micro-circuitry or solar cells, and special glasses and new materials that can be built from vacuum welding. However, there is some debate as to how important space production will be in the near future, and this issue provides the transition between the conservatives and the futurists.

The futurists believe that man's destiny must ultimately be to colonize outer space. This has resulted in the emergence of a new "high priesthood" for the accelerated exploitation of outer space by the United States. The technologies that the futurists have initially pinned their hopes on are solar-power satellites (SPS)—huge systems up to 20 kilometers by 7 kilometers wide that would be constructed in outer space and placed in stationary orbit tens of thousands of miles from the earth. They would display massive solar collecting panels that would convert the sun's rays to electricity that would then be beamed back to earth—probably by microwave technologies. On earth, receiving stations would convert the microwaves into electricity. It has been suggested that up to 30 or 40 of these huge power stations could provide all the electricity the United States needs by the end of the century. The construction of such facilities would require vast amounts of raw material. Since the costs of lifting raw material from earth would be very high given the high escape velocities of earth's gravity, one solution pioneered by Princeton physicist Gerard O'Neill and his colleagues (who include a host of young physicists, engineers, and chemists at institutions such as MIT and Cal Tech) is to make use of moon minerals or even earth-bound asteroids. Moon rocks would be mined and then catapulted into space by a magnetic "mass driver" utilizing the principle of magnetic levitation. In space, the minerals would be "caught" and towed to space factories which would process the minerals for construction. Space construction of this magnitude would require the development of permanent space colonies that would be economically self-sustaining.[28]

Because so many of these ideas have commercial implications, several of the aerospace companies, as well as NASA, have taken an active interest in O'Neill's work and have sponsored their own studies. Hence there is very wide-ranging literature on the subject of space manufacturing, which makes fascinating reading, to say the least.

Although O'Neill and his more strident followers have been dismissed as dreamers, even though their equations seem sound, the political implication of what they are saying has become a serious issue. In 1975, at the Princeton Conference on Space Manufacturing, a group of young space devotees formed the L-5 Society,[29] (L-5 is one of the five Lagrange points equidistant from the moon and earth. At that point, an object would be balanced by gravitational forces of earth and moon and would, therefore, remain stationary.) The L-5 Society aims to set up the world's first space colony and make it economically self-sufficient. In late 1979, the Society hired Leigh Ratiner, former lobbyist for the Kennecott Copper Corporation at the Law of the Sea negotiations, to support them against the proposed Moon Treaty (a follow-on to the Outer Space Treaty of 1967 that was, in part, designed to prevent a colonial race for space).[30] The draft Moon Treaty grew out of the 1979 session of the U.N. Committee on the Peaceful Uses of Outer Space, where consensus was reached on "an Agreement Governing the Activities of States on the Moon and Other Celestial Bodies," which declares that the natural resources of such bodies are "the common heritage of mankind." The Moon Treaty proposes to set up an international regime to manage the resources of the moon and other celestial bodies similar to the proposed regime for sharing the wealth of the seabed.

If the acrimony and squabblings that have arisen at the Law of the Seas negotiations over the ownership of the seabed are any precedent, it is understandable why those who see commercial benefits in the exploitation of the moon have tried to get the Senate to postpone ratification of the Moon Treaty in its present form. For what is at stake is the extent to which U.S. initiative and private industry should be allowed to exploit the undoubted benefits of outer space. Why, it is argued, should the United States tie its hands in the exploitation of outer space when it has an undoubted technological lead? If it were the Soviet Union that had the capacity to exploit the moon in the near future or to develop the commercial benefits of space, then there would be reason to monitor Soviet activities, possibly through an international regime. This is not to say that international cooperation is undesirable for a range of space activities, but that these can be negotiated on a bilateral basis and *should not include statements of principle which have yet to be shown to be either workable or in American interests.*

In the last resort, it must be assumed that if the United States does eventually establish an economic infrastructure in outer space, including space stations or even small space colonies, such activities will have to be monitored and protected against potential problems and threats. Once people work and live in outer space on a routine, protracted basis—just as there are people living on oil rigs in the North Sea and other areas—new legal codes and new forms of justice and law enforcement have to be evolved. Thus, the growth in economic activity in space will eventually have to be paralleled by some constabulary force to patrol and protect sizeable investments. For even if it is ultimately decided to be in U.S. interests to negotiate with the Soviet Union for the regulation of certain military tasks in outer space, such initiatives will not resolve, or even come to grips with, the longer-term commercial competition that will be inevitable if space offers high economic rewards.

Over the long run it may be economic factors that determine U.S. outer space policy. And in many ways this is how it should be. Those who call for new space initiatives bridge the political spectrum and include Governor Jerry Brown, Senators Adlai Stevenson III, Barry Goldwater, Harrison Schmidt, and John Glenn. The urge to exploit the last frontier at a time when America's economic position is losing its competitive edge is compelling and, with the right leadership, could provide new dynamics to American society. A telling comment on the barrenness of current U.S. space policy was made by Norman Cousins who, in chastising those who question whether space exploration is desirable, suggested that: "The world will end neither with a bang nor a whimper but with the strident cries of little men devoted to cost-benefit ratios. If cost-benefit ratios had governed our history Socrates would have become a babysitter . . . and Columbus would have taken out a gondola concession in Venice. . . ."[31]

Notes

1. The next decade could see the development and possible deployment of very large sophisticated satellites that will permit the processing of information to take place in space. This, in turn, will reduce the size and costs of ground receivers which, given advances in micro-circuitry, could literally mean the use of Dick Tracy wrist receivers. The battlefield management implications of these technologies are revolutionary to say the least.

2. *Aviation Week & Space Technology*, June 4, 1979, pp. 47–58.

3. *FY 1980 Arms Control Impact Statements*, Statement submitted to the Congress by the president pursuant to Section 36 of the Arms Control and Disarmament Act (Washington: U.S. Government Printing Office, 1979), pp. 118–126.

4. *FY 1980 Arms Control Impact Statements*, op. cit., pp. 118–126. Initial operational capability should begin in 1985 and the whole system could be fully operational by 1986. To give some indication of the extent to which this system

will be used, upwards of 27,000 user-equipment sets for vehicles, ships, aircraft, and manned portable packs are expected to be ordered in the first instance. The coordinates used by the NAVSTAR will be secure, although it will be possible to use the system for commercial operations as well. Lightweight packs of between 10 and 20 pounds will be possible for Army and Marine troops in the field and for mechanized vehicles. It is expected that the receivers will cost between $10,000 and $50,000 in 1979 prices.

5. *Aviation Week & Space Technology*, September 3, 1979, p. 57.

6. *Strategic Survey 1978*, International Institute for Strategic Studies, London, 1979, pp. 23–29.

7. Malcolm Brown, "U.S. Increases Reliance on Intelligence Satellites," *New York Times*, December 18, 1979, pp. C1 and C2.

8. *The Defense and Space Daily*, October 30, 1979.

9. The history of Soviet tests of ASAT systems is a long and complicated one. In October 1962, *Vostock* 3 and 4 satellites maneuvered within five kilometers of each other. In 1967, the Soviets acquired a capacity to maneuver in space and to dock with manned satellites. In October 1968, the explosion of *Kosmos* 249 after approaching *Kosmos* 248 was repeated with another *Kosmos* (252) and, in 1971, further tests with the *Kosmos* series ended with an interception at 250 kilometers—the distance at which most reconnaissance satellites tend to operate. There was a hiatus in Soviet testing for a while, but testing resumed in 1976 (perhaps as a response to China's ability to place into orbit a 2,000 kilogram satellite). Recent activities have included complex maneuvers involving co-orbiting target satellites and "swooping down" on targets. However, Soviet ability to chase a maneuvering target has not been demonstrated nor can the interceptors take on more than one satellite at a time. So far, there is no public record of any Soviet tests at the high geosynchronous altitudes used by U.S. communication and early warning satellites. However, the Soviet systems could cover the ferret- and electronic-warfare satellites and may well have been originally designed to counter the manned orbiting laboratory (MOL) that the U.S. planned to develop in the 1960s. Certainly the current Soviet systems could be used against the planned Space Shuttle. The Department of Defense expects the Soviet Union eventually to develop an ASAT capability at high altitudes. For more details, see Lawrence Freedman, "The Soviet Union and Anti-Space Defense," *Survival* (May/June 1978), International Institute for Strategic Studies, London; Scoville, Herbert, Jr., and Tsipis, Kosta, *Can Space Remain a Peaceful Environment?*, The Stanley Foundation, Muscatine, Iowa, July 1978; Kim Willenson and Evert Clark, "War's Fourth Dimension," *Newsweek*, November 29, 1976, pp. 46–48. "New Soviet Anti-Satellite Missions Boosts Backing for U.S. Tests," *Aviation Week & Space Technology*, April 28, 1980, p. 20.

10. According to Defense Secretary Harold Brown, the Soviet Union is certainly developing an impressive array of space capabilities, but in the vital area of reuseable space vehicles—which would be essential if a major military space race got underway—their technology might be as much as ten years behind. *New York Times*, February 8, 1980, p. 12.

11. *Aviation Week & Space Technology,* August 13, 1979, pp. 11–13.

12. U.S. satellites usually orbit at four different levels: circular, low eliptical, mid-range circular, and distant geosynchronous.

13. The history of legislation binding the United States to limitations on military activities in outer space began with a 1963 U.N. Resolution adopted on October 17, which called upon all signatories to refrain from introducing weapons of mass destruction into outer space. At the time, both the United States and the Soviet Union issued statements to the effect that neither had an interest in deploying such weapons in outer space. These principles were formalized in the 1967 Treaty on Principles Governing the Activities of States in the Exploration and Use of Outer Space Including the Moon and Other Celestial Bodies. In this Treaty are specific clauses (Article 4) that restrict the deployment of weapons of mass destruction in outer space and also forbid the use of celestial bodies—including the moon—for establishing military bases, testing weapon systems, and conducting military maneuvers. The Treaty did not, of course, completely ban military activities in outer space because at the time, as now, both the countries appreciated the importance of verification and reconnaissance missions that were not yet considered provocative or offensive. The next stage in U.S.-Soviet negotiations was the 1972 ABM Treaty and the ABM Protocol signed in 1974. Article 5 of the ABM Treaty prohibited the development, testing, and deployment of ABM systems or components that are sea, air space or mobile land based. Article 3 of the Treaty prohibited the deployment of ABMs, except two fixed land-based systems and one test site for each side. The Protocol reduced this to one site for each country. Statement E of the "Agreed Interpretation" of the Protocol that was attached to the 1972 Treaty provides that "in the event ABM systems based on other physical principles and including components capable of substituting for ABM interceptor missiles, ABM launchers or ABM radars which are created in the future, specific limitations on such systems and their components would be subject to discussion." It is this clause in particular that has raised questions about the possibility that directed energy weapons could be covered by this Treaty. It is also worth noting that Article 12 of the ABM Treaty permits "national technical means of verification" that could be violated if directed-energy weapons and an ASAT were deployed.

14. *Aviation Week & Space Technology,* July 9, 1979, pp. 18–19. For more details on China's space program, see *Aviation Week & Space Technology,* May 28, pp. 26–27, and June 25, 1979, p. 23.

15. *Aviation Week & Space Technology,* July 9, 1979, pp. 18–19.

16. Reported in *Aviation Week & Space Technology,* September 3, 1979, p. 57.

17. *Aviation Week & Space Technology,* March 28, 1977, pp. 38–48; May 2, 1977, pp. 16–22.

18. Richard Burt, "New Laser Weaponry is Expected to Change Warfare in the 1980s," *New York Times,* February 10, 1980. Burt's article was based on the classified version of the 1979 "Arms Control Impact Statement" prepared by the Arms Control and Disarmament Agency annually for Congress.

19. *Defense Space Daily,* August 6, 1979.

20. Burt, "New Laser Weaponry."

21. Richard Burt, "U.S. Says Russians Develop Satellite-Killing Laser," *New York Times*, May 22, 1980.

22. For details on possible strategic application of these weapons for ballistic missile defense, see *Aviation Week & Space Technology*, October 2, 1978, pp.15–22; October 16, 1978, pp. 42–52. For a skeptical analysis, see John Parmentola and Kosta Tsipis, "Particle-Beam Weapons," *Scientific American*, April 1979, pp. 54–65.

23. See Parmentola and Tsipis, *op. cit.*, and comments by Richard Garwin cited in Burt, *New York Times*, February 15, 1980.

24. Burt, "New Laser Weaponry."

25. There is a third school, the Luddite, that argues that most space programs are too costly to justify in view of pressing alternative priorities.

26. Some space advocates talk of the five phases of space industrialization; the *information phase* (1960s to 1990), during which the main tasks are the collection and transmission of data; the *large structure phase* (1980–2010), when assembly and support technologies will be developed; the *industrial prototype phase* (1990–2025), which will involve the testing and costing of major systems such as Solar Power Satellites that will in turn rely on ground (earth support) for development; the *industrialization phase* (2010–2075), when closed systems (with no direct earth support) will evolve; and the *space habitation phase* (2075), during which space colonies will be established and space energy will be sold to earth. Statement of Klaus P. Heiss in "Symposium on the Future of Space Science and Space Applications," Hearing before the Subcommittee on Science, Technology & Space, U.S. Senate, February 7, 1979. The futurists would not disagree with these stages but would argue that the time-frame is much too conservative.

27. Stephen Gorove, "The Geostationary Orbit; Issues of Law and Policy," *The American Journal of International Law*, vol. 73, 1979, pp. 444–461.

28. For more background, see Jerry Grey, *Enterprise: The Use of the Shuttle in Our Future Space Program* (New York: William Morrow, 1979); Gerard O'Neill, *The High Frontier: Human Colonies in Space* (New York: William Morrow, 1977); Jerry Grey (ed.), *Space Manufacturing Facilities* (American Institute of Aeronautics & Astronautics, 1977), vols. 1 and 2.

29. Grey, *Enterprise*, p. 227.

30. Helen Denver, "Would-Be Space Colonists Head Fight Against Moon Treaty," *Washington Post*, October 25, 1979.

31. Speech reported in *Aviation Week & Space Technology*, February 19, 1979, p. 9.

About the Contributors

Richard K. Betts is currently a research associate at the Brookings Institution. He has taught at Harvard, Johns Hopkins, and Columbia universities and also served on the staffs of the U.S. Senate Select Committee on Intelligence and the National Security Council. Betts has written extensively on nuclear policy, strategic intelligence, and other aspects of defense policy.

Richard Burt is a Foreign Service reserve officer who became director of the Bureau of Politico-Military Affairs in January 1981. At the time his contribution to this volume was written, Burt was the national security affairs correspondent for *The New York Times*, covering foreign policy and defense issues in Washington, D.C. He was previously assistant director of the International Institute for Strategic Studies in London, research associate at the Institute, and advanced research fellow at the U.S. Naval War College.

Robert A. Gessert is a principal scientist at the General Research Corporation in McLean, Virginia. During his sixteen years at GRC and one of its predecessors, the Research Analysis Corporation, Gessert has conducted contract studies on NATO political, military, and economic affairs for the U.S. Department of Defense, the Arms Control and Disarmament Agency, the U.S. Department of State, and the U.S. Army. He also served as an advisor on NATO to the President's Science Advisory Committee and the Defense Science Board. For ten years Gessert taught at a number of universities in the fields of engineering and political-social ethics.

Richard Haass is currently serving as director of regional security affairs in the Bureau of Politico-Military Affairs in the U.S. Department of State. Haass has also been a Defense Department official, a research associate at the International Institute for Strategic Studies, and a legislative assistant for foreign relations to a U.S. senator.

Michael Higgins, who was a member of the National Security Council staff working on European defense problems from February 1974 to July 1976, is a corporate vice-president of Science Applications, Inc., and a member of that company's National Security Studies Office.

Dr. Peter C. Hughes, a defense analyst and consultant, is a frequent contributor to publications on U.S. arms control and national security problems. While in the government, Hughes served as a staff associate to the Senate Armed Services Committee and as a member of the professional staff of the House Armed Services Committee, with primary responsibility for arms control and strategic force programs. During the 1980 presidential campaign, Hughes was part of Ronald Reagan's defense and foreign policy advisory group.

William L. Hyland is currently a Senior Fellow at the Center for Strategic and International Studies at Georgetown University. He served in the U.S. government from 1954 until 1977 and was a member of the National Security Council staff at the White House beginning in 1969. In 1974-75 Hyland was director of the Bureau of Intelligence and Research at the U.S. Department of State, and during the last two years of the Ford administration he was deputy assistant to the president for national security affairs. He also participated in all of the Soviet summit meetings and remained on the NSC staff until the fall of 1977.

Geoffrey Kemp joined the National Security Council at the start of the Reagan administration as senior staff member for Near East and South Asian Affairs. Prior to this appointment, Kemp was a professor of international politics at the Fletcher School of Law and Diplomacy at Tufts University. He has published many studies on national security policy and has travelled and lectured extensively in Europe, the Middle East, the Far East, and Africa.

Benjamin S. Lambeth is a senior staff member of The Rand Corporation, specializing in Soviet political and strategic affairs. He received his graduate training at Harvard University and served previously in the Office of National Estimates and Office of Political Research, Central Intelligence Agency. He has written numerous articles on Soviet military matters and is co-author of *The Soviet Union and Arms Control: A Superpower Dilemma.*

Christopher J. Makins is presently a member of the National Security Studies Office of Science Applications, Inc. He was a senior associate at the Carnegie Endowment for International Peace and director of the endowment's Western European Trends Program at the time his contribution to this volume was written.

Dr. William Schneider, Jr., is an economist and national security analyst. He has served on the staff of the Hudson Institute and as a staff associate to the U.S. House Committee on Appropriations' Defense Subcommittee. During the 1980 presidential campaign, Schneider was also part of Ronald Reagan's defense and foreign policy advisory group; he now serves the Reagan administration in the Office of Management and Budget as associate director for national security programs.

Charles A. Sorrels is currently with a consulting firm. He was a program/budget examiner in the Office of Management and Budget for several years and was later an analyst of defense and foreign policy issues in the Office of the Secretary of Defense and the Congressional Budget Office. In 1979 he was a consultant to the Senate Committee on Foreign Relations and SALT II. Sorrels has written on SALT for the *Wall Street Journal* and *The New York Times* and is the author of a forthcoming book on the cruise missile and its implications for defense and arms control.

Index